THE
BOGEYMAN

Other books by Dr. Sherry L. Meinberg

Be the Boss of Your Brain:
Take Control of Your Life

Into the Hornet's Nest:
An Incredible Look at Life
in an Inner City School

THE
BOGEYMAN

Stalking and Its Aftermath

Dr. Sherry L. Meinberg

Writers Advantage
New York Lincoln Shanghai

The Bogeyman
Stalking and Its Aftermath

Writers Advantage
an imprint of iUniverse, Inc.

For information address:
iUniverse
2021 Pine Lake Road, Suite 100
Lincoln, NE 68512
www.iuniverse.com

ISBN: 0-595-26271-6

Printed in the United States of America

DISCLAIMER

The Bogeyman should be used only as a general guide, since it is based upon the personal experiences of the author. Your own experience may well differ, as stalking is a set of behaviors exhibited by individuals with contrasting backgrounds, differing motivations, and varied psychological disorders. The information and suggestions herein are provided as a public service. Although this is a personal saga, the author includes supporting ideas and data from many sources. The author and publisher make no warranties whatsoever regarding the quality, content, completeness, suitability, adequacy, sequence, accuracy, or timelines, of such information. The ideas, procedures, and preventative measures are meant to supplement, not replace, the advice of trained professionals in any field. Neither the author nor the publisher is engaged in rendering legal, economic, security, self-defense, physical, or psychological services, and shall have neither responsibility, nor liability, to any person or entity, with respect to any damage or loss caused or alleged to be caused directly, or indirectly, by the information herein. Make intelligent choices, applying only those suggestions that appeal to you, and that resonate with your particular situation. Never let a book or a person replace your own thinking. Note the publishing date, since stalking research is still in its infancy, and subject to change. Be aware that laws differ from state to state, regarding both the definition of a stalker and the rights of stalking victims. If you require personal advice, consult with trained professionals. If you require indepth information or additional support services, visit your local bookstores and libraries, consult with experts in the field, use your local yellow pages, and check out the many Internet sites devoted to this subject, while monitoring films, radio, and news reports, in an effort to keep abreast of new safety ideas and stalking research.

If you do not wish to be bound by the above disclaimer, please return this book to the publisher for a full refund.

To my husband, Wayne, for his sustaining love, support, and companionship—who stuck with me, by my side, through thick and thin—for thirty-two years and counting. The third time was truly the charm!

NOTE

Please understand that editoral discretion has allowed me to omit certain names out of sheer politeness.

THE PERSONAL APPLICATIONS

The Bogeyman represents my personal history as it pertains to stalking experiences, related information, and advocacy. It is a sanitized, encapsulated version, condensing forty years of experiences into ten chapters. Since I learned my survival lessons long *before* any stalking facts and figures were available (or said research had even been considered, much less, conducted), this book is not intended as a work of scholarship, and does not present *all* of the information available concerning stalkers. As such, the endnotes are not comprehensive, and are only meant as supportive or reinforcing foundational background material for those who might wish to pursue certain subjects further. Understand that many books and articles about stalking behavior include the same information and/or suggestions, whereas I may have cited only one to three authors or experts per item. The listed sources simply underscore or highlight my own personal experience, and have particular interest for me. The Personal Applications suggested for each chapter are presented in order of the storyline—not necessarily in logical order—and may be skipped entirely, if you are not presently undergoing a stalking situation.

CONTENTS

*We should learn
from the mistakes of others.
We don't have time
to make them all ourselves.*
—Groucho Marx

PREFACE

According to the FBI, I have the dubious honor of being the longest-stalked person in the nation. As such, I learned everything about being a survivor in a trial-and-error fashion—emphasis on error. Most of my survival education has come the proverbial hard way, by making a thousand and one painful blunders. My hit-or-miss method resulted from having received no input from books, magazines, or the media, and with no outside help from individuals or organizations. I was flying blind, always busy making mistakes. After all, I encountered and lived through stalking experiences long before the word was coined, or the research had been collected and compiled. I am now a reluctant expert on the subject.

"How did I get myself into this mess?" you ask. "How could I have made such poor choices in life?" And, you may wonder, "Who was the dumb schmuck who invited him into my life in the first place?" Well, er, that would, uh, be me. I extended him the invitation based on erroneous information. What can I say?

Looking back from the perspective of over forty years distance and insight, the first thing that comes to mind is that I am—and always have been—a bookworm. I love books: the sight, smell, and feel of them, not to mention the treasures within. I while away my time in bookstores, forever buying, reading, high-lighting, discussing, sharing, and donating my volumes. Stories set my pulses racing. As a result, I was always *book* smart, never *street* smart. Indeed, I didn't even know that there was any other *kind* of smart. I am a scholar, not an adventurer, preferring that my knowledge comes second-hand, vicariously. Since I live in my head, dwelling in the abstract, I'd rather *read* about an activity, than take part in it: I'd rather *watch* a snowball fight, than join in. I prefer armchair heroics. It took me years to realize that lessons in print teach through concepts, while street lessons teach through participation; and to be a well-rounded individual, you need both. Reading a book on learning to drive or learning to swim does not replace actually practicing to become skillful. Information and experience are not the same, as I have learned rather painfully.

Protected by my cocoon of books, I thought everyone grew up much the same as I did, with a pretty normal childhood—a sort of Norman Rockwell life. Sure, there was a slight difference in family size and income, with perhaps a different religion, but otherwise, I supposed that everyone's experiences were more similiar than not. In my sheltered environment, I wasn't even *close* to imagining what the real world was like.

My parents were such fantastic role models, always inspiring and motivating. The power of their example was constant. Both were educators, my father having been a principal and school superintendent in the Midwest, and my mother a teacher, so formal education was of supreme importance to them. Although our home life was strictly authoritarian and undemonstrative (affection was shown by an occasional awkward hug), it was calm, predictable, and safe. Everyone acted rationally and respectfully, as emotional displays were off limits. They modeled positive life principles on a daily basis: being honest, virtuous, and moral, while setting similarly high standards of behavior for my younger brother and me: no drinking, no smoking, no swearing, and no outrageous behavior. There was an unrelenting emphasis on hard work, sacrifice, and discipline.

Manners, idealism, and the desire for civic virtue were the norm. I was raised on truth, justice, and the American way. In fact, I lived in such a sane and well-ordered world, I thought *all* adults behaved in such a fashion, with only those few aberrations that I read about in newspapers. I actually thought that by the time one graduated from high school or college, lying, cheating, stealing, manipulation, and the like had been basically drummed out of the vast majority of people—that after twelve, fourteen, or sixteen years of schooling (bouyed by religion) those types of behaviors had virtually disappeared. Right?

Another factor was the era in which I grew up. During the forties and fifties, there was very little talk about *anything* of consequence. Sadly, it was not a time in which to reveal your innermost thoughts or to question the status quo. Nothing of import ever seemed to be openly discussed—mindless chit-chat, superficial observations, whispers and gossip, maybe, but never a conversation about things that were *really* meaningful. Concern with what the neighbors might think, brought about a closed, stiffling, Stepford Wives type of environment.

The narrow vision and inflexible mindset of the times (the rules of etiquette, fashion, grammar, religion, and so forth) left little room for curiosity, creativity, or innovation. I was not to do anything controversial or unladylike, which was tough for me with such a tomboy spirit. My personality traits drove me to hit any barrier head on, in the manner of a hammer driving nails (my father once remarked that I went at life like I was killing snakes, and although accurate, I could do without the visual). In such a bland, peaceful, uneventful life, I resisted the conventional. Drowning from the stress of forced conformity, rigid regulations and restrictions, I was willful, mildly rebellious, and *hated* to be told what to do. It was cataclysmically boring. Dullsville. My normal reaction to the words, "You can't..." was an immediate, "Oh, yeah? Says who?" Then I went right out and tried it. "I can do it!" became the chorus of my lifesong. Refusing to limit myself to one way of life, I was anxious to be on my own, looking for adventures and alternative routes: unpaved paths, unopened doors, and unexplored territories. I wanted to consider other possibilities and opportunities that the adults in my immediate society ignored, or refused to consider.

The soundtrack of my youth was provided by my mother, who played the piano. We sang happy, upbeat tunes: popular songs from the early 1900s, semi-classical, Broadway musicals, Hollywood movies, and *Your Hit Parade!* Classical music was provided through my twice-a-week dancing lessons. So I had a wide-range of musical experience, but as a teen, my record collection was strictly R 'n' R. In my opinion, the only good thing to come out of the fifties was the music, as I was ready to "Shake, Rattle, and Roll."

My biggest problem was that I *assumed* things that weren't necessarily so. Because I was repeatedly told that I was "so smart," I thought that I was able to figure out most things on my own. For instance, when I was six I was given twin dolls—a boy and a girl—for Christmas, with matching bunkbeds and trunks. Because the dolls were not anatomically correct, the only difference between the two was their clothes: a pink dress and a blue jumpsuit. So I decided that all babies were basically built the same, and that when parents went to the hospital for the birth of a baby, the gender was chosen by the type of clothes in which the newborn was dressed. Having never seen family members in any state other than fully clothed, I labored under that misconception for several years.

My parents were somewhat puritanical about sex; the word was never uttered in our household. Even the word *naked* went unsaid. In fact, the first swear word I ever heard was when I was in the sixth grade, while on vacation in Oklahoma. Mother and father were so reserved, and conveyed such a discomfort about demonstrated affection, that the physical aspect of married life was never addressed. And because my parents had separate bedrooms, I thought we were the *richest* family in the whole surrounding community, since everybody else's parents *had* to share a room.

Alas, I knew a little about a lot of things, and a whole bunch about nothing. I was laughingly naive.

Life is what happens to you
when you're busy making other plans.
—John Lennon

Chapter 1:

A SKEWED VIEW

Once upon a time, before DNA testing, nanoseconds, and cyberspace, in the olden days of rock 'n roll and Sputnik, I met Chuck at a dance in 1957, when I was barely seventeen. And as is common in literature, it all began so innocently. I arrived with a date, as did he. Chuck and I wouldn't have even connected if his date hadn't asked me for some mascara as I was walking out of the Women's Room. Apparently, the two of them had been necking, and she needed to reapply her makeup. I loaned her my mascara (nobody thought of health implications in those days!), and waited outside, happily chatting with Chuck.

I'm sure the giddy flush on my face couldn't help but display my pleasure at being in conversation with such a handsome *older* man. Over six feet tall, and slender, his pale white skin, coal black hair, and matching Clark Kent glasses gave him a studious look, while his features were a bit soft, and deceptively vulnerable. His smooth face (devoid of deep-pit acne), and his ready smile (with no orthodontics), were definite pluses. When his date returned, we went our separate ways. Much later, Chuck found me again amid the mass of people, and asked for my phone number. He smiled a lot, and seemed so nice, I thought it terribly romantic. I was thrilled that he had asked. And, since I had never carried mascara in my purse, beforehand, I considered it a sign of kismet.

Then he called! When I had told him my phone number, he hadn't written it down, so that meant that he had actually *memorized* it! Wow! And although he was seven years older, I didn't see this as unusual since my father was eight years older than my mother. I never even considered the age factor as a possible problem. Actually, *because* of the age difference, I knew he was out and about in the wide, wide, world—with a car and a good-paying job—and that made him appear to be mature, sophisticated, and worldly. It never occured to me to wonder why a twenty-four year old man would be trolling for a young, inexperienced, impressionable, high school girl. (To set the tone, listen to the implied lecherousness of the lyrics in "Good Morning Little Schoolgirl" by Muddy Waters, or Jimmy Reed, or the more upbeat version by Jimmy Lang.) I was both pleased and flabbergasted that he had taken a liking to me. Ignorance is bliss!

At first blush, I found Chuck to be visually and intellectually appealing, which just serves to prove that beauty is in the eye of the beholder. *What was I thinking?* It turned out that he wasn't classically handsome, nor was he particularly educated or accomplished, nor had he any appreciable talent or skills; he was a marvel of mediocrity. The razzle dazzle was all in my head. How many times had I been cautioned that you should never judge by appearances? How many times had I heard that you can't tell a book by its cover? How is it that I couldn't remember that sage advice? I was simply overwhelmed by the package, and what I *perceived* to be within. Actually, I couldn't believe my incredible good fortune, in finding someone whose ideas, values, and outside interests were *exactly* like mine.

It took two weeks of dating before he kissed me, which I viewed as a sign that he respected me. *What a total gentleman,* I thought, *so caring and considerate.* Wrong again. He then immediately pushed for exclusivity, which I took to be a declaration of undying devotion. I was totally flattered, and with all the optimism of the innocent, agreed. We then progressed to the handholding stage.

So we became a couple. I was immensely pleased that he wanted to be with me all the time, and go everywhere with me. Our dating consisted of going to the movies, and out to eat. That was the extent of it, as there seemed to be no place to go, and little else to do in those days. But it never presented a problem for me, since I was always going to school or working anyway. Mostly, we spent the bulk of our time at Chuck's middle sister's house, just hanging out.

Her house seemed to be the central meeting place, where their whole family gathered to eat, even though they all lived in different cities. I never found that to be strange, in the least, not knowing how large families operated. I thought it a sign of loving: a *good* sign (think: *The Waltons*). Later, I attributed this extreme togetherness to *financial* problems; a way in which everyone could eat, whether they were working or not, a way to make ends meet and save face, as well as enjoy each other's company. I came to that conclusion, because *all* the men were working but none of the women were; whereas, in my family, the females also had careers, so I decided that there wasn't enough income. I failed to see the blinking red DANGER signs cautioning, "Enter at Your Own Risk," "Petrified Thinking," and "Sexist Traditions."

An odd event happened the first night I met his family. As I prattled on (as is my wont), relating several recent experiences, his sister finally asked, "Who is this *Chuck* you keep talking about?" while the rest of the family members nodded in agreement, also showing their confusion. It turned out that the family had always called him by his given name, *Charles*, or a diminutive of his middle name, and had no idea that he had told me his name was Chuck. Abruptly, the room fell silent as everyone turned to stare at him, while he showed no emotion whatsoever. Meaningful glances were exchanged during this awkward moment, making me feel vaguely uneasy. I wished I understood what the heck was going on. Clearly there were underlying subtexts here that I didn't understand. Mentally giving him the benefit of the doubt, however, I decided that Chuck was just embarrassed about trying to make a fresh start of some sort—a new beginning—and that a new name represented a way of overcoming some difficulty in his recent past: a tragic lost love, or a long-term friendship gone sour, I romanticized. Little did I know.

I was fascinated with the daily interactions of such a huge family, so different from my own. His elderly mother lived with Chuck, directly across the street from the middle sister (another clue that I ignored, chalking it up to his providing needed rent money, while taking care of her). The older brother, with his common law wife (shocking in those times!) and their two sons, lived in Bellflower. His eldest sister, her husband, and several children, lived in Long Beach. The middle sister, with her husband and two boys, lived in Lakewood, while the youngest sister and her husband lived out in Orange County. It was like having a book open before my very eyes. I watched their individual stories evolve in living color, without ever having to actually *read*. Amazing!

This wildly disparate group of characters—with the mood stability of a Texas thunderstorm—was much more entertaining than TV. Here was a different world entirely. With its odd mix of personalities and continual circus of activity, I saw it as one views a spectator sport. I wasted hundreds of hours, watching this daily, twenty-four hour soap opera/situation comedy unfold before my very eyes. It was performance art at its finest. Being a curiosity junkie, I was glued to the invisible screen, watching the daily episodes and reruns, without commercials. Spellbound, I was hooked on the drama of it all. As a result, I totally missed the fact that Chuck was about as vocal as a clam. He responded to others, but rarely initiated a conversation, so he was able to keep the pretense of being a social animal, without really having to interact all that often. *Why couldn't I see that he was socially challenged?* He was so still at times, he could have been a cardboard cutout, while I reasoned that he was having *deep* thoughts. Still waters, and all that. In time I would discover that he was actually a rather dim bulb: sluggish, humorless, and terminally lackluster.

On total, the family seemed to be a little left of the balance beam. It was not, from even a cursory glance, a think tank. Nor was smiling natural for them, reminding me of Grant Wood's *American Gothic*. During the after dinner discussions—when we usually played Canasta—I always learned something new and altogether unknown to me, and slowly pieced together, rightly or wrongly, their highlights of yesteryear:

- Chuck's long dead father, much revered in the family, though rarely mentioned, was more than likely an alcoholic, as well as abusive. An enlarged photograph of him in his coffin was prominantly displayed.

- The youngest of the three sisters was nice, pleasant-looking, timid, and quiet. She was married to a wildly handsome husband, by anybody's standards, who was a binge alcoholic. After years of seemingly wedded bliss, I heard that they slept in twin beds, and had never consummated their marriage, because she was afraid to get pregnant. He could only handle the situation for six or eight months tops, before flying off the handle, drinking, carrousing, and bedding everything in sight. This would last for several days until he was dragged home by the men in the family, with him shouting, "She's too good for me!" and other words to that effect.

- The older brother was both controlling and abusive. He and his partner were long-time, heavy drinkers, which explained the thoroughly mangled physical and mental conditions of their two sons (the term Fetal Alcohol Syndrome, denoting diminished capacity, and permanent, irreversible damage, wasn't to be coined until around 1975, some twenty years hence).

- The oldest sister had a worn, weary, and troubled appearance, that fairly shouted *hard life*. Her husband was also a long-time alcoholic (very controlling and, more than likely, abusive). He is the man that Chuck later blamed for most of his own problems.

- The middle sister's husband dated the older sister before he married her, so sibling rivalry, with some clearly unresolved feelings of jealousy and betrayal, lurked below the surface of the sisters' relationship. They appeared to have ancient axes to grind. It seemed that their caring and intimacy had strings attached.

- There appeared to be no respect for personal boundaries. The older brother tried to convince me to be his girlfriend. When I quietly refused, not wanting a family blowup over his unwanted interest, he said that if Charles "couldn't or wouldn't" take care of me, he'd always be there for me, and look out for me anyway. I thought it odd that he would use those words, as I had seen no signs that Chuck might become disinterested in me. A mental health issue never even crossed my mind.

- The middle sister's husband had had several nervous break-downs as a result of his war experiences, with one lengthy stay in a mental hospital. No one ever expected much from him. Out of the entire family, he seemed the most trustworthy, and the most harmless, to me.

- Although all of the other children from these unions seemed afraid to step out of line, the middle sister's boys were absolute spoiled brats, never having been scolded or made to be respon-sible for any of their negative behavior. After dinner one evening, the two boys, about six and eight years old, were racing through the house, calling each other nasty names while throwing sharp steak knives at one another. I was aghast at everyone's total disregard of the seriousness of the situation. Safety and health issues were running through my mind, not to mention the subject of acceptable, common sense behavior. However, I didn't feel that I could reprimand the children, in the house in which I was a guest, especially with everyone else sitting in the same room. Frustrated with his lack of throwing ability, the older boy ran into the kitchen, by the table at which we all sat, yanked open a drawer, grabbed a knife, and tore out of the room. No one seemed concerned about the boys actions, and carried on as if nothing was happening. I listened in mounting horror as things truly escalated, tracking their sounds from room to room, until they came charging back into the kitchen, and the huge butcher knife zipped across the table where the adults were playing cards together. *That* finally brought an end to such nonsense.

- I was further amazed at the children's low ambitions for their futures. One of the older sister's daughters (about eleven years old) had seen a TV movie, the script of which she decided to use as a blueprint for her own life. It was her plan to be sent to prison, wherein her assigned lawyer would fall madly in love with her, and when she was released, they would get married and live happily ever after. (I wonder if she ever revised the map of her life.) All of their homes held zero encouragement.

Heretofore, I had a mental picture of alcoholics as constantly chug-a-lugging, falling-down drunks, slobbering incoherently, while loudly making scenes. My only reference was what I had seen in the movies. Having no first-hand knowledge, I didn't realize that *any* of these individuals had a substance abuse problem. I never even saw them drinking beer or wine, let alone, hard liquor. It took me years to figure it out. Only the brother-in-law had the honor of being the scapegoat: the Designated Intermittant Drunk.

Because I *gradually* discovered these family facts, their impact was not as pronounced as it would have been, had I heard them altogether. So, with blinders firmly strapped on, I was able to successfully absorb each episode, before the next event presented itself. Since I was dealing with individual stories, I wasn't focusing on the overarching whole of their family behavior and interrelationships, and what that might portend. Instead, I continued shaking my head in wide-eyed disbelief at some of their weird ways, failing to see the overall truth of the situation.

Additionally, because of the large number of family members congregating, with everybody jumping in on others' conversations, with all the inherent noise and confusion amidst the everyday hustle and bustle of life, I never noticed that there were no friends around. Ever. They never even *talked* about friends. So, while I had six very close gal pals, with a much larger circle of friends (from school, work, and church), as well as a handy supply of neighbors and acquaintances that I interacted with on a daily basis, Chuck was a loner. *How could I have missed that?*

At long last, I had finally satisfied my curiosity, having learned far more than I cared to know about Chuck's family. I saw how very different households can be. Yet, all of the disgraceful behaviors I heard about, or witnessed, were things I could handle, because I felt they had nothing to do with *me*.

More than likely I held an unrecognized elitist attitude that I was slumming with trailer trash, although they all had clean houses and well kept lawns. I viewed many of their shenanigans with restrained distaste; they were all so energetically redneck. I knew we were clearly miles apart. Whereas I loved literature, they *never* read; no books, magazines, or newspapers were ever in evidence. I identified with Rodin's "The Thinker," and cutting-edge contemporary art, and looked down upon their cheap knockoffs and enormous yard collections of plastic flamingos and plaster-of-Paris gnomes. Opposites prevailed: chess versus bowling, classical ballet and the theater versus roller derby and professional wrestling. Which, I realize, is just a matter of taste. However, it did not escape my notice that a slightly uncomfortable silence would emanate whenever I would share some exciting things that I had learned in my university classes. A meeting of the minds we had not. So I learned, early on, to curb my enthusiasm for idea-driven thoughts, and began to self-edit, with a sort of inner *pearls before swine* attitude. I stopped expressing my opinions to the family.

With major tunnel vision, I was comfortably blind, seeing Chuck as being separate and apart from their dysfunctional behavior; the only *normal* one in the family. Indeed, he appeared so mentally and psychologically stable, I never considered that he was from the same genetic background. I couldn't see that his family was so interwoven, so braided, that *something* must have rubbed off on him over the years. He was as much a product of his family and his environment as I was of mine. I should have seen the handwriting on the wall, but no-o-o-o, I was too busy being scandalized, amused, and entertained.

The most shocking information came about when it was casually mentioned that Chuck had been the baby of the family, and, as such, had slept in the same bed with his mother until the age of sixteen. *Say, what?* One doesn't have to be a practicing psychologist to know that something is seriously wrong with this picture. That piece of news really jolted me, while Chuck displayed not one whit of emotion. But again, I didn't even know how to broach the subject with him. The whole topic was just too embarassing and uncomfortable, making me slightly queasy. Especially, since they *still* shared a house together. How would one even begin to question such behavior? *So, how did it feel to be sleeping with your mother?* Yuck! This subject was way beyond my comfort level. So, I decided that surely this must be a sick joke, dismissed the thought with a mental shudder, and buried that troublesome item in the lowest depths of my memory vault. Denial, denial, denial.

Chapter 1:

PERSONAL APPLICATIONS

Before becoming involved in a relationship, check out these warning signs for potential stalkers:*

(1) A stalker's most consistent feature is his/her apparent normality.[1] Conventional in appearance, stalkers exhibit a cool, calm, and collected exterior, with superficial charm. They are often excessively neat, extremely cooperative, and well-mannered. Although they blend in well with the crowd, they are not a part of any group. They appear to be average, ordinary citizens, being very good at camouflage. Stalkers know how to make good first impressions, to be friendly, polite, and how to behave when it's necessary (remember Ted Bundy?). Stalking and battering cuts across all ethnic, cultural, social, economic, religious, and educational levels. As such, you must pay less attention to what a person says, than to what a person does. Be aware; be awake to each experience. Stop, look, listen, and *feel*. Keep your eyes as wide open as your heart.

(2) Does this person's smile telegraph warmth and acceptance? Or, do his/her smiles seem to be all teeth and no sincerity: forced, fixed, fake, and manufactured on cue? Do they appear automatic or a little strained?

---

*NOTE: Since many abusers graduate to become stalkers, a number of the signals for domestic violence are the *same* as those for stalkers. Understand that while one person may display only a few of the symptoms, another may exhibit many. Be alert for red flags. Attention and caution are the watchwords.

(3) Does his/her niceness seem plastic at times? Don't confuse niceness with goodness.[2] Anyone can put up a good front. Look for chinks in the facade; look behind the social mask. Meet at a number of public sites, independently, before handing out your address.

(4) A stalker is an expert at mirroring. He/she will agree with all you say, and in the manner of a chameleon, will reflect your values, morals, and judgments. You never know his/her true color. Mimicry is worth a stalker's time and effort because something is to be gained from it later. Check out that which appears to be counterfeit.

(5) Is there evidence of anything important in this person's life? A stalker generally has no outside interests. He/she will present a false image regarding experiences and interests. Does he/she get excited or enthusiastic about anything? Be wary of someone who appears to have *exactly* the same hobbies, pastimes, cares, and concerns as you.

(6) A stalker suffering from antisocial personality disorders will often use aliases. Do you know this person's complete name? Nicknames? Make a note of any permanent identifiers, like scars, birthmarks, tattoos, accent, and anything out of the ordinary.

(7) Stalkers are cunning, persuasive, and manipulative. They tend to be older and smarter than other mentally ill criminals, having more time and resources to effectively stalk their targets.[3] With higher functioning capabilities, they are relentless, determined, and highly motivated, having the wherewithal to travel and carry out a plan.

(8) A stalker is a loner, with no social life. Loners are often socially immature, and unable to establish—or at least maintain—close, meaningful relationships. They often suffer from extreme self-consciousness and a lack of self-esteem, coming from abusive or emotionally distant families. As such, they rarely date, and have few sexual partners. Does this person have any friends? If so, what type of behavior do *they* exhibit?

(9) Although each face has only forty-four muscles, it has the ability to show 7,000 expressions. Do you see a variety of expressions, or does

this person display a deadpan, poker face? Do the eyes register any emotion at all? Does he/she ever get excited, or only exude a funeral director seriousness? In situations where the normal person would act scared, angry, horrified, or worried, stalkers display no emotion, anxiety, or nervousness. They do not react as you might react to shocking things,[4] showing a detached interest, at best. Psychopaths are known for their lack of anxiety. Indeed, the most dangerous person is considered to be the one who's rage is quiet and cold.[5] Watch for inappropriate responses.

(10) Have you observed a *genuine* sense of humor, or does the laughter sound artificial? Does this person's eyes match his/her laughter? Is the laughter presented on cue, or possibly a few beats after the fact?

(11) Stalkers were often mistreated as children, either through neglect, growing up in dangerous situations, watching repeated violent acts, or receiving physical and emotional abuse. Carefully consider his/her family members. Explore family trees. Abuse is a learned behavior. Experts tell us that dysfunctional childhoods excuse nothing, yet explain many things.[6] Know that when you marry, you're marrying history.

(12) A stalker will frequently show signs of trouble—displaying an antisocial streak—at an early age: being seen as odd or *different* by peers; problems at school; difficulties with neighbors; bullying younger children; playing with matches and/or arson; abusing or torturing animals; truancy; running away from home, and the like. What do you know about this person's childhood or adolescent years? Are youthful experiences ever even mentioned? I heard only one childhood story about Chuck: When he was ten years old, a truck hit him while he was bicycling, knocking him sixty-six feet through the air. He landed on his head, which swelled to four times the normal size. People thought it might burst like a overinflated balloon. Later, when he awoke from his drug-induced haze in the hospital, he immediately dressed and went home, refusing further health services. Does this person seem to have a

secret childhood or adolescence? Even if you feel rude or ridiculous, *ask*. Remember, the only dumb question is the one you don't verbalize. If no answers are forthcoming, experts encourage you to *guess*. Realize that children who do not receive love in normal ways, become adults who seek love in other ways.[7]

(13) Overwhelming evidence shows that stalkers are likely to have a history of psychiatric difficulties: thought disorders, mood disorders, substance abuse disorders, or personality disorders.[8] Research indicates that at least 50 percent of stalkers suffer from some form of mental illness,[9] with some experts placing the figure between 80 and 90 percent.[10]

(14) A stalker has a history of physical violence, displaying a reckless bravado and a total disregard for safety.[11] Understand that past violence is the best indicator of future violence.[12] Experts tell us that it *is* possible to predict the dangerousness of erotomanic stalkers, with an accuracy of 88.9 percent (multiple delusional objects and a history of serious antisocial behavior).[13]

(15) Does this person's history include any police encounters? Ample evidence shows that a stalker generally has prior criminal offenses, both related and unrelated to stalking behavior.[14] It would never occur to the average person to question a new acquaintance as to whether he/she has previous offenses on record: threats, assaults, battery, or stalking. Ask anyway. Before you begin dating, check it out. You'd better learn what kind of fight you're in, before you climb into the ring. Research shows that stalkers have battered and stalked in former relationships. In the absence of such information, consider his/her *attitude* toward the police and the courts.

(16) Be alert: Have you noticed any smoldering resentments, unreasonable ill will, unswerving animosity, or racist attitudes? Look for out-of-balance emotions: an Achilles' heel.

(17) Does this person have very traditional ideas concerning the appropriate roles and behavior of women? Are women considered to be

second-class citizens? Are you expected to follow orders and advice without question? Are you expected to read your partner's mind, and anticipate his/her wants? Are you worried that you might aggravate your partner unnecessarily?[15] Are you considered to be his/her property?

(18) Does this person give credit where credit is due? Does he/she show appreciation and thank people for their efforts, or only criticize? Does this person always have to be right about everything, blaming others for problems of his/her own making? Stalkers refuse to accept responsibility for their actions. They blame other people, as well as external factors, such as alcohol or stress,[16] for their violence, having the social conscience of Marie Antoinette.

(19) Experts and common sense tell us that an active mind evolves. Normal thought is forever being reviewed, recycled, and renewed. Changing your mind is a sign of an evolving consciousness. Does this person display an Archie Bunker mindset? Does he/she seem close-minded, stuck, unable to bend? Too set, too rigid, too inflexible?

(20) A stalker often grows up in an addictive home, and may also have a substance abuse problem. Is this person difficult to live with, inconsistent, and moody? Have you seen evidence that he/she is enamored with alcohol, or is working up the pharmaceutical ladder, from pot to glue, to crystal meth, to acid, to cocaine, to heroin? Know that the most frequently used drugs of abuse or dependence for stalkers are alcohol, marijuana, amphetamines, and cocaine.[17] Research family history in this regard—if you are considering having a family—to determine genetic predispositions. If you hear gossip such as,"There's a drinking streak/drug problem in that family a mile wide," you'd be wise to follow up on it. Scientists tell us that genetic factors, when linked to the emotional and behavioral conditioning operating within addicted families, practically assures that some type of addiction will be present in succeeding generations.[18] Keep an eye out for bad genes

and bad parenting. Understand that most incidents of battering and sexual abuse occur in addicted families.[19]

(21) Recognize that you *see* things not as they are, but as *you* are.[20] You place your own interpretation on everything, large, small, and trivial. You view the world through your personal expectations, and the filter of your ideals, purely through your own projections. Experts say that a kind of fog or snow-blindness is developed, where you actually cease to see what you're looking at. Realizing this, you need to look into all those cracks and crannies that have gone unnoticed. Maintaining your illusions can be hazardous to your health. It's what you don't see that can hurt you. Now that you're an adult, there's no need to play Make Believe or Let's Pretend. See each experience as it *is*, rather than what you would like it to be, or think that it should be. ("There was no way around the fact that when it came to men I'd been a darn fool. My judgment had been horrible, my motivation worse, and I'd been completely naive." Georgette Mosbacher)

(22) The process of romance is that of choosing *not* to see faults, or minimizing them, or denying flaws altogether. Newly dating couples tend to look for the good, and overlook the rest.[21] Reports indicate that romantic love lasts about two years.[22] (Note the quote from Judith Martin, known as Miss Manners: "When you're in love, you put up with things that, when you're out of love, you cite.") Don't rationalize or make excuses for poor behavior ("He/She's going through a little adjustment period.") See without putting your own spin on it. Your idealized motives may not even be close; they may not be in the same zipcode, or even the same time zone. What you perceive to be a heart of gold, may prove to be like the Rolling Stones' "Heart of Stone." Know that you may be ascribing positive motivations where none exist. At all.

(23) If answers to your direct questions are always on the other side of vague, make the commitment to put forth the effort to get clear, specific, accurate information. Be diligent about tiny clues. By choosing to ignore the facts, you may be putting yourself at risk. Is there something

that doesn't seem right? Something that doesn't quite track? Something that seems a little off? There's a lot to be said for testing the waters. (Refer to your local Yellow Pages for investigative services, or check the Internet for companies that provide personal profiles and background checks: **WhoisHe.Com** or **WhoisShe.Com, backgroundchecks.com,** or **firstinc.com,** and the like. There are around 300 choices, at various prices. Your first search category: background checks.) Think of it as research and insurance. Do your homework. Make informed decisions. While the dinosaurs never saw it coming, you can. Give yourself a fighting chance. Know what's coming down the pike.

Chapter One Endnotes:
A SKEWED VIEW

1. Judith Lewis Herman, *Trauma and Recovery: The Aftermath of Violence—From Domestic Abuse to Political Terror* (New York: Basic Books, 1992), 75.

2. Gavin De Becker, *The Gift of Fear: Survival Signals That Protect Us From Violence* (Boston: Little, Brown, 1997), 57.

3. Doreen Orion, *I Know You Really Love Me: A Psychiatrist's Account of Stalking and Obsessive Love* (New York: Dell, 1997), 38.

4. De Becker, ibid, 51.

5. J.R. Meloy (ed), *The Psychology of Stalking: Clinical and Forensic Perspectives* (San Diego: Academic Press, 1998), 148: L.E. Walker & J.R. Meloy, Chapter 7: Stalking and Domestic Violence, citing J.M. Gottman, N.S. Jacobson, R.H. Rushe, J. Wu Short, J. Babcock, J.J. La Taillade, & J. Waltz, *Journal of Family Psychology*, (1996): 9.

6. De Becker, ibid, 49.

7. ibid, 179.

8. American Psychiatric Association, *Diagnostic and Statistical Manual of Mental Disorders*, (DSM-IV-TR), 4th ed, rev. (Washington, D.C.: American Psychiatric Association, 2000), 463-468.

9. M. Zona, K. Sharma & J. Lane, "A Comparative Study of Erotomanics and Obsessional Subjects in a Forensic Sample," *Journal of Forensic Sciences*, JFSCA 38 (1993), 894-903.

10. Orion, ibid, citing D. Ellis, "Nowhere to Hide," *People*, 17 May 1993, 63; R. Harmon, R. Rosner, & H. Owens, "Obsessional Harassment and Erotomania in a Criminal Court Population," *Journal of Forensic Sciences* 40 (1995), 188-196.

11. Meloy, ibid, 73; De Becker, ibid, 50-51.

12. Meloy, ibid, 146: Table 2.

13. Robin P.D. Menzies, J.P. Fedoroff, C.M. Green, & Kari Isaacson, "Prediction of Dangerous Behaviour in Male Erotomania," *British Journal of Psychoiatry*, 166 (1995), 529-536.

14. Meloy, ibid, 296: Stephen G. White & James S. Cawood, Chapter 15: Threat Management of Stalking Cases, citing: R. Harmon, R. Rosner & H. Owens, ibid, 188-196; J.R. Meloy & S. Gothard, "Demographic and Clinical Comparison of Obsessional Followers and Offenders with Mental Disorders," *American Journal of Psychiatry*, 152, (1955): 258-263; and P. Mullen & M. Pathe, "Stalking and the Pathologies of Love," *Australian and New Zealand Journal of Psychiatry*, 28, (1994): 469-477.

15. Dawn Bradley Berry, *The Domestic Violence Sourcebook* (Los Angeles: Lowell House, 2000), 244.

16. Melita Schaum & Karen Parish, *Stalked: Breaking the Silence on the Crime of Stalking in America* (New York: Pocket Books, 1995), 61.

17. Meloy, ibid, 73: Michael A. Zona, Russel E. Palarea, & John C. Lane, Jr., Chapter 4: Psychiatric Diagnosis and the Offender—Victim Typology of Stalking.

18. Robin Norwood, *Why Me, Why This, Why Now: A Guide to Answering Life's Toughest Questions* (New York: Carol Southern Books, 1994), 145.

19. *ibid.*

20. Philosophers, poets, and psychologists have pointed this out over the years, as have more recent experts: De Becker, ibid, 32; Deepak Chopra, *Unconditional Life: Discovering the Power to Fulfill Your Dreams* (New York: Bantam, 1992), 23, 33, & 80; Neale Donald Walsch, *Moments of Grace: When God Touches Our Lives Unexpectedly* (Charlottesville, VA: Hampton Roads, 2001), 70.

21. De Becker, ibid, 183.

22. Sonya Friedman, *Smart Cookies Don't Crumble: A Modern Woman's Guide to Living and Loving Her Own Life* (New York: Putnam, 1985), 129, citing the Kinsey Reports.

*Oh, life is a glorious cycle of song, A medley of
extemporanea; And love is a thing that can never
go wrong; And I am Marie of Roumania.*
—Dorthy Parker

Chapter 2:

THE TIE THAT BINDS

Back then, when couples dated for a good length of time, getting married was just the expected thing to do, like going to school. You never questioned it, you just did it. (Sing the 1955 happy hit, "Love and Marriage," by Cahn & Van Heusen, which later became the ironic theme for the TV show, *Married, With Children*.) Given the times, Chuck and I also never discussed family values or the future, other than, "After we get married, I want a house like that." I just *assumed* that everyone who got married wanted the same things: a loving, lifetime relationship, common goals, and an expanding family. I looked at our future together with wonder and promise. I saw our nuptials as the start of something great. I don't know how I could have been so off the mark.

On the day of our wedding, there was a window of opportunity—well over an hour—that presented itself, in which I could have called the whole thing off. But, of course, the wedding and reception were already paid for with my parent's hard-earned money, the guests had all arrived, and I had been conditioned to believe that *this* was the day every girl dreamed about. (All six of my closest girlfriends from high school were long-since married, with several children each, by the time I finished college, and began my teaching career. Although all had agreed that I would be the first to marry, I was the last, by far, and felt excluded from their shared homemaking and childrearing experiences). Knowing what I know now, I would have left the church in a fingersnap, but as we all realize, life is lived forward and understood backward. So, I let this golden opportunity slip through my fingers, obviously having the preservation instincts of a lemming.

The wedding that was scheduled before ours had run long over the expected time limit. It seems that the groom, a psychologist, was having a hard time making a commitment. Everytime it came to the point in the ceremony where he was to say "I do," he would promptly faint. His buddies would dutifully haul him out the side doors, slap his face around, and give him a cigarette. Then they would give him a quiet pep talk, until he finished smoking, and composed himself enough to try again. It obviously never occurred to him that he had a problem. *Physician, heal thyself!*

Feeling somewhat superior in that commitment was not a problem for us, I was actually *relieved* when that ceremony was, at long last, completed, and we could finalize our own vows. So there I was, walking down the aisle, just strolling on down the railroad tracks, blissfully unaware of the freight train racing at full throttle, right towards me. Our wedding went off with hardly a hiccup in the arrangements other than the fact that my beautiful sister-in-law had cut and dyed her hair, and no one recognized her. Without a pinprick of apprehension, I figured things were off to a good start. I was happily unaware of anything unusual.

I entered our formal union carrying the baggage of my hopes and idealistic expectations: In my happy dreams, marriage represented home, hearth, and safe harbor. I expected an emotionally loving, supporting, and caring partnership, where understanding, tolerance, and respect abounded on a daily basis. Reality wasn't even close, and I was soon disappointed: the understatement of the century.

While driving back to my studio apartment after our wedding festivities were completed, Chuck, my brand new husband of only a couple of hours duration, delivered a one-two punch that left me reeling:

(1) He claimed that he lost his wallet, so we couldn't go on a honeymoon. (Yeah, right. But who wants to start their marriage with a king-size argument that would be remembered forever after? Since I was never too direct or too confrontational with anyone—being reluctant to give offense—I gave him a long, dark look, but said nothing, while trying to *understand* this turn of events); and,

(2) Further on down the road, Chuck informed me that he had quit his job to play the *horses* full-time. I was stunned. Not only could I feel future waves of disapproval coming from my staunch anti-gambling family, but I was now the sole support for the two of us, and everyone knows that teachers are underpaid. *What to do, what to do?* I couldn't decide whether he'd been *fired*, and just said that he quit to save face, or if he had actually turned in his resignation on his own initiative. Again, I simply didn't know how to respond, and said nothing.

Then, while still trying to come to grips with these revelations, he followed with the knockout blow. His third statement paled the first two into insignificance, and changed my life forever:

(3) He gravely announced that if I ever had a baby, he'd drown it in the bathtub. Upon hearing this chilling news, my brain became a series of short-circuits that rendered me incapable of processing what I'd just heard. I was struck dumb, *unable* to respond. My heart leaped into my throat and blocked my breathing, my head felt kicked in by a buffalo, and my vocal chords seemed paralyzed. My mouth opened and closed like a beached fish, making no sound. I couldn't breathe, I couldn't think, I couldn't talk. It was impossible to absorb. I searched for a response to a situation that was completely incomprehensible to me. *How could anyone reply to such a statement?* With that one sentence alone, I suffered an instant compound fracture of the heart, realizing

that I had married a man with a head full of bent spaghetti wiring, and had just made the biggest mistake of my life.

How could things go so wrong, so fast? I was overwhelmed at the speed in which my life had gone to hell in a handbasket. The train that I had been ignoring, hit before we even got home from the church, and the fall-out from the accident was just beginning. It was clear that Chuck had been on his best behavior when I met him, when I dated him, and when I married him. He had suddenly shed his choirboy image, and I was finally meeting the *real* Chuck, in the manner of a ship sailing under false colors. Talk about camouflage! I had entered this marriage in good faith, and felt waylaid by a stranger in the street: betrayed, duped, and defrauded.

The I-accept-you-warts-and-all wording of the traditional wedding vow suddenly took on a whole new, sinister meaning. I was unprepared for the reality of the situation. With the phrase "for better or worse," I assumed the bad times would be transitory, and the good ones per-mananent. As "for richer or poorer," I wasn't expecting our *double* income to be less than I was accustomed to on my own, and, as far as "in sickness and in health," I wasn't thinking *mental* health. And I equated sickness with the elderly.[1] This was not good.

So much for my One True Love. Having severe second thoughts, I was desperately trying to sort it all out, realizing that I was seriously unprepared and ill-equipped to handle this turn of events. I knew exactly how Alice felt when she fell down the rabbit hole. The ride home lasted for several aeons. As I contemplated this day of gargantuan disappointment, the absolute enormity of the situation pressed down on me like the stone lid of a crypt. And things went downhill from there.

After these revealing disclosures, there was no chance of consumating our marriage that night (or *any* time, if I had my way about it). "Don't touch me. Don't even *think* of it. Keep your hands to yourself!" I snarled. So we slept on my two studio couches, which turned into extremely uncomfortable twin beds. Several weeks went by in much the same manner. *How many other couples have sham marriages? Is this a common experience that no one talks about?* I constantly asked myself, but was afraid to ask others.

Emotionally hurt, mentally exhausted, and majorly stressed, I had no idea how to handle the situation. I was stumped for ideas, yet, discussing anything of private import simply wasn't done, and, trust me, the library was no help. I was too embarassed to discuss my dilemma with family members, let alone, strangers. After all, this was the man who was supposed to *love* me, and therefore the situation was a thousand times more offensive. I would have been hard-pressed to even *find* a psychologist, counselor, or therapist, even if I knew what they were for, and could actually afford their input. As such, I wasted a lot of time worrying about *society*—instead of myself—just dangling in the wind, reacting to events, instead of making things happen. Confusion, resentment, frustration, and persistent sadness, were a constant reminder of my shattered illusions.

I had never even heard the word annulment, and divorce wasn't considered an option, due to family and cultural norms. A divorcée was considered beneath contempt and looked down upon by civilized society. I never expected to be divorced. Ever. I felt stuck, akin to touching a tar baby.

As many people come to the conclusion sooner or later, unquestioned rules of right and wrong relieve us of thinking. Sometimes strength means holding on, and sometimes strength means letting go. After much soul searching—reexamining my priorities and motives—I finally came to the realization that *marriage for life* is a theoretical, hopeful, and worthwhile goal to strive for, but in my case, it was not realistic. And no matter *what* my family, friends, neighbors, or colleagues might say, I did not want to continue living a lie. So, after much weighing of the pros and cons, I decided to give up this asinine charade, and obtain a divorce.

And told him so.

Chuck's reaction was not even in the realm of what I considered a possibility. With demented Charles Manson eyes, he dispassionately explained in gory detail, that he would *kill* my whole family if I ever left him, with weapons prominantly mentioned. And by this time, he had shown enough disturbing features of his personality, and displayed enough weird behavior, that I thoroughly believed him. I was shaken to the core. My marriage became a kind of indentured servitude, with all the romance of a gynecology examination.

Years later, I realized that the interesting point in his position was that he did not threaten to kill *me*. It would have been a forgone conclusion that I would duke it out, toe-to-toe, and fight to the finish in such a situation.He probably knew that if I ended up in the hospital, *he* would end up battered and broken in the bed next to me. Being a coward and a manipulator, Chuck didn't want an opponent, so trying to scare me with bodily harm was not the way to go; but threatening my family had definite possibilities. Although brave for myself, I feared for my family, and took the bait: hook, line, and sinker.

When I approached the police with my problem, I was told that it was a "family matter," and they couldn't get involved. Threats weren't against the law. They couldn't intercede until something physical actually happened. I found this lack of police support disheartening. So, I made the conscious choice to stay in the marriage, thinking not if, but *when* the violence actually happened, it would be too late, and one or all of my family members could be dead. I could see no way out of my predicament, with no alternative options. At that point, I took what I considered a permanent residence in the Twilight Zone.

Experts tell us that women who are held captive are rendered so by economic, social, psychological, or physical force.[2] Fitting this pattern, my complete and total enslavement was brought about solely through threats and intimidation. Even so, I became the same as other hostages, political prisoners, concentration camp inmates, religious cult members, and battered women. Although each situation is unique to the individual, research clearly shows that all are remarkably similar.[3] And like Tigger, I thought I was the *only* one.

The methods employed included techniques of disempowerment and disconnection, through the systematic, repetitive infliction of psychological and sexual trauma. Such methods were designed to instill terror and helplessness, and they worked, as Chuck began administering misery on the installment plan. Although it took awhile for me to realize what happened, the cumulative effect was that I was slowly cut off from all other relationships, and effectively made a prisoner in my own home.[4] The blinds were always closed, my friends were subtly persuaded to not return, the phone was for outgoing calls only, and so on. Gradually alienated and isolated, I didn't see the pattern until it was too late. I felt like a figure in an Edward Hopper tableau.

The sexual violence was actually used infrequently at first, but nevertheless, it kept me in a constant state of extreme duress. I knew that my family's lives depended upon my complete and total compliance, and as such, I was forced to violate my own principles.[5] Perversion and deviance were words I learned about firsthand, the hard way. Without getting into excruciating details, suffice it to say that I was coerced into sexual practices in which I endured a great deal of humiliation and demoralization, not to mention pain. First, he insisted that I shave my pubic hair, assuring me that if I didn't do it, *he* would. Since I didn't want him anywhere *near* me with a razor, I complied. Besides being embarrassing, it was time-consuming, a total and complete bother, and it itched. Apparently, I wasn't *young* enough for him.

Whenever Chuck would place a blanket on the living room floor, I knew I was in for another disgusting and degrading experience. It turned out that he couldn't handle the missionary position, as he wasn't, uh, up to the task; for lack of a better expression, he couldn't complete the evening, as he didn't seem to be a finisher. Instead, he had bizarre, medieval, sexual inclinations—involving instruments, bottles, and the like—after which I always felt bent, folded, stapled, and mutilated. He was into some heavy S and M, being light years beyond different, as twisted as a doorknob. His personal role model turned out to be Fatty Arbuckle. *Who knew?*

Feeling dirty, both inside and out, my Snow White image was tarnished; so I worked hard to be Spic and Span sparkling clean—stain free to the core—by taking two baths a day. *Rub-A-Dub-Dub.* This lasted for years, and I never even questioned the need for such behavior. Freud would have had a picnic. Another side affect that developed was a high tolerance for abuse and pain, as one more bruise hardly mattered one way or another. I became utterly used to it. Now that I had some physical evidence, however, I contacted the police again. You can imagine how uncomfortable *that* was. Outnumbered and surrounded, engaging such a totally macho culture made me extremely nervous. After all, women weren't really police officers in recognizable numbers, until the late eighties and early nineties. My shameful secrets were not something I wanted to openly talk about. When I forced myself, I was too embarrassed to give eye contact, looking only at the floor, which didn't help my credibility, I'm sure. It was a most intimidating experience, confronting an endless succession of contempt, disbelief, and outright hostility.

"Uhhh, that's highly unlikely," one unsympathetic officer remarked, giving me a *You've got to be kidding* look, after I haltingly presented my case. His coworkers sneered, and rolled their eyes, making rude remarks at my improbable story, clearly convinced that I was either looking for attention or trying to get back at my husband for some minor reason or another. All I got for my efforts was a trainload of indifference.

Apparently, it couldn't be proven that my wounds and scars were not self-inflicted, although no one expressed an interest in actually *looking* at them. I could logically see how they might misinterpret vaginal scarring as being self-induced, but deep scratches and cigarette burns on my *back?!* I don't think so. The angles and the pressure applied would have been totally different. And bite marks? (*Grandmother, what big teeth you have!*) Even a cursory examination would have revealed that those were not *my* teeth prints. However, it couldn't be proven that I wasn't a *willing* participant (a classic he said/ she said situation, a simple case of my word against his). The policeman sounded so accusing as he questioned my credibility. My complaints were considered too minimal to pursue; the facts and my scabs were conveniently ignored, and I was all but called a liar. My tale of woe was apparently too farfetched to be taken seriously, engendering raised eyebrows and fishy stares all around.

It became abundantly clear that no help would be forthcoming, when I continued to hear the words "family matter." Now I ask you: Why were criminal acts *not* considered to be criminal when they were perpetrated against family members? Why were strangers considered to be more important than loved ones? It just *never* made sense to me (a rose is a rose is a pansy). The laws were definitely repressive to women,[6] and I dispaired of them ever changing, certainly not soon enough to do *me* any good. I gave up all hope for rescue from the police or the courts.

Instead of channeling all of my anger at Chuck, I again displaced it on society: *Why didn't anyone tell me that sex hurt so much?* I questioned. *If young women knew of all the pain involved, they would never get married, there would be no children, and civilization would cease to exist as we know it.* I felt extreme anger at everyone, who helped to perpetrate this lie of omission upon girls and young women. To say that I was unsophisticated, is putting it mildly.

Over a period of time, the pain became so intense that I couldn't sit down without difficulty. I finally went to see a doctor, which I had heretofore avoided like the plague, given my prudish background. In a climate in which women were devalued and always considered at fault (suggestive clothes, vivid make-up, come-hither looks, sexy walk, "always asking for it"[7]), I was at a loss as to how I could share my sense of stigma and defilement. Finally, screwing up my courage, and blasting through the sexual taboo, I revealed my confidences. It was hard to even find words to *name* my experiences. The words *rape* and *implements* made me feel not only used and violated, but dishonored in the extreme. It was shameful enough to even *think* about, and I didn't want those words attached to me in any way, shape, form, or fashion. Upon hearing my complaints, through hiccups and tears, this elderly man's comment was—and I kid you not: "You made your bed, now lie in it." Mr. Empathy. I received no sympathy, no support, and no suggestions or medical advice, whatsoever. Not only was it an extremely embarassing experience, but it did not help matters, and it cost me sorely needed money. In addition, it put me off doctors again, for a number of years.

I had no one to talk with. I would have welcomed companionship with Elwood P. Dowd's 6 foot 3 inch invisible rabbit (from the movie *Harvey*) if given the chance. Much later, in yet another effort to retain my sanity, and get out from under the suffocating fear, I opted to take psychology courses at the local university (teachers are required to take classes, to keep their skills up to date). While taking an Abnormal Behavior class, I first heard the term *psychotic schizophrenic*. Imagine my surprise when the *classic behavior* presented was exactly the same kind that Chuck had been recently displaying.

For instance, on several occasions, Chuck loudly maintained that the *problem* with our marriage was my *wardrobe*. So he would announce that he was going to rip my clothes into shreds, to save our relationship. At which point I would physically charge into him, holding him away from the closet doors, in order to save my clothes. After all, how could I work and bring home a paycheck, if I didn't have anything to wear? A pushing and shoving match would then commence, with us wrestling around, until he got tired of the effort. Sometimes, late at night, when he was in such a mood, I would sleep on the bedroom floor, with my back against the sliding closet doors, so I could jump up and protect my clothes, if need be.

Then one night, after he started the same routine again, he suddenly reversed his position, saying, "No! I'm *not* going to rip your clothes up! I'm not going to *rip* your clothes! People would think I was *crazy* if I ripped up all your clothes. They would think that I was having some kind of *fit;* that I was out of *control,* or something. No! I want everyone to understand that I'm *serious* about our love. So I'm going to take these scissors, and carefully *cut* your clothes into little squares." (How's that for logic?) Brandishing sharp scissors in his hand did not have a calming affect.

While the rest of the class was laughing hysterically about similar examples, it seemed I could hear the distant Dopplered echo of a train. I was stunned to realize that Chuck's strange behavior not only had a name, but was formally recognized as a mental illness. This course had revealed a truth that I should have tumbled onto much sooner: Chuck was not just *sick,* he was *certifiable.*

Schizophrenia,[8] I learned, is an illness of severely distorted thinking and behavior, in which symptoms such as delusions, hallucinations, and disorganized speech are often present. Paranoia rules, and those who have the condition experience *untrue,* unshakable, unsupportive, fixed beliefs. Chuck's heroes were gangsters in general, and in his delusional state, he was convinced that he was a hit man for the mafia. Definitely a psycho: no two ways about it.

Understanding exploded in my mind like Fourth of July fireworks. Small incidents suddenly began to make sense. For instance, while Chuck was married to me, and had the appearance of being normal, his relationship with his mother went basically unchanged. She couldn't, or wouldn't, relinquish her maternal role, and refused to let go of her last child. So she continued to wash and iron his clothes, among other things. I consciously excused her behavior as simply her need for a reason to get up in the morning, and to continue being useful. In addition, consumed with pent-up anger, I was more than willing to let her do his dirty laundry. I figured that I had enough to deal with: the grubby givens of each day. Besides, I abhor housework. Martha Stewart, I'm not! Therefore, I did not complain, nor did I try to change the situation. It was a Norman Bates sort of place.

One day, I had to drive him to a dental appointment for major root canal work. I didn't even know Chuck was having problems with his teeth, as his mother had made the appointment for him. I was expecting a wait of several hours duration, and settled in with a big, fat book, in the waiting room. Apparently, he was all set up in the dental chair, when the dentist told him that he was going to use sodium pentothal. Chuck leaped out of the chair, strode into the waiting room, and rushed me outside. He kept shouting that "truth serum" was being used.

"*So?*" was my immediate response. "What kind of secrets could you possibly have, that anyone *else* would be interested in?" I was thoroughly irritated with this turn of events. I assumed he was afraid of the possible pain involved, and was just using the knock-out drug as an excuse. *What a big baby,* I groused, to myself, of course. Wrong again! Not only did he have fantasy secrets, but real-life secrets, as well.

Chapter 2:

PERSONAL APPLICATIONS

When involved in a relationship, check out these warning signs for potential stalkers:*

(24) Is an unstable job history evident? A strong work ethic is not high on a stalker's list; career-related ambition and accomplishment are not personal goals. Stalkers have difficulties reacting to normal stress, and may consequently perform poorly, having troubles on the job: showing up for work late, expending little effort, displaying a negative attitude, and the like. There may be serious performance incidents on record, as well as documented insubordination, since stalkers have a problem with authority figures. Although they typically have more education than most law-breakers, they often work at jobs that are menial, that are lacking in respect, and offer little opportunity for advancement.[9] Elevated rates of unemployment or underemployment allow more time to plan and execute stalking behavior, enabling them to become full-time professional stalkers,[10] since their crimes are premeditated.

(25) Are unsuitable role models obvious? Who are this person's sacred idols? Who has been promoted to demigod status? If Bonnie and Clyde, Jack the Ripper, Lizzie Borden, Bluebeard, Ivan the Terrible, Stalin, Eichmann, Pol Pot, Jeffrey Dahmer, or Hannibal Lecter, represent his/her

---

*NOTE: Since many abusers graduate to become stalkers, a number of the signals for domestic violence are the *same* as those for stalkers. Understand that while one person may display only a few of the symptoms, another may exhibit many. Be alert for red flags. Attention and caution are the watchwords.

heroes, get out fast. This is one reason that bosses ask potential employees to name their personal heroes.[11] Don't just assume that your friend will value the same people you do. (Whereas Chuck's heroes were gangsters in general, and Fatty Arbuckle in particular, my sheroes were Wonder Woman, Susan B. Anthony, Eleanor Roosevelt, and other likeminded, inspiring people. Could we have been any further apart? It just never occurred to me to *ask*.)

(26) Is there a fascination with violent people in the news? Does this person justify the violence of others? Does he/she identify with the perpetrators? Is there a rush to defend their actions, whether knowing them or not? Any justification, defense, or identification with violent people is a sure tip-off to potential trouble.

(27) Domestic violence is not just one act that is quickly over—unexpected slammed doors, an uncommon outburst, or an occasional loud argument—but a prominent theme of power, control, and domination. It is a systematic pattern of physical, sexual, and psychological abuse.[12] Six million women are believed to be beaten in their homes each year, in the U.S. alone. That number is shocking enough, until you realize that The National Coalition Against Domestic Violence estimates that up to 90 percent are never reported.[13] And according to former U.S. Surgeon, General C. Everett Koop, "Battery is the single most significant cause of injury to women in this country."[14] Realize that commitment and masochism are not synonymous.

(28) A stalker's intimidation, promises, and threats to harm you or kill you, are initially meant to frighten you, to convince you of his/her power, and to control your behavior, rather than to hurt you. Although research differs on this issue, know that even though most threats are *not* followed through—he/she is favoring words over action[15]—the risk of violence increases with an articulated threat.

(29) In order to force a victim to toe the line, stalkers often direct their threats toward others: parents, family, extended family members,

friends, and even their own children.[16] It is an effective method. If someone is intimidating you in this way, seek help immediately.

(30) Oddly enough, research shows that threats about you, spoken to an uninvolved second party, are actually more serious than face-to-face threats.

(31) When threatened, do not show fear. Understand that the value of any threat is determined by your reaction. Stay calm. Do not become defensive.

(32) When threatened, do not make a counterthreat, as that only makes a bad situation worse. Do not make this a contest or a war of words. Take some advice from a fortune cookie: Never contend with anyone who has nothing to lose. Experts stress reacting calmly, silently asking yourself, "Am I in danger, right *now*, this very minute?"[17]

(33) Does there seem to be an irresistible attraction with weaponry? Weapons are important to stalkers and batterers, as instruments of power. They are often fascinated with weapons, beyond any reasonable explanation, such as hunting, collecting antiques, or going to historical reenactments. They consider guns, knives, and blunt instruments to be suitable for intimidation and control,[18] where bombs are more likely to be seen as weapons of revenge. They talk about weapons, and often collect them. Do you see evidence of such a fascination with weaponry, such as magazines, books, posters? Know that weapons are used in 30 percent of domestic violence incidents.[19]

(34) Does he/she overlook and override other people's feelings? Does this person lack empathy or concern for the welfare of others? Can he/she identify with others? Is *any* kind of social consciousness apparent? Does he/she show signs, expressions, or words that express remorse? Or does this person lack a sense of guilt?

(35) Paranoia, the belief that everyone is against or conspiring against one, is characteristic of stalkers. Does this person project strong feelings onto others, with no evidence of such emotions?

(36) Does this person need to be in charge? Stalkers often had a chaotic upbringing, which explains their compulsion to dominate. Is this person a control freak? Does he/she tell you what to do, what to say, what to wear? Does he/she seek to impose ideas, rules, and choices upon you, attempting to control your activities, purchases, and outside friendships? Know that it isn't love if you can't express your ideas and feelings freely.

(37) Do you feel smothered? Does he/she guard you like a rottweiler? Does he/she demand that you account for your time, in an accusing tone? Is he/she suspicious of those you spend your time with? Does this person expect you to prove your loyalty by sacrificing all other relationships? Is he/she out to destroy your ties with others? Does this person expect you to give up your beloved pet(s)? If nothing else, any of the above serve as a revelation of selfishness and deep problems. Know that possessive attention is not a sign of passionate love. Do not feel flattered or comforted by this excessive interest and domineering behavior. When attention is too insistent, it pushes loved ones away. One does not aid love by depriving it of oxygen,[20] as he/she simply strangles the life out of the relationship.[21] Again: It isn't love when another can't give you the space to make your own decisions, express yourself freely, and live your own life. Understand that social isolation is the most effective method of control. (Listen to B.B. King's rendition of "Don't Open the Door.") Realize that a batterer crosses the line and becomes a stalker when overpossessiveness, excessive monitoring, and constant surveillance enter the picture.

(38) Animal cruelty is another red flag to watch for. Stalkers have little use for animals, and can torture or kill them for no reason. (Chuck would aim the car at dogs or cats on the road.) Does this person have pets? How does he/she treat your pets? How does he/she treat animals in general? According to experts, cruelty to animals is one of the strongest signals of danger. There is a definite link between cruelty to animals and other forms of violent or antisocial behavior.[22] (My

friend's husband shot and killed her three cats, and promised that her horses were next. She fled the ranch with her two children, and no money whatsoever, leaving their belongings and vast property behind. All these years later, he continues to stalk her.)

(39) Stalkers and batterers are often seen to be chronic failures in sexual situations. Know that rape is a regular form of abuse in approximately 50 percent of violent relationships,[23] and less than one-in-ten is reported.[24] Understand that sexual assault at home (in marriage or a committed relationship) is no different than acquaintance rape, date rape, street rape, or any other violent crime.[25] Rape is a three-pronged physical, psychological, and moral violation of the victim.[26] It is an act of control, a means in which to gain power, to punish, and to inflict pain.

(40) Know that people do not rape because they can't find a willing sex partner. Their goal is not an expression of affection, desire, or love, in any way whatsoever. Rape isn't sex. A rape is meant to hurt and degrade; it is an act of violence, pure and simple. It is about hatred, humiliation, and terror.[27] According to the U.S. Department of Justice, someone in the nation is sexually assaulted every two minutes.[28] One out of every six American women have been the victims of attempted or actual rape,[29] and one in every ten rape victims are male.[30]

(41) Mental health practitioners tell us that many sexually assaulted women have difficulty even *naming* their experiences,[31] much less describing them. So the first task of any consciousness-raising is to actually use the proper words: rape, sodomy, and so on.[32]

(42) Betrayals by family and friends are doubly damaging, more so than assaults by strangers, since it violates the victim's sense of trust, safety, and love.[33] It is reported that over half of all rapes are assaults by those who know their victims,[34] while the U.S. Bureau of Justice Statistics places the number closer to 68 percent.[35] Call a rape crisis hotline, or visit a rape center for services, such as the Long Beach local SACA: Sexual Assault Crisis Agency[36]. Find a shelter that will comfort

you, and detoxify your sense of defilement, shame, and stigma.[37] Shelters are where you will find safety, guidance, support, and understanding.[38] Join a support group or get individual counseling.

(43) It is reported that rape survivors have more nervous breakdowns, more suicidal thoughts, and more suicidal attempts than any other group.[39] So it's important to seek support, whether you think you need it or not.

(44) Does chronic lying seem to be a pattern? A stalker is deceitful, and lies, even when no gain is involved. Is this person into serial exaggeration, needlessly embellishing or embroidering stories? Does he/she deliberately misinterpret, slant, or change the facts to make him/herself look good?

(45) Stalkers tend to experience mood swings, even without alcohol or drugs in evidence. Be wary of anyone who is usually moody, sullen, depressed, or angry about something. Is there a chip on his/her shoulder? Are petty annoyances cause for WWIII? Do you spend a lot of time anticipating this person's moods?

(46) Does this person minimize abuse, or act like it never even happened? Stalkers and abusers have no conscience when it comes to hurting others. Realize that violence is a process evolving over time: progressing steadily from unkind remarks, to minor faultfinding, to harsh criticism, to intermittant abuse, to heavy abuse, to severe attacks, and sometimes death. It began *long* before you two met, and will only get worse. Experts remind us that violence is always the *choice* of the person doing the hurting.

(47) It is not uncommon for victims to blame themselves in stalking or abuse situations. Since no one wants to feel helpless, if you believe you may have, in some minor way, caused or contributed to what is happening, then you might think that you can also make it stop.[40] Understand that with most stalkers, it is the *first* contact that cements and focuses the target behavior.[41] Realize that you aren't at fault: you didn't want it, you didn't ask for it, and you definitely don't deserve it!

Dr. Sherry L. Meinberg 37

Victims of stalkers and abusers *are not to blame*, any more than the victim of a fire is to blame for using a stove, or the victim of a carjacking is to blame for driving a vehicle, or the victim of a burglary is to blame for owning a computer.[42] Likewise, spouses do not abuse their partners because the laundry isn't done, or the house is a mess, or the dinner is burned. They do it because they are in need of an excuse to behave violently.[43] In any case, that is not a fair penalty for bad choices.[44] Clearly, our society is consumed by victimhood. It is assumed that victims are to blame for being scammed, beaten, raped, or murdered; that somehow we *asked for it* or at least allowed it to happen.[45] Put the blame where it belongs: on the perpetrator. Granted, you may have provoked someone's anger. But you didn't provoke the violence. That was his/her choice, and his/her problem.[46]

(48) Victims recovering from stalking or battering experiences have often disowned their bodies. This splitting from your physical self, by freezing your emotions or numbing your body, may have been a protective device at one time, but you need to get reacquainted with the parts of your body that have been blocked.[47] Do whatever you can to reconnect: manicures, pedicures, and facials; bubble baths or mud baths; Swedish, shiatsu, or therapeutic touch massages; herbal wraps and scrubs; reflexology, and the like. Experts agree that paying attention to your body, and caring for your body, are essential to a high quality life.[48] Pamper yourself on a regular basis. You need and deserve to have your body well taken care of. Bodywork should not be considered a luxury for you, it must be standard.[49]

(49) Whereas most people strive to be productive, to be useful, to be of service, and to live a life that matters, a stalker will focus on one goal: *you*. This person will stay fixated on you to the exclusion of everything else, deriving much of his/her identity by feeling connected to you.[50] He/she is not devoted, but obsessed with you, spending a disproportionate amount of time thinking about you, talking about you, watching, following, and harassing you. Wishing to become the

most important thing in your life, by terrorizing you, this wish becomes true.[51] The resulting stalking pursuit becomes the center of his/her life. Is there an obvious fixation on you?

(50) Regardless of your input on the matter, does this person expect the relationship to last forever, and ever, amen? No matter *what* he/she does to you? Relationships change. Understand that you can never have a loving reciprocal relationship with an abuser. Do *not* feel trapped to a vow that your partner had already abandoned. Most religions today recognize that a violent marriage is the absolute opposite of a holy institution.[52]

(51) Your feelings of fear, distrust, and isolation may be compounded by the disbelief and incomprehension of family members and friends that you turn to for help.[53] They may accuse you of lying or overdramatizing your situation,[54] since they know both parties involved, and have a hard time believing the situation. Adding insult to injury, they may become hostile toward you, claiming that you are the reason the family is tearing apart. Don't shoulder the blame. Don't let their lack of understanding stop you from getting the care and nuturing you need. Check your newspaper's weekly Health Calendar for times and locations of public lectures, seminars, and free screenings. Find a local support group or crisis center. Take care of yourself.

(52) By the year 2000, women comprised only 10.9 percent of sworn law enforcement employees nationwide. Women held 13 percent of the jobs with those agencies of over 100 officers (up from one percent in 1972), and an even smaller 7.1 percent in agencies with fewer than 100 officers. A recent 2001 status report of Women in Policing shows slow gains and low representation of women in both large and small police agencies, over a twenty-eight year span.[55] A 2002 Feminist Majority report echoes those findings, due to bias in police hiring, selection practices, and recruitment policies, alongside that of widespread harassment encountered by women in law enforcement.[56] Even though the gains have been slow to include women in the police force, experts

suggest that your request to speak to a female officer can be easily granted in the larger cities. Ask.

Chapter Two Endnotes:
THE TIE THAT BINDS

1. Melody Beattie, *Codependent No More: How to Stop Controlling Others and Start Caring for Yourself* (San Francisco: Hazeldon, 1992), 131, citing Janet Geringer Woititz, "Co-Dependency: The Insidious Invader of Intimacy," in *Co-Dependency: An Emerging Issue* (Hollywood, FL: Health Communications, 1984), 55.
2. Judith Lewis Herman, *Trauma and Recovery: The Aftermath of Violence—From Domestic Abuse to Political Terror* (New York: Basic Books, 1992), 74.
3. ibid, 74-75.
4. ibid, Chapter 4: Captivity, 74-95.
5. ibid, 83.
6. ibid, 72.
7. George Lardner, Jr., *The Stalking of Kristin: A Father Investigates the Murder of His Daughter* (New York: Atlantic Monthly Press, 1995), 172.
8. American Psychiatric Association, *Diagnostic and Statistical Manual of Mental Disorders* (DSM-IV-TR), 4th ed., rev. (Washington, D.C.: American Psychiatric Association, 2000), 298-316; J. Reid Meloy (ed.), *The Psychology of Stalking: Clinical and Forensic Perspectives* (San Diego: Academic Press, 1998), Chapter 4: Psychiatric Diagnosis and the Offender—Victim Typology of Stalking, 69-84; Kim T. Mueser & Susan Gingerich, *Coping with Schizophrenia: A Guide for Families* (Oakland, CA: New Harbinger, 1994); Kayla F. Bernheim & Richard R.J. Lewine, *Schizophrenia: Symptoms, Causes, Treatments* (New York: Norton, 1979); Daniel G. Amen, *Change Your Brain, Change Your Life: The Breakthrough Program for Conquering Anxiety, Depression, Obsessiveness, Anger, and Impulsiveness* (New York: Three Rivers Press, 1998), 115, 126-127, 200, 217.

9.   Doreen Orion, *I Know You Really Love Me: A Psychiatrist's Account of Stalking and Obsessive Love* (New York: Dell, 1997), 38.

10. ibid, 182.

11. Frank Pacetta & Roger Gittines, *Stop Whining—and Start Winning: Recharging People, Reigniting Passion, and Pumping Up Profits* (New York: HarperBusiness, 2000), 191.

12. Meloy, ibid, 158, citing American Psychological Association (1966). *APA presidential task force on violence and the family report.* Washington, DC: Author.

13. Dawn Bradley Berry, *The Domestic Violence Sourcebook* (Los Angeles: Lowell House, 2000), 7.

14. ibid, 93, citing Patricia Murphy, *Making the Connections: Women, Work and Abuse* (Winter Park, FL: GR Press, 1993).

15. De Becker, ibid, Chapter 7: Promises to Kill, 103-118.

16. Herman, ibid, 77.

17. De Becker, ibid, 112, 169.

18. Berry, ibid, 245; Meloy, ibid, 17.

19. De Becker, ibid, 95.

20. David Wolpe, *Making Loss Matter: Creating Meaning in Difficult Times* (New York: Riverhead Books, 1999), 133.

21. De Becker, ibid, 207.

22. Lardner, ibid, 100, 104.

23. Berry, ibid, 8.

24. Herman, ibid, 73.

25. ibid, 31; Melita Schaum & Karen Parrish, *Stalked: Breaking the Silence on the Crime of Stalking in America* (New York: Pocket Books, 1995), 141.

26. Herman, ibid, 57.

27. Berry, ibid, 144.

28. Rape, Abuse and Incest National Network (RAINN) website http://www.rainn.org/statistics.html: RAINN calculations based

on "2000 National Crime Victimization Survey," Bureau of Justice Statistics, U.S. Department of Justice.

29. ibid, citing "Prevalence, Incidence and Consequences of Violence Against Women Survey," National Institute of Justice and Centers for Disease Control and Prevention, 1998.

30. ibid, citing 2000 National Crime Victimization Survey.

31. Herman, ibid, 67, citing M.P. Koss, "Hidden Rape: Sexual Aggression and Victimization in a National Sample of Students of Higher Education," in *Rape and Sexual Assault*, vol. 2, ed. A.W. Burgess (New York: Garland, 1987), 3-26.

32. The basic struggle with a rape victim's definition of the experience is reflected in the titles of many recent works on rape. Herman, ibid, 248, citing: S. Estrich, *Real Rape;* Koss, *Hidden Rape;* & Warshaw, *I Never Called It Rape.*

33. John Barnhill & R.K. Rosen, *Why Am I Still So Afraid? Understanding Post-Traumatic Stress Disorder* (New York: Dell, 1999), 36; Berry, ibid, 143.

34. ibid.

35. Violence Against Women. Bureau of Justice Statistics, U.S. Department of Justice, 1994.

36. SACA: Sexual Assault Crisis Agency, 1703 Termino Avenue, Suite 103, Long Beach, CA 90804. Office: (562) 494-5046; Fax: (562) 494-1741; TDD (562) 597-5121; 24 hour hotline: (562) 597-2002 or (800) 656-HOPE

37. Herman, ibid, 68.

38. Check out your city, county, and national shelter and resource center information. I first became affiliated with my local WomenShelter of Long Beach (besides English, this shelter offers Cambodian, Chinese, Hindi, Korean, Punjabi, and Spanish language help, as well as handicap services); Then I became involved at the county level in the Los Angeles Commission on Assaults Against Women (LACAAW) through Peggie Reyna, when she and I

were on several cable shows together. Her position is concerned mostly with Self Defense and with the Deaf and Disabled Services; and, I also became a Board Member of the national Survivors of Stalking (SOS), founded by Renee Goodale in Florida. Search their websites.

39. Herman, ibid, 50.
40. Orion, ibid, 66.
41. ibid.
42. Schaum & Parrish, ibid, 114.
43. Barnhill & Rosen, ibid, 85.
44. De Becker, ibid, 183.
45. Lardner, ibid, 172,
46. Berry, ibid, 247.
47. Beattie, ibid, 131,
48. Cheryl Richardson, *Take Time for Your Life: A Personal Coach's Seven-Step Program for Creating the Life You Want* (New York: Broadway Books, 1999), 157.
49. ibid, 161.
50. Berry, ibid, 245.
51. Lynda Edwards,"Trespassers of the Heart," *Details*, December 1992, 40.
52. ibid, 109.
53. Herman, ibid, 61.
54. Schaum & Parrish, ibid, 124.
55. National Center for Women and Policing, "The fourth annual 2000 Status of Women in Policing Survey," *Feminist Majority Report*, Vol.13, No. 2 (Summer, 2001), 8. The full report is also available online at www.feminist.org.
56. Elizabeth Koenig, "Gender Gap in Police Brutality: Men Cost More," *Feminist Majority Report*, Vol. 14, No.1(Spring, 2002), 4. Visit www.womenandpolicing.org for information.

*From ghosties and goulies, long-leggity beasties
and things that go bump in the night,
Good Lord, deliver us.*
—old Scottish prayer

Chapter 3:

WHEN THINGS GO BUMP IN THE NIGHT

Things escalated. My prolonged and repeated abuse became so bad, and my fear was so great, that my stomach began shaking. Constantly. I didn't like the feeling of being unable to control my own body. That seemed like the last straw, especially since I couldn't control anything else in my life. I felt overwhelmed with the burden of it all. It became readily apparent that, in order to function even minimally, I had to completely compartmentalize my life. Repression, dissociation, and denial, were now operating full-time with me. Indeed, the ordinary response to atrocities for *anyone* is to banish them from consciousness.[1]

My days and months went by in a fog of numbness; unnoticed, and unappreciated. I was totally out of touch. Each day slowly drifted into a monotonous repetition of the day before. Gradually, my world became constricted.[2] I couldn't deal with anything other than my trauma, as my survival instinct overrode my brain. I was not in the mood to notice my physical surroundings, seasonal changes, or the weather. I no longer took note of how light and shadows change colors, shapes, and textures. I was no longer interested in art, architecture, history, philosophy, or comparative indigenous cultures. I no longer went to movies, museums, or art galleries, nor followed the latest fads, fashions, and furnishings. I stopped reading poetry, working crossword puzzles, and listening to my favorite music. Food had no taste. My curiosity, which heretofore knew no bounds, dwindled to nothing. I refused to open books, and ignored my own research, which had always been a personal passion. I had lost the ability to recognize beauty or feel any sense of wonder or awe.

We moved. Our new apartment was not a place in which I felt centered, focused, or balanced. It was sorely lacking in decor, as well as creature comforts, being furnished in early monastic: no paintings, posters, photos, or mirrors, no sculptures, plump pillows, or plants. There was nothing ornamental about it whatsoever. No bright colors or patterns jostled for attention; no contrasting textures could be felt. No fresh flowers, scented candles, incense or potpourri competed for fragrance. No books or magazines were in evidence. There was no sparkle or glow, no zip or whimsy anywhere. In short, it contained not a shred of meaningful connection.

The furniture was utilitarian, with no personality whatsoever. Even though we had plenty of chairs, Chuck's favorite sitting space was on the living room carpet, his back rigidly pressed against the wall. From there, with all the charisma of a dead mackerel, he would stare at me in a trancelike state, with such absolute coldness and emptiness that my very being was chilled. It occurred to me more than once, that if looks could kill, it would be all over but the shouting. Although I never once saw him perspire, the wall behind him became permanently discolored: stained with his sweat.

My Bleak House, as I dubbed it, was utterly without song. To my way of thinking, complete and total silence should be reserved for those in cemeteries. As grim as the lives we led, our place felt lonely, alienating, and depressing. With a motel feel to it, our apartment held the sense that it was not fully lived in.

My world was getting narrower and narrower. I felt constricted, shut down, and sensory deprived. Talk about a straitjacket! Everything that had once spun my dials up to ten, were totally turned off, as I disengaged from everything I held dear. The lyrics, "These are a few of my favorite things," no longer played in the background of my mind. They seemed like a faraway memory, as if they had happened to a doppelgänger in another lifetime, on a different planet, from a distant galaxy, in an alternate universe. I did not lament their passing, however. I reasoned that Chuck had contaminated my life, and if I ever got out of this mess—if I ever found an escape hatch—I never wanted to remember him in connection with *any* of my interests. I wanted no reminders, no link whatsoever, between Chuck and the things I loved. So I let them all go by the wayside, withdrawing without a fight. In any case, I had no energy to pursue them.

The thing that really got to me was the fact that I had done this to myself. I had simply exchanged one kind of prison for another. I had walked right in, and shut the barred door behind me. I obsessed over this thought at great length, internalizing my rage. It filled me with self-loathing. I played endless self-recrimination and self-justification tapes through my head, the usual double feature. He was fatally flawed. *How could I not have seen that?* My self-esteem plummeted. It was difficult to reconcile in my mind the fact that although I lived in the most well-established democracy the world has ever known, I was putting up with conditions of dictatorship in my own private home. *How could this be, in this day and age?*

Although there was no quality in my life anymore, I had more immediate concerns. I was simply too busy juggling my thoughts about home and work, moving through each week in robotic motion. *One day at a time,* I reminded myself, as my goal for each day was simply to get *through* it. I didn't even know there was a group called AA, much less that it had a motto. Just staying alive—in a somewhat functioning state—was a major accomplishment. *What kind of existence is this?* I repeatedly asked myself, which brought about a rehashing of *why* I was allowing this to happen. I regressed to the simple bare survival stage; a life full of physical threats, danger, and inner turmoil. A great sense of sadness prevailed. I can testify that Abraham Maslow was right, when he argued that humans have basic physical and emotional needs that *must* be satisfied before we're able to pay attention to outside stimuli, social, or spiritual concerns.[3]

All of the gloom and doom and trauma that was taking place in my personal life came as a surreal counterpoint to my professional career, where I was a take-charge, in control, highly successful teacher, skilled in making things happen. Indeed, I was continually asked to be on the fast track for a principalship, during my first three years of teaching. My principal said that he would support my efforts, and be my mentor; and I was courted by those in administration.

My homelife, however, was in sharp contrast to my educational life, and was such a profound embarrassment to me, that I refused the offer (as if being a teacher should automatically mean that I was insulated from getting into such a predicament). To my way of thinking, teachers weren't supposed to make mistakes, or show weaknesses like terror or rage. We were to be seen as above it all. I felt that if anyone found out that my private life was such a troubled mess, it would reflect poorly on my confidence and my intelligence. I would be revealed as bad, defective, and inferior. How could anyone with any *brains* get into such a quagmire? And even worse, it might very well torpedo my entire career. So, ashamed and self-blaming, fearing disapproval, ridicule, and rejection, I let that chance of a lifetime slide. Eventually, my superiors stopped offering their plum prize.

Whenever I went to work, by an extreme act of will, I developed the capacity to mentally wall off my home situation from ordinary consciousness, so that I could actually teach. I became adept at altering my consciousness through minimization, dissociation, and outright denial. Deliberately putting my fright and anger on hold, I would mentally click into teacher/earth mother mode. With this voluntary suppression of thoughts,[4] I could avoid my emotional distress,[5] and totally focus on my students and *their* needs. I was able to alter my reality enough that I could not only function, but function well. Since it was probably the only place where I felt a measure of safety, I gave it my best. After all, just because *I* was having my own private crisis didn't mean the whole world would have to suffer along with me.

The minute I got off the school grounds, however, my stomach resumed its jumping. I was so frightened. On several occasions, the tremors traveled down my leg, and I couldn't keep my foot solidly on the gas pedal, having a staccato affect. It felt very weird not to have conscious control of specific body parts. Even so, I clung to my daily tightwire balancing act, always teetering on the edge of a headlong plunge, conscious of the fact that there was no safety net below.

Into what circle of Hell have I descended? I often wondered, as I tried to shake off the feeling that too much was wrong in my world. I understood that one can learn to value harmonious emotions by first experiencing turbulent ones, but this was ridiculous. Tears were always alarmingly near the surface. It was clear that I needed a respite from the turmoil that dominated my thoughts. And it came, via a stranger.

While shopping one day, a man rushed up to me, and asked if I could use a part-time job at a well-known franchised gym. He said that I was "made" for the position, being the "perfect size, perfect shape, and perfect weight." And I *was,* thanks to a genetically endowed athletic ability and fifteen years of ballet. In addition, I had been conditioned through the combined efforts of the fifties culture and the advertising industry that one's looks were of *primary* importance, and that the outside presentation was of more importance than one's inner being. So I was cosmeticized to the nth degree; my hair was never out of place, and my wardrobe would rival that of a movie star. As such, I became a walking advertisement for the gym. Vanity, vanity.

Seizing this opportunity on the spot, I later explained to Chuck that it was a way to bring more money into the household (translation: more money for him to play the horses). In reality, I was opting for diversion. It was a way to evade him for another four hours a night, so I could be my usual upbeat self. My main way of handling stress, and keeping memories at bay, was to always be on the go—in perpetual motion, with the flurried activity of the Keystone Kops—while delivering edgy fast-talk, allowing few silences to intrude: the perfect avoidance technique. (Cue: Rimsky-Korsakov's "Flight of the Bumble Bee")

So now, with two jobs—and the compartmentalizing of my life—I could avoid actual contact with Chuck, as well as refrain from obsessing on the depths of my discomfort, for longer periods each day: times in which I could savor the delight of the moment, when I could laugh, learn, and engage in stimulating conversation. Events of my interior life rarely matched my activities.

Working at the gym took no effort whatsoever. I showed clients how to use the various machines, and kept track of how many sets they had accomplished each session. It wasn't brain surgery. Although I thoroughly enjoyed joking around with everyone, internally I was shaking my head in judgment, regarding the amount of weight some women had allowed themselves to accumulate. I just couldn't understand how they could let themselves go like that. I was so young. A little escapism worked wonders. I maintained an Alfred E. Neuman,""What, me worry?" attitude, while at my second job. "Whistle While You Work," became my theme song. Although always appearing social and gregarious, I obsessively guarded my privacy and my inner world, so my deepest issues and fears never showed on the surface. Because I jabbered on endlessly, radiating a perky, bouncy, upbeat delivery—seemingly open about anything and everything—my listeners thought they knew *all* about me (a happy bubblehead), which was just the way I wanted it. My continual shield of words[6] helped to keep me hidden. They protected me. Small talk deflected my exposure,[7] while at the same time, burned off stress.

I preoccupied myself with a thousand different matters to avoid thinking about what weighed so heavily on my heart, scattering my focus, and laying waste my energy. So work represented a little island of safety. Moonlighting became a habit, thereafter, and from that point on, I have juggled two or three jobs concurrently, whether I needed them or not. Old habits are hard to break.

Chronically traumatized, I became hypervigilant, anxious, and agitated, the only crack in my outward facade. An exaggerated startle reponse became obvious. Normal everyday sounds, such as the dryer buzzer, a door slamming, thunder, a car back-firing, something falling, sirens, or *any* loud or unexpected noise, caused me to literally jump and flinch. A flash of movement caught from the corner of my eye would cause me to gasp and jerk away, with raised arms to ward off blows, to avoid whatever might be coming my way. It was like having a real-live bogeyman forever sneaking up behind me. *Watch your back* became my motto, while I was feinting, and jabbing, and jumping at shadows like a crazed ninja. The feeling of urgency was overwhelming. My conditioned response happened so often, onlookers would laugh at my bobbing and weaving, saying, "Your nerves are shot, Sherry!" and words to that effect, never realizing the significance of what they were witnessing. I was constantly on guard, always on the cusp of crisis, moving instantly into an adrenaline rush, ready to fight or run. Potential doom and danger always seemed just around the corner.

Working longer hours, and sleeping less, I never got enough rest. Unable to relax, it took forever for me to fall asleep at night. My sleep patterns changed, and I became an extremely light sleeper, alert to the tiniest sound, causing me to awaken frequently. Sounds that I had heretofore merely found annoying, and could easily ignore, became a major problem. I simply could no longer tune out or adjust to repetitive stimuli: clocks ticking, birds singing, crickets chirping, traffic sounds, planes, beeps, bleeps, buzzes, whirs, chugs, hums, or white noise of any kind. Winken, Blinken, and Nod were nowhere to be found. Neither was the Sandman. I took to roaming aimlessly around the apartment in the dark. Insomniac city.

You need sleep to be normal, and I wasn't getting it. Eventually, of course, my deprivation resulted in low energy, fatigue, and colds, mixed in with headaches. My irritability and stress became the breeding ground for overreactions, losing perspective, and poor decisions. I lost all interest in my appearance. I began losing weight, and swam in my clothes. My bloodshot eyes—bruised by worry and fear—became permanently pouchy with dark half-circles, as I held that thousand-yard stare. I was unconcerned when my nail polish chipped, and I nervously began to tear at my fingernails, chewing my cuticles and nails to the quick, turning them red, inflamed, swollen, and sore. My bruises began showing in greater frequency; some were black and blue, some purple, and some were green and yellowing, as if I'd contracted a bad case of hepatitis, giving me the look of an odd patchwork quilt. I felt like a circus freak on display, and took to wearing long-sleeved blouses and dresses.

I began hearing comments like, "What the hell have you done to yourself?" Ask me: *Did I care?* So much for the importance of keeping up appearances. Anyway you viewed it, I was not at my best. I looked a little frayed around the edges, showing that washed-out, bottomed-out, burned-out feeling. I felt shaky, shabby, and double ugly, with a seemingly permanent role in a Grimm's fairy tale. It's a good thing that the gym went bankrupt when it did, because that probably saved me the further embarrassment of being fired. I no longer looked like the perfect *after* poster girl representing the company. I was a physical mess.

I could see questions arising in other's eyes, some showing concern, while others glistened with a need for all the sordid details. Only a few actually inquired about my bruises. Of course, I lied through my teeth. I just didn't want to talk about it. I was determined not to wimp out: no moaning, groaning, complaining, or carrying on would help matters. I am not the type to cry in public. After all, if the *police* couldn't help, what could anyone else do?

And then there came a time when the Night Train chugged into my life, and my vaguely threatening anxiety dreams graduated into full-blown nightmares. Heretofore, the dreams of my youth had been beautiful, life-enhancing experiences, from which I awakened renewed, refreshed, and revitalized. Now the creepy-crawly terrors of the night took hold, and I slid into the world of Hieronymous Bosch. Later, I dreamed a series of operatic dramas, including voice-overs, flashbacks, and fantasy sequences—two or three each night—in which I was *murdered* in the culminating scene. Each in a different manner. By Chuck. These dreams were brilliantly intense and colorful, with accompanying sound effects, while the disturbing strains of Chopin's Opus no. 35 ("Marche Funebre"), played solemnly in the background: Dum, dum, da dum, dum, dum, dum, da dum, da dum. It was all too gothically spooky.

Although each murder was creatively different from the next, the final scene was *always* the same. My coffin was slowly lowered into the ground, and after thumping to a stop, I could hear the dirt shoveled in on top of it: thud, thud, thud. Jolted wide-awake, freaked out and jittery, with my heart hammering wildly in my chest, a warped recording of "The Worms Crawl In" ominously scratched into my awareness. Of course, with 31 flavors of fear coursing through my mind, I was afraid to go back to sleep. It was most disturbing. *Wasn't it enough that my days were a shambles?* I continually asked myself. As my existence seemed barren beforehand, it simply didn't seem fair to add nightmares to the mix.

So, now I had something new to stew about: *What was the message I was missing here? What was this repeated nudging from my neural wiring all about? What was the night side of my mind trying to say?* I suddenly had a real interest. Whenever I get involved with something, I *really* get involved. So, being a champion researcher, I plunged heavily into the subject of dreams, in a determined effort to scratch this mental itch. Like a junky on a binge, I absorbed every printed word I could find on the subject, reading dozens upon dozens of books and articles, in an attempt to understand my situation. It was writ so large you could have read it from the Skylab, but I ignored the obvious, of course. I found many items of interest. The most useful for my immediate purposes were:

(1) Dreams tell us not only what we want or desire, but what we *need*, as well.

(2) Dreams involve showing what we may not be seeing: directing attention to whatever we are most in danger of ignoring, or rejecting, in our everyday affairs.

(3) When our outlooks becomes too rigid or limited, dreams can give the other side of the picture.

(4) In a crisis, when our lives are threatened by outside circumstances, we will have the most vivid and meaningful dreams.

Aha! Eureka! Excelsior!

And, because one dream often throws light on another, experts suggest that far more satisfactory results can be obtained by trying to interpret them in *groups,* rather than looking at each one in isolation. Realizing that I had a problem of not seeing the forest for the trees, I decided to start recording my dreams in a diary, which I maintained for seven years thereafter.

Consciously, I hadn't a clue as to what was going on, but luckily, instinct and intuition lent their guidance. Thank goodness I was picking up the information subliminally, so I finally got the message: I was being sized up for a chalk outline. Chuck was *literally* plotting my imminent death.

Then I started reconsidering all of the near misses and the variety of unusual incidents I had encountered over a number of months. For instance, Chuck would drive like a maniac, taking foolish chances, getting to within inches of creaming dogs or cats. Was he hoping to scare me to death via a heart attack? He would speed and stop, speed and stop, repeatedly slamming me into the dashboard. (This was in the days before seat belts.) He followed this with a series of deliberate near misses. He would aim the car at a telephone pole, street lamp, parked vehicle, tree, or whatever, driving as fast and as close as possible, before jerking away at the last moment. Of course, the object in question was always on the *passenger* side. I just thought he was a *sicko*, playing chicken with inanimate objects, and didn't see a more sinister plot.

For a number of weeks, he worked at trying to make me think I was losing my mind, but he couldn't pull it off. I wasn't going for it. He'd make statements out of the blue, apropos of nothing, as if we'd been in the middle of a long conversation, or having no relationship whatsoever to what we'd actually been discussing, acting like I couldn't remember what had just transpired. *Give me a break, Wacko.* He finally gave up on that plan, since I couldn't be convinced.

One night, as I was getting out of the tub, always an intensely modest experience for me, he barged in and *unintentionally* bumped my radio into the bathwater. I was more concerned with the lack of privacy than the fact that I just missed being electrocuted. My brakes were tampered with on another occasion. And so on, and so forth.

Taking another look at the string of bizarre *accidents*, and putting them altogether, the light finally dawned. *Duh.* One needn't be a member of Mensa to guess his intentions, but I'm obviously a slow learner. As the cold breath of reality sank in, the background beat of a headache began, that rarely went away thereafter. I'd never been afraid of dying, but dying before my time, at the hands of another, was an entirely different matter. I realized that under the circumstances, caution was definitely in order from there on out.

At length, I accused him of planning to murder me. Breaking into a malevolent grin, Chuck happily answered in the affirmative, taunting me in exuberant glee, *"A wife can't testify against her husband!"* This sentence became a mantra to him. I heard that spousal privilege line over, and over, and over again, delivered with undisguised hilarity. *"A wife can't testify against her husband!"* Those seven words were etched on the front of my mind like the carvings on Mount Rushmore.

Chuck was very open about trying to get his hands on my insurance death benefits. Again, I knew I'd get no help from the police, because, after all, *planning* a murder didn't count. Truly, I understand that intentions don't always translate into action, but it seems to me that a *pattern* of behavior was apparent. He had a history. The intensity of his thoughts and schemes should say something. What was I supposed to do, just stand around twiddling my thumbs, waiting for the Grim Reaper? I always seemed to be circling the drain, racing toward oblivion, with one foot firmly planted in Forest Lawn. Continually anticipating my *final exit* was not condusive to good mental health. And trust me, the wedding vow phrase, "'til death do us part," came to have an altogether new meaning for me.

My life settled down to never-ending shades of abandon-all-hope gray: shifting from dove, to iron, to lead, to zinc, to dull pewter, to battleship, in which I identified with Ansel Adam's theory that the world could be represented in nine zones of gray. ("Life is made up of moments, small pieces of glittering mica in a long stretch of gray cement." Anna Quindlen) I called these my *gray mist* days, where everything was shadowy, unreal, and potentially threatening. I was always on the outskirts of panic. *What could I do with my anger?* I was having more than a slight upthrust of aggression and hostility, and had nowhere to go with it. I had no outlet.

The insurance situation left such a lasting imprint, that I have purposely refused to carry life insurance on myself since that unhappy experience well over forty years ago. Years afterward, when I was a corporate director for an international business, the president of the company suggested an increase in the board members' *individual* insurance coverage from one million to two million dollars, whereupon I considered resigning, rather than deal with the temptation issue in a logical manner.

Chapter 3:

PERSONAL APPLICATIONS

When involved in a relationship, check out these warning signs for potential stalkers:

(53) Some dangers are less obvious than others. Understand that your instinct and intuition speak to you long before your brain grasps the situation. Intuition is knowing without knowing how or why you know.[8] And it is now official: neuroscientists estimate that your unconscious database outweighs the conscious on an order exceeding ten million to one.[9] So pay attention to your survival signals, and listen to them without debate.[10] Does this person make you the least bit uneasy? Is there something that feels a little off-kilter, or not quite right about the situation? Do you feel apprehensive, suspicious, or threatened for seemingly no reason? Do you feel the need to be on guard, without knowing exactly why? Listen to your hunches. Pay attention to your gut feelings. Heed your private blinking yellow light, and proceed with caution. Your inner expert knows when you are in the presence of danger. Do not disregard your built-in alarm system. Do not minimize, deny, or ignore these warning signs. Trust, honor, and respect your inner signals. Always make the effort to identify your discomfort. Look for the hazard.[11]

(54) The Post-Traumatic Stress Disorder[12] found in war veterans is essentially the same as that for battered women, victims of child abuse, rape, and stalking in civilian life.[13] It was recognized in the 1970s, that the most *common* PTSD is not experienced by men in war, but by women in civilian life.[14] Eight percent of the U.S. population will have PTSD at some point in their lives: about 20 million people.[15] PTSD

results from massive trauma that causes intense fear, helplessness, or horror,[16] involving immense danger which could be life threatening. Traumatic events are those that are outside the range of normal experience: sudden, unexpected, and catastrophic.[17]

If you are still suffering from a trauma that happened years or decades ago, you can receive relief by getting some form of post-traumatic stress counseling. Call RAINN, the Rape, Abuse and Incest National Network, at 800-656-HOPE or 800-656-4673. This service will connect you to the crisis center nearest to you.

(55) The intensity of the trauma, the severity, frequency, and duration, determines who is likely to get PTSD. If your trauma was brutal, has lasted a long time, and has been repeated, know that you are at risk.[18] While the average person may experience two traumatic events in a lifetime, a person with PTSD may experience an average of twenty-three traumatic events.[19] When you can no longer absorb the trauma, your defenses will shut down until you can later deal with the experience. In war, when under fire too long, *every* front line soldier, in a state of continual stress, will eventually go into shell-shock or battle fatigue.[20] Research shows that between 200 to 240 days[21] exposure to combat conditions will break even the strongest person, resulting in extensive and enduring changes. How long have you been in your stressful situation?

(56) Everyone afflicted with post-traumatic stress disorder has symptoms from each of these three categories: over-arousal, reexperiencing, and avoidance/numbing.[22] They suffer from a combined generalized anxiety, as well as from specific fears. Are you always on the alert for danger? Are you in a constant state of vigilance?

(57) Is it more difficult for you to tune out annoying repetitive sounds, than it is for other people? Such distracting sounds can shatter your concentration, allowing your thoughts to bounce from pillar to post.

(58) Do you have an extreme startle response to unexpected or loud sounds? If you are suddenly surprised, do you seem to jump out of your skin? Is your reaction noticable to others?

(59) A common physiological reaction to constant trauma is a persistent shaking. Are you always in control of your body?

(60) Are you just going through the motions of living? Do you feel numb, detached, or disconnected from life? Do you sense that something is missing? Does your spirit seem crippled? Is an inner deadness apparent? Do you feel that a part of you has died?[23] This reaction is akin to that of a shell-shocked war veteran.

(61) A core symtom of PTSD is the effort to avoid anything related to the event(s): thoughts, people, feelings, or memories.[24] Psychogenic amnesia, or short-term memory loss, can occur when you are under too much stress. Are you experiencing a narrowing of consciousness? Do you voluntarily suppress your thoughts? Know that when you suppress anything, you are refusing to look at the situation because you fear your feelings about it. Are you afraid of something in your life? Suppression is an ineffective way to interact with your world. Be willing to see the truth in your experience. If your field of interest begins to wane, or your focus of life constricts, take steps to care for your physical and emotional needs. Show initiative by taking action: plan something for your future, and find things to look forward to.

(62) The altered state of dissociation sets atrocities aside. This keeps those overwhelming experiences walled off, or disconnected from ordinary consciousness.

(63) Are you working several jobs? Day or night, or both? What are you feeling? What are you avoiding?

(64) Has your sleep pattern changed? Does it take you longer to fall asleep? Do sleeping pills or tranquilizers give you little relief? Are you more sensitive to noise? Do you awaken frequently during the night? Are you afraid to go to sleep, in an unconscious fear of traumatic

dreams? Insomnia, agitation, and pacing have a direct link to prolonged trauma.

(65) Do specific sounds, smells, places, or insignificant reminders trigger terrible memories for you? Do you keep reliving your trauma? This will happen through the first few weeks following a traumatic event, but it should taper off within six months, and then slowly weaken thereafter. However, the longer you've been in the situation, the longer it takes to recover.[25] Expect persistent flashbacks and extreme reactions over the years. (A family friend was a veteran of the Vietnam war. The man was strolling through a mall, enjoying Christmas shopping with his entire family, when several balloons unexpectedly burst in unison. He immediately dropped to the ground, crawling frantically through the crowd, yelling, "Medic! Medic!" at the top of his lungs, finally hiding behind a huge cement planter. His family was embarrassed and dismayed, not knowing what to think, because the war had been over for twenty years. Certainly, the war had ended for the rest of the world, but not for many of its veterans.)

(66) Throughout history and around the world, ancient shamans, the Senoi tribe in Malaysia, Aboriginals, and native groups, as well as Freud[26] and recent dream researchers, all remind us that dreams are an important part of our lives. Jung also believed that dreams were messages from the soul, and could be premonitions, warning people of dangers and impending disasters, and even death.[27] Although you spend a third of your life sleeping, you only dream approximately two hours each night: four or five dreams a night, spending about 20 percent of your total sleep in the dreamstate, so by the time you turn seventy, you will have spent about six years of your lifetime in a dream state.[28] You dream more than one thousand dreams a year, whether you remember them, or not. Dreams are meaningful.[29] Pay attention to your dreams, and respect them. Keep a notebook or tape recorder, a flashlight, and some pens by your bed, to record your dreams in the night, or directly upon awakening. Immerse yourself in the subject of dreams. What is

each separate meaning? What is their collective message? Dreams are not meant to conceal, but to reveal,[30] and important dream messages will be repeated, in varying ways, until you finally get the idea.[31] Honor your dreams by paying attention, and gaining deeper insights into your fears, needs, and truths.[32] Calvin Hall, a dream research pioneer, said, "A dream is like a personal document, a letter to oneself."[33] So, take a tip from an old Yiddish proverb: "A dream which has not been interpreted is like a letter unread."

(67) Panic attacks, night sweats, and nightmares, with themes of danger and violence, are universal responses of chronic trauma, and may persist.

(68) Understand that you were doing your best in a no-win situation, and that it is normal to have deep feelings of guilt or self-blame. Know, however, that *both* are forms of revictimization, as you continue to inflict emotional pain and punishment on yourself. Don't feel guilty about feeling guilty.[34]

(69) It wasn't until 1995, in *People v. Carron*, that a stalker's *intent* could be considered by the court. In 1996, *People v. McClelland* ruled that a stalker's *prior history* became relevant and admissible in a trial. (Either or both of these laws would have helped me immensely from the sixties on.)

(70) Eighty percent of homicides are committed by those who are related to, or know, the victim.[35] Each year, it is estimated that at least fifteen hundred women are killed by a current or former husband, partner, or boyfriend.[36]

Chapter Three Endnotes:
WHEN THINGS GO BUMP IN THE NIGHT

1. Judith Lewis Herman, *Trauma and Recovery: The Aftermath of Violence—From Domestic Abuse to Political Terror* (New York: Basic Books, 1992), 1.
2. ibid, 42-47.
3. Abraham H. Maslow, *Motivation and Personality* (New York: Harper and Row, 1954, rev. 1971); Dan Millman, *Everyday Enlightenment: The Twelve Gateways to Personal Growth* (New York: Time Warner, 1998), 6.
4. Herman, ibid, 46, 87.
5. ibid, 42.
6. Deepak Chopra, *Unconditional Life: Discovering the Power to Fulfill Your Dreams* (New York: Bantam, 1992), 194.
7. David Wolpe, *Making Loss Matter: Creating Meaning in Difficult Times* (New York: Riverhead Books,1999),100-101.
8. Gavin De Becker, *The Gift of Fear: Survival Signals That Protect Us From Violence* (Boston: Little, Brown, 1997), 26.
9. Michael J. Gelb, *How to Think like Leonardo da Vinci: Seven Steps to Genius Every Day* (New York: Delacorte Press,1998), 160.
10. De Becker, ibid, 278.
11. ibid, Chapter 2: The Technology of Intuition, 25-41.
12. American Psychiatric Association, *Diagnostic and Statistical Manual of Mental Disorders* (DSM-IV-TR), 4th ed, text rev. (Washington, D.C.: American Psychiatric Association, 2000), 463-467; John Barnhill, & R.K. Rosen, *Why Am I Still So Afraid? Understanding Post-Traumatic Stress Disorder* (New York: Dell, 1999); Dawn Bradley Berry, *The Domestic Violence Sourcebook* (Los Angeles: Lowell House, 2000), 55-60, 93; Herman, *Ibid*, 119-122; Frank M. Ochberg, (ed.), *Post-Traumatic Therapy and Victims of*

Violence (New York: Brunner/Mazel, 1998); Melita Schaum & Karen Parrish, *Stalked: Breaking the Silence on the Crime of Stalking in America* (New York: Pocket Books, 1995), 129-131.

13. Daniel G. Amen, *Change Your Brain, Change Your Life: The Breakthrough Program for Conquering Anxiety, Depression, Obsessiveness, Anger, and Impulsiveness* (New York: Three Rivers Press, 1998), 90-91; Herman, ibid, 32.

14. Herman, ibid, 28.

15. Barnhill & Rosen, ibid, 17.

16. ibid, 23, 29.

17. ibid, 30.

18. ibid, 18.

19. ibid, 14.

20. Deepak Chopra, *Ageless Body, Timeless Mind: The Quantum Alternative to Growing Old* (New York: Harmony, 1993), 151; Barnhill & Rosen, ibid, 16.

21. Herman, ibid, 25, citing J.W. Appel & G.W. Beebe, "Preventative Psychiatry: An Epidemiological Approach," *Journal of American Medical Association* 131 (1946), 1468-1471, quote on 1470.

22. Barnhill & Rosen, ibid, 3.

23. Herman, ibid, 48-49.

24. Barnhill & Rosen, ibid.

25. Herman, ibid, 48.

26. Sam Keen, *Hymns to an Unknown God: Awakening the Spirit in Everyday Life* (New York: Bantam, 1994), 263; Sigmund Freud (translated by A.A. Brill), *The Interpretation of Dreams* (New York: The Modern Library, 1994); Sigmund Freud, (translated by James Strachey, in collaboration with Anna Freud, assisted by Alix Strachey & Alan Tyson), *On Dreams* (New York: W.W. Norton, 1989).

27. C.G. Jung (translated by R.F.C. Hull), *Dreams* (Princeton, NJ: Princeton University Press, 1974; C.G. Jung (translated by Richard

Winston & Clara Winston), *Memories, Dreams, Reflections* (New York: Vintage Books, 1965).

28. Salli Rasberry & Padi Selwyn, *Living Your Life Out Loud: How to Unlock Your Creativity and Unleash Your Joy* (New York: Pocket Books, 1995), 86. Chapter 7: Wake Up to Your Dreams, 86-98; Phyllis R. Koch-Sheras, Amy Lemley & Peter L. Sheras, *The Dream Sourcebook and Journal: A Guide to the Theory and Interpretation of Dreams* (New York: Barnes and Noble Books, 1998), xx.

29. ibid.

30. Barbara Hoberman Levine, *Your Body Believes Every Word You Say: The Language of the Body/Mind Connection* (Fairfield, CT: Aslon Publishing, 1991), 159.

31. ibid, 160.

32. Rasberry & Selwyn, ibid, 91.

33. Koch-Sheras, Lemley, & Sheras, ibid, xv.

34. Barnhill & Rosen, ibid, 82-84.

35. De Becker, ibid, 23.

36. Berry, ibid, 7.

…when sorrows come, they come not single spies
but in battalions.
—Shakespeare

Chapter 4:

A MATTER OF SOME URGENCY

Late one night, while speeding down the street, almost three years into this ghastly marriage, Chuck finally snapped. Big time. Acting crazy and disoriented, he informed me, in no uncertain terms, that it was to be *my* decision as to which family member he was going to kill: my mother, my father, my brother, his wife or new baby daughter, since it made him no nevermind. He was simply in a trigger-happy mood. *Do it or die*, his eyes suggested.

This was it! The time was now! He had finally gone off the deep end. When I shrieked that I *couldn't* make such a decision, he showed his displeasure by backhanding me, while shouting, "Make a choice!" Various colors exploded in my head, as my cheek and mouth went numb, and began to sting. Blood gushed from my nose, as it began to swell.

"Make a choice!" he chanted out of control, continuing to strike my face. The resulting bump on my nose is an indelible reminder of this experience. Although he was yelling right next to me, his voice seemed to come from a great distance, as if from the end of a long tunnel. "It's up to you! Make a choice!" Smack!

Without even consciously thinking about it—refusing to take further part in his mental derangement—I opened the car door to jump out. Unfortunately, he grabbed the back of my blouse. So there I was, with my right hand holding onto the car seat, my left hand holding onto the open door, and my feet dragging along the street pavement, as he continued yelling at me. Finally, my zipper broke, and Chuck lost hold of me, as I fell onto the street. Rolling over and over, I cracked my head. As a thousand excruciating pin-lights of pain lit up my brain, I momentarily blacked out. I revived after he managed to hit the brakes, and was roaring back in my direction, with tires squealing. As my brain alarm began blinking, *Condition red!* CONDITION RED! I shook my head to clear it. *Don't lose it,* I demanded. *Not now, not now.* Realizing that I had the life expectancy of a fruit fly, I finally understood the acronym FEAR: Fuck Everything And Run, as every functioning brain cell in my head screamed at me to vacate the area. Spinning into action mode, I jumped up, and ran for cover.

I crouched behind some bushes in front of a house, teeth clenched, neck craned, muscles rigid. My heart felt like a kettledrum. When Chuck didn't feel the expected bump as he rolled over the spot where I had been laying, he got out of the car, and looked underneath it, his expression a perfect blend of confusion and incredibility. I could almost see the question marks dancing above his head, as he stood up and slowly scanned the area, his features reeking of homocide. (*Come out, come out, wherever you are!*)

I was so scared, my chest heaved in great gasps of air, and I was certain he'd be able to hear the rasping of my breath if he got any closer. With an air of icy determination, he returned to his car to park it, as my panic reflex kicked in. I took that opportunity to flee: feet flying, arms pumping. My heart beat in triple time, as I hightailed it around to the back of the house, and pounded on the door. But in the quiet of the night, the noise seemed magnified a millionfold, and I knew Chuck could easily find me. So I left, and ran to the next backdoor. I hammered on the backdoors of numerous houses, but I was so spooked by the echoes, that I wouldn't wait for anyone to answer them. I was utterly freaked out of my mind.

At the end of that row of houses, I ran into an overly tall chainlink fence. My heart continued to throttle up, realizing that I was trapped, as a hundred thoughts streaked through my brain. My breathing was fast, hard, and becoming progressively more erratic. The phrase "Armageddon: The Final Frontier," neoned in my mind. I closed my eyes. *Slowly breathe in, breathe out*, I ordered myself, recognizing that as long as I was alive, I still had a chance to see another day. Digging below the terror for elements of rational thought, I hastily surveyed the area, and focused on the fence at ground level, where the dirt seemed somewhat uneven and disturbed. Upon closer inspection, I was elated to find a humongous hole directly underneath one section, resembling a tunnel to China, that had obviously been freshly dug by a very large dog. I was so thankful that no one had taken the time to fill in the crater. I didn't even have to *think* about it, as I automatically scrambled under the fence, and sprinted down another street. Seeing a light on in the last house, I headed straight for it. When I got to the front door, I grabbed hold of the door knob with one hand, as I began to knock with the other. Imagine my surprise as I went barreling through the unlocked door, right into a living room! My peripheral sight registered an older couple, with eyes round, mouths open, and faces blank with amazement, sitting on their couch together, watching TV. Hysterical at this point, I turned back, slammed and locked the door, sobbing, "Don't let him in! Don't let him in!"

Leaning against the door, and gasping like a landed fish, it finally registered that the couple was frozen in disbelief. Here was a totally wild-eyed stranger, *in* their house, unannounced. At length, with a scowl on her face, the woman slowly shuffled across the room. "Honey," she said disapprovingly, "put your clothes on," as she yanked my blouse up over my shoulders. *I beg your pardon?* This was the first indication I had that after my full-length zipper had broken, my blouse had fallen off, held only by the long sleeves which were simply hanging inside-out from my wrists. So I had been essentially running around the neighborhood with my bra on display. This bothered me more than the fact that I had been bleeding profusely. When I had shimmied under the fence, the blood mixed with the damp dirt, bark chips, and minced vegetation, forming a kind of mud, that clung to my body. I looked horrible: like an escapee from an insane asylum or some sort of swamp creature. No wonder they seemed reluctant to help.

It became immediately apparent that I was interrupting their entertainment for the evening. They were in the midst of watching the classic, "Red River," starring John Wayne, and I was causing them to miss part of the dialogue. I felt terrible to be intruding, yet I refused to go back outside; this place represented sanctuary to me. Not knowing what else to do, I sat down beside them on the couch, and as my pulse and breathing slowed, finished watching the movie. Of sorts.

Yippy-ti-yi-yay, I thought. *I need to circle the wagons around my life.* Clearly, I wasn't concentrating on the film, as silent tears blurred my vision, and I was alert to every little outside sound, straining to identify each potential threat. I was afraid that any minute, Chuck might crash in, and all hell would break loose. *There are no "Happy Trails" here*, I noted.

During one of the commercials, the woman gave me a washcloth and a Band-Aid, and pointed toward the bathroom. As I went through the door, I was frightened to see myself in the mirror. Yow! (*Mirror, mirror, on the wall...*) My face was Kabuki white, my eyes seemed to be popping out of my head in the manner of a cartoon character, and my tangled hair was in total disarray, giving me the look of Medusa. I thought it best to avoid the visual. I tried to wash off the blood, but the washcloth was instantly dyed red from the first wound I tried to clean. I felt terrible about ruining it. The only injury that was small enough for the Band-Aid to cover, was a place at the bottom of my thumb, about the size of a quarter.

Social training instilled from the cradle dictated that one should not inconvienence others for the sake of one's own personal comfort or ease. Since it was the middle of Sunday night, I didn't want to concern my parents with a late-night phone call, because I knew they had to get up early and go to work, both being teachers, as well. I had played the martyr role for far too long, so busy taking care of others' needs that I neglected my own. I just thought I was being *nice* and *considerate*. So I was thankful that this was a two-bedroom house, and that the couple offered me the extra room for the rest of the night.

Exhausted and overstimulated, I couldn't fall asleep, of course, as there was nothing to relieve the ache in my heart, and the tension in my body. In addition, I needed blankets, because I was shivering uncontrollably from the combination of cold and fear. But I couldn't even handle a sheet against my body, because of the weight on my wounds. I was simply too wired, as all ten thousand of my brain cells were listening intently to every magnified sound. Barely breathing, tracking with my ears, every fiber of my being was fixated on auditory input. When the tree branches scratched against the window screens, or the dogs from the surrounding properties started barking, my well-known hyper-imagination went into overdrive. I was convinced that Chuck was creeping around just outside the bedroom wall. Getting closer, and closer, and closer. I was stressed to the max.

In the midst of my terror, I marveled that I had been a willing prisoner all those months, to save my family members, and that Chuck had elected to kill one anyway. I couldn't quite grasp the fact that he broke his own rule. It just didn't compute. Why hadn't I realized, early on, that I was in an agreement with someone who couldn't be relied upon to honor it? How could I have trusted him to act normally? How could I have expected straight thinking from crooked and scrambled brains? I alternated between extremes: thrilled to be finally out of my predicament, but furious that I had been in this situation far too long.

Intermittently, I tried to use the bathroom. Unfortunately, that required that I pull down my pants, which were matted and stuck to my body. When I tried to peel them off, I fainted from the effort. Twice. The first time, I was surprised to find that I had slid down, when I awakened on the tile floor: the clue being the wide swath of blood left behind on the wall, looking like a macabre Rorschach test. The next time, I toppled into the tub, headfirst, my body drapped over the side. Although it represented a state of blessed anesthesia that kept me out of harm's way for a little while, I decided to leave the room. I was hurting too much, making too much noise, and might awaken my hosts. This convinced me to control my bladder by whatever means necessary. I was in agony.

Unbeknownst to me, Chuck got tired of looking for me, and went seeking my brother, instead. Knowing that Terry, his wife, and new baby, lived in one of the three apartment buildings next to the bowling alley, Chuck began his search. Looking in all of the attached parking lots for their car, circling around the front and sides of the buildings, he was scanning the area for a distinctive vehicle: a mint-green 1955 Thunderbird convertible hot rod. It shouldn't have been hard to find. It wasn't there.

Unfortunately, as he drove back up the alley, Terry was driving down the alley, returning from a late movie. Pleased to see Chuck, thinking that he thought enough about them to come over for a visit, he began rolling down the window. That happy thought was short-lived, however, as Chuck shouted that he had just *killed* me, and had come to kill them also. Shoving Maureen's head down, in anticipation of flying bullets, Terry stomped down hard on the gas pedal, and laid rubber through the parking lot. Pulling into the carport, he sent her running into their apartment, to lock herself in, and call the police. Being nineteen and hot-headed, he sped over to our parents' house, and grabbed his old hunting rifle. Mother freaked when she saw Terry load it, and storm off. She and my father also called the police, hurriedly dressed, and zoomed to my apartment.

Arriving at my place, he found the door already open. Chuck was calmly sitting in a chair, inviting him inside."Hey there, Terry, how *good* to see you! Come on in," he gestured, with a smile on his face, as if nothing in the world was wrong.

Upon seeing this odd behavior, Terry refused go in, suspecting a trap of some sort. "Where's Sherry?" he demanded. Chuck widened his grin. *"Where's my sister?"* Terry reiterated, as Chuck gave him a smile that should have put him on penicillin. After shouting back and forth for a bit, the first squad car pulled into the parking lot.

In a last ditch effort, still trying to lure him inside, Chuck matter-of-factly said, "Come on in, and I'll kill you." As Terry was about to enter, two policemen had slowly walked up behind him. Terry was happy to see what he considered to be backup, reinforcements coming to help him. Not so. Terry was knocked unconscious by the first officer, who upon seeing the rifle, surmised that *he* was the bad guy, and confiscated the rifle.

The police then engaged Chuck in conversation, who feigned perfect innocence and lied without compunction, spreading his hands in a practiced manner, palms up, eyes wide, saying that he didn't know *why* his young brother-in-law had come after him. He calmly explained that yes, he and I had had an argument, but that I had taken off in a hissy fit, so he didn't know *where* I was. He then attacked my family's credibility, *complaining* that my whole family was weird, and all this nonsense was finally getting to him. He just didn't know how to *deal* with them, he added, as my parents arrived on the scene. Of course, my mother and father were hysterical, seeing Terry on the ground, and not finding me anywhere. Their reactions fed right into the storyline Chuck had been fabricating, so it was easy to see who the officers believed. The good news is that they did not arrest Terry; the police released him to our parents' care.

Later, when Mom and Dad finally got home, they called all of my teacher friends, who got dressed, went outside to places they thought I might be, and literally beat the bushes. Here I had deliberately not called anyone—why put everyone in a tizzy?—and they were all out in the middle of the night looking for me anyway.

Then the phone calls to my parents started coming. Chuck just wouldn't let the situation alone. Everytime my mother or father answered, he used insulting and repulsive language, calling them foul names, taunting them by saying he had killed me, and there was nothing they could do about it. The minute they would hang up, he'd call again. Dozens upon dozens of calls came in, one after another, in a matter of minutes. My parents were afraid *not* to answer the phone, in case I was trying to call them for help. So they felt they had to endure his rantings.

Chuck's Academy Award performance had been so believable that the police actually became concerned about *my* crazy family. He had laid it on so thick, after Mom, Dad, and Terry had left for home, that the officers actually *believed* my father had a vast gun collection in the house, stockpiled with tons of ammunition, and that he had vowed to kill Chuck! The officers sped into the driveway, and rushed into my parents' house, with their guns drawn! My mother kept pleading with the police to listen to Chuck's vile and threatening phone conversations, and then they would know who to believe. On cue, the phone rang again, and she answered, immediately handing the receiver over. The first officer blanched, upon hearing such an explosive burst of obscenities, as he passed the receiver on to his partner, who had the same reaction. Both seemed stymied and unsure about the situation. Stunned into silence, they left shortly thereafter, shaking their heads in confusion.

Meanwhile, in my neck of the woods, centuries seemed to have passed before morning arrived. I slept fitfully, and awoke headachy and disoriented, unsure where I was, or why I was there. Every bone, every muscle, and every square inch of my body was shrieking. In addition, my brain cells seemed to be on strike, as it was too early to get my head in gear. I stumbled into the front room, just as the woman went off to work: *at the police station.* I still can't get over that fact. It seems that she was a dispatcher, and didn't consider my problem worthy of official attention. She probably dealt with similar situations all the time, just not inside her own house, on a Sunday night, her time off. *Kind of like a busman's holiday*, I surmised.

I called my school secretary, to inform her that I needed a substitute, and to pass the word on to a teacher friend that I wouldn't be going to our university class that night. I hung up too fast to get the message that everyone had been out looking for me earlier, and that they needed to know where I was.

Next, I called Terrell, my closest childhood friend (someone that Chuck had never met), to come and get me. I told her that I didn't know the name of the street, or the address, but I gave her directions. Since I obviously didn't express that this was a matter of some urgency, she leisurely took her daughters to school, and went to a couple of stores, before picking me up. The wait seemed to go on forever: oceans rose and fell, continents formed, dinosaurs died.

I planted myself on the front porch, because my lecherous host had blatantly suggested a romp-in-the-hay, and was staring at me with less than wholesome interest. I guess that once a Dirty Old Man has seen your bra and some bare skin, he thinks you *want* him. Sure. "You old perv," I muttered under my breath. Now his wife's initial reaction to me made perfect sense. *Horny ol' goat*, I huffed and puffed. As if I didn't have enough to deal with.

Upon her arrival, Terrell got out of the car to meet me, as I gingerly stood up from the steps to greet her. The pain was nauseating. She took one look at me, and knew that something had hit the fan somewhere. Putting her hand out in front of her like a traffic cop, she yelled, "Stop!" and hurried back to her car and took two Valiums. She brought me one, and when I refused to take it (never having heard of Valium before), she gulped that one down, also.

Figuring that my parents were at work, and not wanting to take the chance that Chuck might be waiting at their house, Terrell took me to her house. She immediately put me in the bathtub, to soak my clothes off. It was heaven, just to be able to use the toilet again. Then she cleaned my scratches, scrapes, and gaping wounds, putting some kind of salve all over them, applying gauze over that. When she was done, I looked something akin to a mummy. She dressed me in one of her voluminous muumuus, since all of my ripped and bloodied clothes had to be thrown away. I was so thankful for her efforts on my behalf, but don't remember if I expressed those sentiments at the time. Probably not, given my state of mind.

My shock was genuine and bone deep. I definitely wasn't thinking clearly about what to do next. Later that afternoon, Terrell and her husband, Bob, both suggested that I check into the hospital, but I didn't think that was necessary. "I feel fine, just fine," I said, taking the path of least resistance. And, discounting the ache in my head, back, arms, shoulders, chest, stomach, and legs, I *was.* "Fit as a fiddle, top-drawer, first class, thank you very much," I assured them, tightening my jaw so they wouldn't see the pain, while nodding to show how fine I was. "Especially since you've taken such good care of me," I added for good measure. Truth be told, I'm not a fan of hospitals. The sharp smell of formaldehyde alone sends me right over the edge. As such, I will not willingly place myself in such unpleasantness. "I'm all right. I'm *fine,* really." I was a million miles from fine, unless you consider the acronym: Fucked up, Insecure, Nervous, and Emotional. But I felt fortunate just to be alive.

I still had no idea that everyone was worried about my whereabouts. I just wanted to lay low, where Chuck couldn't find me. So, I stayed overnight in their guest bedroom. I was unaware that my brother had spent Monday night, as well as Tuesday night, on the CSULB campus, looking for me and interviewing other students, or that friends and family members were frantically searching for me.

Tuesday afternoon, my mother finally figured out where I was staying. Blowing in like a hurricane, she was understandably furious that I hadn't called. When she finally wound down, she took a good look at me, and said, "Get in the car. We're going to the hospital." *Excuse me?* I'd had enough of being ordered around, and I had determined that I was never again going to do anything until I was damned good and ready. I really wasn't able to discern the difference between loving concern and controlling behavior at that point. My brain seemed to be functioning with all the agility of sludge.

Since I had already gone through this conversation with my friends, I was adamant about not going, and stuttered and sputtered as we argued a bit. Then, in a voice of reason, she said, "You know, Sherry, it will help you get a *divorce*, if you have to stay in the hospital." Aha! With those magic words, I was out the door in a flash. My friends piled in their car, trailing ours.

Although I was slowly shuffling along, stiffly and carefully, we all walked through the hospital door together. The nurses, as well as those manning the check-in counter, took one look at me and yelled, "Stop!" "Freeze!" and "Don't move!" in unison. "Hold it right, there!" another nurse yelled, as she quickly pushed a wheelchair up to me. I couldn't figure out how everyone knew that *I* was the prospective patient. I kept protesting that I was fine, and that the staff was overreacting. Disregarding my objections, they put me in the chair, and wheeled me away, leaving my mother to fill out the forms, and my friends to explain the situation.

Of course, it turned out that I was still in shock: my eyes seemed to be bulging out of their sockets like Ping-Pong balls. The hospital personnel insisted on checking me very carefully, to make sure I didn't have broken bones or other injuries, and they administered a number of x-rays and tests. One doctor didn't like the look of my brain x-rays—concussions are tricky—and I was told I would probably have a two week stay for observation, so he could keep an eye on whatever it was that was bothering him. It all sounded like so much mumbo-jumbo to me. "Oh," I said, intelligently. I definitely wasn't processsing things clearly.

Finally, their pushing and prodding over, I was placed in a room with three other patients. A veritable parade passed by to visit them, rattling on like castanets. There was a sense of barely restrained frenzy in the air. Words sprayed around the room like a lose high-pressure hose, while the volume constantly changed. But all meaning was lost, as everyone appeared to be speaking some unfamiliar language: Old Norse, Gaelic, or Frisian. Raucous laughter, snippets of gossip, and good-natured teasing came whirling across the beds like a confetti tornado.

What I needed was a place to lick my wounds in private; to be comforted in quiet with a good slug of endorphins. I was tired. Bone tired. I found it hard to concentrate, much less, rest, what with all the merry-making. Especially, when those around the far bed began drinking champagne, and clinking their glasses together. I don't know *what* they were celebrating, but they were sure happy. I knew on some level that I should be celebrating with them; rejoicing that I was convalescing, instead of decomposing. But no, not yet. I wondered if I would ever get to be that joyful again. I doubted it. In the extreme.

For the first time, the police were supportive, the Bellflower PD, that is. A squad car was parked outside my window during the night. It made me feel safe and secure, at last. I fell asleep, almost overwhelmed with nostalgia for plain vanilla boredom.

The next morning, a different set of nurses came on duty, and it was clear that I had entered the Red Queen's world. The supervisor pitched a fit when she saw that I was supposed to have been placed in a private room; and then, to make matters worse, when she saw the bandages that Terrell had lovingly administered two days prior, she went into orbit. It was "off with their heads" time, since no one had changed my bandages when I checked in. As a result, they had to *tear off* all of the gauze, that was again matted to my wounds. Talk about hurt! My physical healing had to start all over again. I was *not* a satisfied customer.

Later that afternoon, Bob came by, to check on my progress, on his way home from work. In another room now, I could hear many raised voices in the hallway. Recognizing his voice, I crawled down to the end of the bed, and looked out the doorway, to see if it was really him. He walked by my room in a frantic state, and I called out to him. He doubled back, took one look at me, and yelled back over his shoulder, "Here she is! I *told* you she checked in last night!"

Bob walked right in, and asked how I was doing, so he could report my current situation to Terrell. As he stood at the bottom of the bed chatting with me, about a dozen doctors' and nurses' heads jammed in the doorway like olives in a jar, watching us. Never realizing that they were concerned about my welfare, and that they thought he was Chuck, I considered their behavior rude and intrusive. "Can't anyone get some *privacy* around here?" I complained. I couldn't fathom why everyone was being so ill-mannered, which goes to show that my thinking still wasn't up to par.

There was one more week of school left, but it was apparent that I wasn't going to make it back in time for any farewells with my students or colleagues. To this day, I don't know who packed up my things, and closed up my classroom for the summer. With my mind thoroughly targeted on my trauma, school was the least of my worries, so I gave it short shrift. The range and complexity of my thinking process was next to nil. I simply focused on the need for a change of scenery, to get out of town for awhile. There was a Winslow Homer-like painting of a peaceful countryside on the wall, representing a warm, calm refuge, into which I gladly crawled in and stayed. I must have had some heavy duty medication, because I kept fading in and out, like plop-plop, fizz-fizz, aaahh.

Like Humpty Dumpty, I suffered a great fall, and shattered so completely that I couldn't put myself back together again. My grasp of time was blown to smithereens, something akin to Salvador Dali's *Soft Watch At The Moment Of First Explosion*. There is a definite break in my memory here. So much so that I remember next to *nothing* about that stay, only a few camera-click impressions. A combination of my emotional state, exhaustion, and heavy sedatives induced total repression: a complete blank. I never even realized that anyone came to see me during visiting hours. It never seemed important to even *ask* about that period of time, since my analytical skills were substantially diminished. As far as I was concerned, I checked in one day, and checked out a couple of days later, and little of import had happened, since I was just recuperating: from exactly what, I still don't know. Thirty-some years after the fact, while writing this book, I found that, in addition to my physical ailments, there was concern over my fragile mental condition. I was on a suicide watch. Say what? *Me?* Apparently, I was on the verge of, or had experienced, a nervous breakdown.

Terry had been so frantic about my emotional condition, that he stayed with me as much as possible, holding my hand and listening to my babbling and blubbering, while I claimed that I had no reason to live, et cetera. Being so concerned about this new preoccupation of mine, he was kicked out of the hospital on two occasions because of his hovering. Terry then took up station on the grounds, patrolling on his own, just in case Chuck should make an appearance. *How could I not remember ranting and raving about something of this magnitude?* Talk about selective amnesia!

At the end of that week, my mother checked me out of the hospital, against the doctor's wishes. She had her station wagon packed with everything I would need to stay in Las Vegas for six weeks. That was the time required to establish residency in order to obtain a *quickie* divorce. She and my father had a tough time getting my things, because Chuck wouldn't let any of my family in the apartment. They finally appealed to the manager, who allowed them to take *only* my clothes, nothing else, because of the legality of the situation. They had to leave my car, and personal items, but I didn't care. I was outta there! With a whoop of uncensored gratitude, I was almost overwhelmed by a sense of freedom and escape.

And so we were off! I imagined Chuck in my rearview mirror, getting smaller, and smaller, and smaller, until he was permanently out of my life. The "Hallelujah Chorus" rang out in my head as my heart did a little dance, which was extremely unnerving, but I was filled with euphoria: sheer, uncut, unabashed euphoria, thrilled with the notion that at last, at long last, I was definitely packing up, getting out, and moving on. And I would never have to see Chuck again.

Famous last words.

Chapter 4:

PERSONAL APPLICATIONS

Consider these facts and safety measures when dealing with a stalker:

(71) It is not uncommon for threats to be made against the victim's family, because all of the members are seen as obstacles standing between the stalker and the victim, and must be eliminated.[1]

(72) Always keep a few emergency phone numbers, and some coins in your pockets or shoe. Alert your family and friends to the changing situation, so they can be prepared for the fallout.

(73) Believing that a stalker will think as you would, and act as you would, is dangerous thinking. Nothing you say will be heard in the way you mean it. Stalkers are completely oblivious to logical arguments.[2]

(74) In order to escape accountability for his/her crimes, a stalker will deny ("It didn't happen that way"), rationalize ("They made me do it"), and outright lie about the events ("It *never* happened").[3] As a last resort, he/she will attack the credibility of the accuser.[4]

(75) Take care of your own needs, in whatever way you can. Practice self-acceptance, self-compassion, and self-nuturing.

(76) There is truth to the old saying: *Fine* is a four-letter word for denial.[5] Locate your feelings, good, bad, or neutral. Don't censor them, block them, run from them, or repress them. Don't pass judgment on them. Name them correctly, face them, and experience them deeply. Then communicate what needs to be said, take appropriate action, and deal with them.[6] You need the full range of your feelings, just as you need the full freedom of your thoughts.

(77) You may find that your sense of time may be altered, experiencing a surreal slowing down or speeding up.

(78) You may experience serious memory gaps, having blocked all memory of certain events. You may have only murky recollections or vague physical feelings.[7] Aftershocks of traumatic events will continue to be felt over time. Expect odd memories to bob to the surface of your mind. Sometimes whole scenes will be revealed at once, while more often, you will grasp only glimpses, something akin to strobe flashes in a dark room: sketchy, confusing, and disjointed. It might take you years to put all of the pieces together. Explore the maze of your memories. It has been long understood that *dwelling* upon stressful situations can negatively inpact you. Doctors now tell us that simply *thinking* such thoughts can release the same amount of destructive hormones as the original stress itself.[8] Don't let it throw you off balance.

(79) Get outside emergency services whether you think you need help or not. You may have sustained far greater damage than is readily apparent. This is not the time to feel guilty or embarrassed. You may feel disoriented, and may not be thinking clearly. How you think or feel directly after the event, may not be how you think or feel later. Just do it: get help. Know that this is simply one more indignity you have to endure, to bring the perpetrator to justice. If assaulted or raped outside your home, immediately get to a hospital. If at home, call 911 for the police and an ambulance. Don't shower, clean yourself up, douche, change clothes, or straighten up the area. Keep everything just as it is, for evidence. When sex is nonconsensual, there are physiological differences that doctors are able to recognize: signs of forced entry, lacerations around the labia, tears in the vaginal wall, traces of sperm and DNA, et cetera. Realize that a medical report can provide powerful evidence, even if there is no serious physical injury involved, which immediately becomes a police or court issue.[9]

According to the American Medical Association, one million women a year visit physicians or emergency rooms due to beatings alone. At least one in five perpetrators are current or former husbands, partners, or boyfriends. In 1992, the U.S. Surgeon General reported abuse by a husband, a partner, or a boyfriend as the leading cause of injury to American women.[10]

Chapter Four Endnotes:
A MATTER OF SOME URGENCY

1. Doreen Orion, *I Know You Really Love Me: A Psychiatrist's Account of Stalking and Obsessive Love* (New York: Dell, 1997), 118.
2. Gavin De Becker, *The Gift of Fear: Survival Signals That Protect Us From Violence* (Boston: Little, Brown,1997), 115, 126, 139; Orion, ibid, 300.
3. J. Reid Meloy (ed), *The Psychology of Stalking: Clinical and Forensic Perspectives* (San Diego: Academic Press, 1998), 9, 155; Dawn Bradley Berry, *The Domestic Violence Sourcebook: Third Edition* (Los Angeles: Lowell House, 2000), 245.
4. Herman, ibid, 8.
5. Gay Hendricks, *Conscious Living: Finding Joy in the Real World* (San Francisco: Harper, 2000), 26.
6. Melody Beattie, *Codependent No More: How to Stop Controlling Others and Start Caring for Yourself* (San Francisco: Hazelden, 1992), Chapter 13: Feel Your Own Feelings, 141-150.
7. Joan Barnhill & R.K. Rosen, *Why Am I Still So Afraid?: Understanding Post-Traumatic Stress Disorder* (New York: Dell, 1999), 2.
8. Deepak Chopra, *Ageless Body, Timeless Mind: The Quantum Alternative to Growing Old* (New York: Harmony, 1993), 5, 148; Dharma Singh Khalsa, *Brain Longevity: The Breakthrough Medical Program that Improves Your Mind and Memory* (New York: Warner, 1999), 121; Gary Small, *The Memory Bible: An Innovative Strategy for Keeping Your Brain Young* (New York: Hyperion, 2002), 63-64.
9. Berry, 143-144.
10. ibid, 8.

I personally think we developed language
because of our deep inner need to complain.
—Jane Wagner and Lily Tomlin

Chapter 5:

PREDATOR ON THE PROWL

The passing desert appeared harsh and brutal. This was not the world of Georgia O'Keefe. The oppressive heat, hostile vegetation, odd creatures, desolate rocky plateaus, and endless sand, seemed an apt comment on my life. Everything seemed poised to prick, sting, bite, or kill me, while the ground continually shifted underneath my feet. *Just like home,* I observed silently.

In the midst of a triple-digit heat wave, Mother and I arrived in Las Vegas, steamed, baked, and deep-fried. After spending all day looking, we finally found a reasonably priced apartment for me to reside in, just off the strip, behind the Sands Hotel and Casino. Unfortunately, the electricity couldn't be turned on until Monday, so to escape the 110 degrees at midnight, we found ourselves in the local drugstore, enjoying the air conditioning. I was bedraggled, but hopeful. I had been sprung from the prison of marriage, and in my mind I did a whirling dervish routine. The relief was exhilarating.

The apartment manager had assured us that he would testify in court that I had established the requisite state residency for a quickie divorce. *Six weeks,* I thought happily, *six weeks!* I wanted this marriage over and done with, finished and forgotten, dead and buried. Kaput. So, this seemed the fastest and safest way to go. After Mother was convinced that I was settled, she left.

That was a strange time for me. The euphoria soon vanished. After hanging out at ground zero for so long, it was difficult to wrap my mind around the fact that I had actually *survived*, with my whole family intact. What had happened was a blur, an unreal torquing of reality. I alternated between utter numbness and a vivid reliving of excruciating events. I seemed to be convalescing from a long illness, shuffling into each day with all the enthusiam of a zombie.

A chilling sense of isolation prevailed. I needed a massive support system, and had no one. At a time when I needed love and protection the most, at a time when I needed TLC and touchy-huggy-feely friends around, I was left to my own devices. I felt utterly alone, abandoned, and disconnected (my "Eleanor Rigby" days). Hungry for company and conversation, I still made few attempts to make new friends, since my general trust in people was shattered. Submerged in the swimming pool, I listened to the adventures of my neighbors, but kept silent about my own. My long love for blues music began there in Las Vegas, starting with Jimmy Reed and Muddy Waters. It fit my mood.

My ego had taken a major broadside. My self-esteem was shot, and I was extremely self-critical. Doubt and guilt kept me anxious and uncertain, uneasily adrift. Swamped with self-loathing, I kept questioning myself, *How could I not have known?* and *Is there something I could have done differently?*[1] Of course, dwelling on my mistakes was unproductive, but that didn't stop me from worrying.

I was detached from the world I understood. I no longer stood within a shared cultural belief system. I was emotionally cut off, estranged, and totally out of the loop.[2] I felt as separate from the crowd as if others were a different species, while the words from a childhood song, "The cheese stands alone..." played over and over in my head. Everything seemed odd, strange, rearranged. Vascillating between anger and indifference, outrage and dispair, I was suddenly unsure about everything. I felt dizzy and unmoored, having lost my balance, as well as my center. I trembled with fury at the perceived treachery and betrayal all around, making the usual curses at a world so indifferent to the needs of others.[3]

It was an experience of such devasting emotional impact that it rocked the foundation of my being, and I continually railed at all organized religions.[4] I saw the universe as a cold, lonely place, and all promises of divine help as a cruel joke, leaving me with a hole in my being. I wanted a faith that didn't require the abandonment of my brain, but found that neither religion nor atheism offered respite. (It took years to climb out of that deep, dark place of emptiness, and regain a sense of the spiritual in my life.)

I was simply drowning in depression. Inbetween bouts, however, I was able to glimpse small slivers of sunshine. I recognized that soon I would have a new beginning; a fresh start; another chance to get it right. It was a considerable comfort.

Then, somehow, Chuck found out that I was staying in Las Vegas. Somehow, he was able to obtain my address. So he embarked on a journey to find me. In kamikaze mode, he was apparently driving too fast, crossed over the center line, and collided with a cement truck in the middle of a bridge. He ended up in the hospital. Somehow, his family was able to obtain my phone number, and the calls started coming in, one after the other. I became jumpier than a basket of grasshoppers, as they pleaded with me to return home. They cited an ungodly number of broken bones, and multiple injuries, itemizing them in gross detail, and emphasizing that Chuck was soon to die.

Well, boo and hoo. I just couldn't seem to work up a decent regret, and lacked the depth of character to offer much sympathy. Truth be told, I couldn't even scrape up the grace to feel *concerned* about it. Needless to say, I bypassed the Hallmark cards. I'd been around that dysfunctional family far too long, and didn't believe a word they said. They wanted me to visit Chuck in the hospital, because it was his one last wish. Failing that, they wanted me at the funeral. As trustworthy as the Borgias, I had the sneaking suspicion that they just wanted me to break my Nevada residency, so I remained in exile. (*I'll get you, my pretty, and your little dog, too!*) Finally the calls tapered off.

It later turned out that Chuck had apparently come through the accident with barely a scratch, comparatively speaking. Why was I not surprised? *My* car, however, was a total and complete loss, with photos to prove it.

After copious amounts of sun, sand, and Coppertone, I returned to California with divorce papers clenched tightly in hand, resisting the urge to turn a self-congratulatory somersault. I was rested, as relaxed as possible under the circumstances, deeply tanned (in those days, no one thought about skin cancer), and looked like my old self again. But it is simply not possible to walk away from extraordinary events unchanged. No one goes through a divorce entirely unscathed. There is no way I could have remained untouched by such pain and ugliness.

Even in the midsixties, the times were restrictive. Marriage was considered a *forever* experience (hum along with Natalie Cole and Nat King Cole's "When I Fall In Love"). There was a large-scale cultural prejudice against divorce. The word itself was considered "dirty," and was only spoken in hushed whispers. In the eyes of polite society, a divorcée was a hussy, a fallen or scarlet woman, used or damaged goods, tainted, and so forth. I was not prepared for the ostricism I had to endure—like a leper or pariah—feeling that I was walking around with a Hester Prynne-like tattoo emblazoned on my forehead. Heads turned and whispers followed wherever I went. The uncomfortable feeling in the air was most disconcerting, as if people mentally took a step backward, to remove themselves from such wickedness. You'd have thought I had a contagious condition, or I'd been fraternizing with the enemy. It was a flaming wonder that they hadn't run me out of town, or tried to stone me. "Before You Acuse Me" became my personal theme song.

What I couldn't fathom was the clear, if subtle, change in those I knew *well*, as I walked a daily gauntlet of disapproval. My friends' and colleagues' tones turned businesslike, at arm's length, without personal warmth, in a kind of guilt by association attitude. The women seemed to edge away, distancing themselves more each day, as I was clearly a daily reminder of their own vulnerability and what *could* happen to them.[5] Most appeared afraid to have me around their boyfriends or husbands. They were fearful, I suppose, that I was suddenly a rival, and that I might leap upon their guys, tempting them down the garden path, or luring them onto the rocks in the manner of Sirens from days of old. What rubbish! I needed another man like I needed a brain tumor. An emotional porcupine, I all but *bristled* with Do Not Disturb, No Trespassing, Stay Away spines. Why couldn't they see that? So much for sisterhood.

Everybody needs to talk to somebody; it's a basic human necessity. The mere sight of a friendly face would have done wonders for my morale. *Ignore them, ignore them, ignore them*, became my mantra, while I concentrated on the business of getting my life back in order. I bought another car, and lived with my parents, while I looked for an apartment. "Onward and upward," I would mutter to myself with mock enthusiasm. I wanted to do nothing more than fill the moat and raise the drawbridge, but instead, I worked at rethinking, revising, and repairing my attitude. I struggled with my out-of-kilter feeling. I focused on reestablishing autonomy and self-control, while mourning my losses. At first, I skittered from task to task, as organized as a tossed salad. My thoughts jumbled together like colored glass in a kaleido-scope, but I worked hard at damage control. I struggled to regain a sense of normalcy, and eventually began to make my recovery. Yahoo! With time and effort, my mind stopped sizzling in its habitual static. The knockdown doll was bouncing back.

When the new school year began, I started teaching again, and my life finally returned to something approaching normal. The jubilant strains of "Zip-a-dee-do-dah" happily encircled my mind and heart each day, as I looked forward to a new life without Chuck. How could I know that the fun had just begun; that I had embarked on an odyssey that would span over four decades, and that this fiasco would never be allowed to die a natural death? In keeping with the Las Vegas tradition, I held onto the *illusion* that obtaining a divorce was a fast and simple solution to my problem; a quick and easy fix, a Band-Aid to cover my hurt. In fact, it was merely a stopgap measure, a short-term solution to a very long-term problem.

Unfortunately, Chuck didn't take rejection well. He wouldn't let go, and refused to be ignored. He found a way of ensuring that we would always be a part of each other's lives; that we would always be connected, and that I'd always be *thinking* of him, whether I wanted to, or not (sing along with Sting's lyrics, "Every breath you take, Every move you make…I'll be watching you."[6]). He would show up at my elementary school, just before class was over for the day, and wait outside in his car. I found this profoundly claustrophobic, and monumentally disturbing. Terror swiftly returned like a swarm of bats. I seemed to regress to the perpetual FALLING ROCK zone of my previous existence. Potential trouble was everywhere. My life was once again, full of landmines. The old, familiar, Pavlovian response resumed its place in my life, as my whole body started shaking like a quivering mold of Jell-O every time I saw his car. My head felt like a jackhammer in overdrive, and my stomach rebelled, ready to do a Krakatoa. It was only by the sheerist act of will that I was neither shrieking nor jabbering senselessly.

My self-improvement and up-and-at-'em efforts came to an abrupt halt. I knew this situation was going to have a BAD ENDING, if the police wouldn't do something about it. Worries decended upon me like a murder of crows coming to roost. Their constant cawing distracted me, shattering my ability to think clearly. I fully expected to be hunted down, and wasn't convinced that I was going to survive the experience. Each moment had the possibility of a close encounter, and it took willpower to keep from constantly look over my shoulder. Just stepping outside was an act of bravery.

And so began an ugly downward spiral. Being hit by numerous jolts of adrenaline daily, my heart had too many power surges to the system, and I became utterly unable to gear down and return to normal. The energy of continual alarm and rage contaminated my thinking, and I backslid emotionally. Large areas of feeling were left unexpressed, and unexamined, closed off in self-protection. Sleeping alone at night, as comfortable as a bed of cacti, my paranoia ran unchecked. Reasoning with myself did no good whatsoever. Fear ruled. I could feel Chuck hanging around out there, just beyond my vision, waiting for the perfect moment to pounce. Inwardly, I felt like Edvard Munch's *The Scream*. Being strung out, sleep deprived, and fueled by caffeine and junk food, I was living on copius amounts of industrial strength Excedrin. Returning to that tired-out, worn-to-a-frazzle look, I became a Nervous Nellie, in mental gridlock, staggered by the speed at which I had fallen.

I finally regressed to the point where I wished bad things would happen to Chuck, like blowing him away like a dandelion, or planting him deep below the topsoil, or dancing the fandango on his grave, but I was so appalled that I had even *considered* such ideas, that I could never quite get into specifics. I didn't know that I was even *capable* of such a thing, as it was hardly Gandhi-like. I just wanted some kind of justice. I was shocked at myself, pretending that I never thought about it, having always felt I was more civilized than that. I worried that I wasn't as *nice* as I always considered myself to be.

Intermittently, other teachers would walk me outside as a group, casting dirty looks at Chuck, waiting until I got into my car, before disbanding. A mad chase would then ensue. Whenever he'd catch me at a signal, he'd shout out, "Don't worry! You have nothing to be concerned about!" and similar words, none of which inspired confidence in what he was saying. I had the overwhelming desire to hold up my fingers in the shape of a cross, as if to ward off Dracula, while shouting "Back! Back!"

Thereafter, whenever Chuck would follow me, I'd head for the Sheriff's Department, to wait in their parking lot, until he'd get tired and go on home. Long after he departed, I would leave in the opposite direction, and take a circuitous route going back to my place. It was flat-out scary.

Terrified, and out of my depth, I didn't know what to do. The police again refused to get involved over a "family matter," even though we were no longer a family, and his stalking behavior started *after* our divorce. I couldn't convince anyone of the seriousness of the problem. I would hear remarks like, "A pretty girl like you? Who *wouldn't* want to follow you around?" or, "With your looks, what do you expect?" or, the ever popular, "You should feel flattered!" Similar sentiments were delivered along with mental pats on the head. There, there. They just couldn't see why I was so uncomfortable, or what all the fuss was about. (Over three decades later, my primary physician said to me, "Don't you wish your husband paid as much attention to you as your stalker?" Proving once again, no matter how highly educated, there are people who *still* don't get it.) Talk about a blind spot. I could see the door slamming in my face so fast, I both heard, and felt the resulting reverberations.

My concern was approaching critical mass, while both the Long Beach Police and the Los Angeles County Sheriff's Departments continued to maintain that they couldn't do anything until Chuck actually, physically, did something to me. In those days (the sixties, as well as the seventies, eighties, and early nineties), according to the law, continually following me, harassing me, phoning me, and threatening me, did not count as criminal behavior. I was left with the burden of unexpressed rage at all of those who failed to help me, and remained indifferent to my plight.[7]

Then he actually, physically *did* do something. Growing weary of our game of hide and seek, Chuck finally decided to escalate matters. After wildly chasing my car down the street one evening, he pulled up alongside of me, and sideswiped my car. I felt like I had been rammed by a runaway freight train, as he shoved my car up into a parking lot, ultimately slamming it sideways against a cinderblock wall. He jumped out of his car, ran around it, ripped open my door, and grabbed me, my fingers still clutched in a death grip on the steering wheel. He dragged me out by my long hair, tearing hunks out of my scalp in the process. Dazed, I was kicking, screaming, and fighting, although somewhat incapacitated by the blood streaming into my eyes. I probably did little more than thrash and flail both arms around, due to dizziness from the knock on the head. As my strength waned, he threw me into his front seat (think: Grade B movie), tore around to the driver's side, leaped in, and stomped on the gas pedal. The car lurched out onto the street, fishtailing and burning rubber, as we shot off like a rocket. It all happened so fast, it was hard to believe it had actually taken place.

Craning my head over my shoulder, I could see that my car rested at an angle—catercornered against the cinderblock wall—two tires resting *over* the cement tire stops, the windshield cracked. The windows and driver's door were left wide open, with the radio on. My purse was lying open inside the car, and a few miscellaneous items had spilled out and were rolling on the asphalt. Chuck had abducted me right off a main street, and nobody saw or did anything about it.

As we caromed down the street, a la Mario Andretti, Chuck leaned over, and retrieved two bottles of liquor from the floorboard in front of me. He opened both, placing a bottle of whiskey between his inner thighs, and gripping a bottle of vodka in his right hand. He commenced to chug-a-lugging liquid courage as he drove. Having never seen him take even a sip of alcohol before, I was astounded at the number of bottles, of all shapes, kinds, and brands, that were rolling around under my feet.

My head was thundering as little twinkle lights spread across my field of vision. Since I was unaware that head wounds bleed copiously, often looking far worse than they really are, I was more than a bit concerned about the status of my injury.

With pinwheel-like eyes, and a demented "Here's Johnny!" look about him, he informed me that he knew I *still* loved him and wanted to continue our relationship. He knew that I *really* didn't want the divorce, and that I had been *forced* into getting one by my family. He maintained that they had *poisoned* my mind against him, and that he was proving the depth of his love for me by *rescuing* me from the clutches of my family. Uh huh.

He appeared to truly believe his projection, and, trust me, I didn't contradict him, knowing that arguing was not in my best interest. I wanted both his hands on the steering wheel and his eyes on the road. Chuck then explained that we were headed for Mexico, where we could just be by ourselves—without interference from others—and we would live "happily ever after." He continued to rattle on about what we were going to do after crossing the border, how we were going to live, and so forth. He said he couldn't wait until I cooked and cleaned for him, without anyone else to bother us. (Me? *Surely you jest.* My kitchen is a minimalist masterpiece, as I am rarely in it. This guy didn't know me from Adam's ox.)

While visions of domestic bliss danced in his head, I was in emergency mode, knowing that if we ever crossed the border, I'd never live to tell about it. For the first time in my life, I appreciated the infinite series of traffic signal red lights, seeing them as providing more opportunity for escape. My heart seemed to be trying to thump *out* of my chest, as I was red-lining in the adrenaline department.

Finally, after traveling a good length of time, I spied a black-and-white, idling just off the highway, hidden back amongst some enormous bushes. I figured that this might be my one and only chance, and that I had to get out of the car. *It's now or never,* I thought. But remembering the *last* time I tried leaping from a moving car, I wasn't keen on doing it again. Luckily, a set of railroad tracks crossed Pacific Coast Highway, and like a good driver, Chuck actually stopped. I was out that door in a second!

Instantly, I switched into go mode, kicking into a turbo charge, shouting and gesturing for the police, when with unbelievable timing, the police unit shot across the road, lights swirling, siren shrieking, and headed back in the other direction. They didn't even *see* me, and I knew my chances of being saved ranked right around zero.

Chuck, had, by now, also jumped out of the car, and was chasing me down, leaving his car—with both doors wide open, and the engine running—sitting in the middle of PCH. He was fast gaining on me, and lunged forward, only to grab the heels of my shoes. I stumbled, but managed not to fall completely, and regaining my balance, I shot on down the road, with adrenaline pumping into my system at warp speed. He hit the ground heavily, and slid. I could hear him howling for me: "Come back! Come back! *I love you!* COME BACK!" A high-pitched keening followed, providing an eerie sound track for the scene.

A pick-up truck traveling in my direction, sped across the opposing lanes of traffic. Angry horns blared on all sides, as the driver pulled in front of me, shouting, "Get in! Get in!" I ran around, ripped open his passenger door, and found three small children frozen on the seat, their eyes as big as beach balls. My no-nonsense teacher voice instantly took over, as I ordered, "Everybody up!" They stood up, I slid in, they sat down, and we were off.

"I saw you trying to get to the police car!" the driver yelled. "Don't worry! We'll catch up to it!" He blasted back across the opposing traffic, ignoring cursing, gesturing drivers, as we sped on up the road in an apparent effort to break the sound barrier. We finally caught the squad car, as it no longer had its siren on—the emergency being over—and explained matters to the officers. They said that they would gladly help me, so I thanked the good Samaritan, said goodbye to his children, and they left.

The police spent some time looking for Chuck, while I, in a state of high anxiety, cowered, hiding below the window level. But both he and his car were long gone. Then the officers drove me back to their city line, and called the Seal Beach police, who sent a squad car for me. The SBPD officers were so nice and courteous. They were genuinely caring and helpful, while I displayed the upset, devastated, confused demeanor of a person in crisis.

Unfortunately, when the SBPD drove to their boundary line, and called the Long Beach Police Department, all public service came to a screeching stop. This was the city in which I was raised, and continued to live and work and pay taxes, and the response of the police that had sworn to protect me was: "We aren't a taxi service!" They refused to help.

Obviously shaken, wigged out and disheveled, I resembled a bad Picasso immitation: my complexion was the shade of Cream of Wheat, my make-up was smeared with streaked mascara and blood, my hair was ripped out in places and looked as though I had jammed a wet finger into a light socket, my torn blouse was missing a couple of buttons, my hose were in shreds, and my high heels were mangled. Clearly, I'd been through an ordeal, and couldn't walk home. In addition, I had no money to even *call* for a cab. Considering my situation, the two SBPD officers didn't want to leave me alone in the middle of the night, in a dark, deserted area.

The two police departments argued back and forth about the matter, but the LBPD was adamant. They would do *nothing* for me. The Seal Beach officers were clearly put out by this turn of events, and profusely apologized to me. Explaining that they weren't allowed to drive into another city's jurisdiction without permission, they did the next best thing and called for a cab. They even waited until the driver arrived, just in case Chuck came back on the scene. My mind was still rattling around like a pinball machine. Alternately I jabbered on like a DJ on speed, in disjointed and unconnected phrases, and stalled midsentence, staring vacantly off into the Distance. An airplane droned overhead, going east. I wished I was on it. I seemed to have mislaid the ability for coherent thought. I had lost it.

Once in the taxi, I tried to make sense out of events that made no sense whatsoever. My thoughts were dark. Anger and fear[8] rose together inside me in a billious stew. On a scale of one to ten, with ten being the most disastrous, this rated about four million to me. How could the LBPD not see the seriousness of the situation? Didn't Chuck just do something *physical* to me? Wasn't deliberately causing an accident against the law? Wasn't kidnapping a crime? Didn't police promises count? *Didn't I matter?* Laws mean nothing if they are enforced selectively. It was long past Cinderella time, and my disenchantment with my local police department was complete.

Hurt and outrage swelled at the outrageous one-sidedness of it all. Talk about gender discrimination! There were no protection laws or justice for females. I was living proof! I was absolutely, positively sure of it now. I was appalled to realize that women believed we had much greater status and freedom than was actually the case.[9] My world felt suddenly unrecognizable, unfriendly, and foreign. Surreal. I was 57 varieties of mad. It was difficult to recognize, much less accept, that in the best democracy the world has ever known, women were living in conditions of total dictatorship,[10] and we didn't even recognize it. So there I was in the midst of personal trauma, railing at society. Again. I felt isolated and invisible before the law,[11] and totally out of sync with what I had always believed to be true.

With my sense of justice offended, I began to worry about my students. How could I continue to tell my young girls to go find the police in times of trouble? Losing respect for the law leads to anarchy—a giant step backward in our social evolution—and I fretted over which side of the line I was now standing upon. My thoughts were odd misfires, lost in a vortex of spiraling feelings and emotions. Cursing had never been my strength, so I was at a loss for words. Anger was a lump in my throat.

It took two days for me to get up the nerve to go back and retrieve my car. I was reluctant to return to my vehicle, unless accompanied by a Sherman tank or special forces of some kind, such as a heavily armed platoon of Green Berets or Navy Seals. My parents drove me to my car, with obvious apprehension, since there was no hope of police involvement anywhere on the horizon. I found it basically unchanged, although the door was shut, and the radio was turned off. On the driver's seat, however, was the white shirt that Chuck had been wearing during my abduction. It was ripped and filthy, embedded with dirt, oil, and grime. Safety pinned to the front, was a torn note that said: See what you made me do!

Chapter 5:

PERSONAL APPLICATIONS

Consider these facts and safety measures when dealing with a stalker:

(80) Stalking is a distinctly unusual crime with its own dynamics and special hazards,[12] with psychological terror being the primary weapon. It is disordered, sick, and abnormal behavior, clearly abusive, violent, antisocial behavior that isn't justifiable under any circumstances.[13] After centuries of stalking behavior being observed—and ignored!— progress is slowly being made. Consider the quote made by California Senator Sheila Kuehl, when she was the co-founder and managing attorney of the California Women's Law Center: "I think we're undoing thousands and thousands of years of human history…Women's voices are just beginning to be heard in the law, and the law is very recalcitrant, whether it's judges or lawyers or the police."[14]

Stalking has only recently been considered a crime (the first anti-stalking law in the U.S. was passed in California, in 1990: Penal Code Section 646.9). There are now specific stalking laws in all fifty states, as well as the District of Columbia. (Check the penal codes of your state through websites, such as **FindLaw.com**). There are also supportive stalking laws at the federal level: The Violence Against Women Act of 1996, and The Interstate Stalking Punishment and Prevention Act of 1996.[15]

(81) Stalkers have many similarities. They are generally older than other law breakers, but often younger than their victims. They my be unemployed or underemployed. They have had severe disruptions in childhood primary relationships via emotional separation, such as divorce, incarceration, or death. They are often socially incompetent,

with failed intimate relationships. Prior criminal, psychiatric, and substance abuse histories, are in evidence. They are considered to be smarter—with more schooling, high school or college—than other criminals.

(82) Even so, stalkers are, in reality, a diverse group, drawn from all different demographic groups: racial, ethnic, religious, socioeconomic, educational, and occupational backgrounds. There is no single "one size fits all" profile. They display a broad range of motivations, behaviors, traits, and a variety of mental disorders. Professionals in mental health and law enforcement advise that *all* stalkers should be considered extremely dangerous.[16]

(83) One in twelve American women will become stalking victims at some time in their lives.[17] It is estimated that over one million adult women and 371,000 adult men are stalked annually, in the U.S. alone.[18] You are not alone. And it is worth mentioning that for every actual stalking victim, untold other family, friends, neighbors, and coworkers are affected. So many stalking cases are handled now, that experts have made discription distinctions: intimate-partner, casual acquaintance, stranger, juvenile, celebrity, cause, revenge, electronic, and serial stalkers.[19]

(84) The most common form of stalking involves those who have been sexually intimate in the past, with 75 to 80 percent emerge from domestic situations,[20] although acquaintances, and less often, strangers are targeted. Another source says 83 percent are comprised of spouses, ex-spouses, or former significant others.[21]

(85) The stalker forms a lovesick fantasy, idealizing the one admired, that links the stalker to the victim, in his/her mind, forever. The target is seen to be the answer to all of the stalker's problems, the person to fill the hole in his/her heart.[22]

(86) The chosen victim is usually thought to be of a higher social status. Since the stalker has a poor self-image, he/she looks to the victim for approval and validation. When it is not forthcoming, it affects the

stalker's identity and self-worth, stirring up old rejection and abandonment issues, bringing about jealousy, anger, and, sometimes, revenge.

(87) Experts tell us that the primary motivation for stalking is not sexual. The obsessive pursuit of the victim both alleviates his/her grief, while venting anger and hostility: by acts of intimidation, power, and control. Stalkers and abusers often have the mindset that you *belong* to them, and are theirs to control or punish. They rationalize their invasive and violent behavior by blaming you for some minor or imagined misdeed.

(88) Memorize the Big Three: (1) You are not to blame, (2) You deserve support, and (3) You are not alone.[23]

(89) A stalker is unable to cope with loss. He/she can't take rejection, and refuses to be ignored, because of the threat to his/her identity. Don't feel sorry for him/her, or display sympathy; Don't worry about hurting his/her feelings. Don't try to reject that person by letting him/her down slowly and easily. There is nothing you can do that the stalker won't interpret as an invitation.[24] None of that kind of thinking will make a difference, and it will just prolong your connection.[25]

(90) In an effort to keep the contact open, a stalker will make small requests, that seem very reasonable, such as asking for a lost phone number or address of someone else, information, *anything* to continue the attachment. Know that any type of connection—even negative—is seen as progress. Avoid any contact whatsoever.[26]

(91) A stalker does not relish being dismissed, ignored, or rejected, which is tantamount to being erased,[27] and will use guilt, insults, harassment, and anything else to provoke a response. Do not respond. Experts explain that by telling someone ten times that you don't want to talk to him/her, you *are* talking to that individual: nine times more than you said you would.[28] And furthermore, each contact, ensures another six weeks or so of continued annoyance.[29] A stalker will try to wear you down, knowing that persistence pays.[30] Besides guaranteeing further contact, spouting off about how you feel will probably establish an

adversarial atmosphere, which may even escalate his/her negative behavior. Responding with an explosive reaction most always hurts more than it helps.[31] Remember the old saying: Anger is one letter short of danger.[32] Even though a stalker would much rather be your pretend friend or fantasy lover, he/she will just as easily accept being your enemy.[33] View your stalker as an addict, detoxing from an addiction to your relationship. Experts advise that you give *one* explicit rejection— making clear that his/her approach is inappropriate, unacceptable, and counterproductive—and have no contact after that. Do not discuss matters, do not argue, and never try to explain. Once is enough.[34]

(92) Make no mistake: You are in a high-risk situation. Do not underestimate a stalker. Do not minimize or ignore the problem. Do not argue with your intuition.[35]

(93) Know that both children and adults are stalked prior to being abducted.

(94) There is a high rate of violence with stalking, compared to other crimes. Research clearly shows that the traditional upbringing of women virtually guarantees that they will be surprised by such harassment, totally unprepared for danger of any kind, and poorly trained to protect themselves.[36]

(95) Doctors say that those who suffer the loss of love show changes in their brain chemistry that influences every cell in their body.[37] Numbness is a defense mechanism to protect yourself from feeling too much, so you won't be overwhelmed. This pendulum effect in Post-Traumatic Stress Disorder rotates between feeling too little, and feeling too much.[38]

(96) Realize that stalking is not be a brief encounter; it is a long drawn-out intrusion in your life.[39] You are in it for an extended length of time. Stalking behavior is an excessive preoccupation with a specific person, taking place over a period of months, years, and decades. Indeed, erotomanic delusions last on the average of slightly more than a decade.[40] In my case, however, I've dealt with stalking behavior for four

decades. Since experts maintain that the longer a victim is stalked, the higher the risk of violence, this does not bode well for me.

(97) Stalking lays a heavy psychological burden on the victim's shoulders. Substantial emotional distress is apparent. One former police captain, and current stalking expert, calls it terrorism, likening the experience to living in Beirut, since the victim can't get away from the stalker, and is at risk no matter the time or place.[41] One of the worst aspects of stalking is its unpredictability: a stalker can suddenly appear at any time, any place, anywhere.[42] That uncertainty, coupled with its long-term nature, makes it one of the most severe life-changing and emotional scarring experiences an individual can face.[43] Terror can be the most exhausting, difficult, and debilitating experience for the victim to deal with.[44] Psychologists have identified the most severe types of stress as those that are repeated, extreme, unpredictable, and unavoidable. This pattern has been termed Inescapable Shock (I.S.).[45] Struggles over your own issues of trust, safety, and intimacy are normal, as are bouts of anxiety, personal depression, and recurring symptoms of trauma. You are responsible for your own well-being. Contact other stalking survivors. Join a support group. Get individual counseling.

(98) Make mental awareness a part of your daily life. Consciously confront the mental obstacles in your path of self-safety and self-care. In a stalking situation, it will be easy for you to feel outraged, furious, and terminally resentful. Justifiably so. But if given free rein, your mind will constantly leap from one thing to the next, in a state of total distraction. You need to stop the mindless merry-go-round that restokes your anger, and take control. Rein in those continually looping thoughts and mental temper tantrums. Get your mindset off the injustice of it all, and focus on *surviving*. Think, focus, concentrate. Pull your awareness back each time it wanders.

(99) Get that "Poor, Poor, Pitiful Me" song out of your head. Bannish the inner voice that whines, *It's not fair! Why me?* Fight against using victimization as fuel for self-pity. Rise above this character flaw. It is a

negative indulgence, a seductive excuse, that can easily become habitual. ("Self-pity in its early stages is as snug as a feather mattress. Only when it hardens does it become uncomfortable." Maya Angelou)

(100) Pay close attention to how you talk to yourself: *I'm too tired. It's too hard. I don't have time. I can't. It's not going to help. I never win. I'll never make a difference. It won't matter anyway. I'll never change,* et cetera. You are not only what you think, feel, and say about yourself, but what you believe about yourself.[46] How you talk to yourself determines what you achieve.[47] Doctors now say that every single cell in your body is vitally aware of how you think and feel about yourself.[48] Push through any negative patterns. Clear the fog in your head, and silence the excuses and the distractors. Suspend self-criticism. Attitude is all important. Understand that how you think and talk about yourself and your life is a key component to a quality life.[49]

(101) Your social health is just as important as your mental, physical, and emotional health. Do not neglect your social contacts. ("The best time to make friends is before you need them." Ethel Barrymore) Your family, friends, neighbors, and coworkers can provide valuable help and needed support for you in times of crisis.

(102) Virtually every stalking victim has experienced some form of disbelief, or minimizing of intrusive events, by those around them: family, friends, neighbors, colleagues, and strangers, as well as those in law enforcement.[50] Don't let it throw you. Expect it.

(103) When a stalker refuses to let go, he/she will often enlist the aide of relatives. Becoming involved, family members will make phone calls, write letters, assist with surveillance, and generally do anything to help recover the relationship. Some provide assistance because they want to keep their basic family unit intact. Others buy into the illusion, or help because they've been given misleading information about the situation. It is best not to interact with *any* of them. Often, they too, will continue their efforts, long after you have told them to stop.

(104) Stalkers are identified as being in one of three broad categories: Simple Obsession (47 percent), which are ex-spouses, ex-lovers, and co-workers; Love Obsession (43 percent), which are generally strangers who use harassment as a way to make the victim aware of their presence; and, Erotomanics (9.5 percent), who display a delusional belief that the stalker is *loved* by his/her victim.[51]

Erotomania, or de Clerambault's syndrome,[52] is a fixed belief, seemingly set in cement, because there is no way to convince a delusional that he/she is not experiencing reality. Experts contend that one should never argue delusions with the delusional,[53] as they firmly believe that if only they persevere, they will eventually win the heart of their seemingly indifferent loves.[54] It has little to do with sex, and more to do with idealized romance, a *pure* relationship, or *true* love. The stalker has an intense need to feel special, to be wanted and loved by someone considered to be *better*. (Croon along with Dean Martin, what might be considered the erotomanic's anthem, "You're Nobody 'Til Somebody Loves You"[55]). The targeted person is seen to be a nice, friendly, girl or boy-next-door type, one who is open, nonthreatening, and approachable. The intended victim is *perceived* to have superior looks and intelligence, to be on a higher social scale or socio-economic level, and have some kind of authority position, or fame. But of course, it's not necessarily so, and can simply be a figment of the stalker's imagination.[56] Research shows that the very first contact is what catalyzes the bond. However, that, too, can simply be a delusion.

Erotomania is considered the most bizarre disorder connected with stalking, as well as the most tenacious, chronic, and difficult to treat. Unfortunately, those with the disorder do not respond to medication, and never seek help because they don't think they have a problem. Erotomanic behavior even persists through lengthy interventions—prison terms and/or forced hospitalization—and according to the experts, only ends if and when another love object is found. Even though research shows that about 17 percent[57] of erotomanics have stalked more than one victim, it's still difficult to think that the victim will only cease to be stalked, if *another* victim is targeted. *Who wants to wish that upon someone else?* Although the Erotomania disorder has a history harkening back to the days of ancient Greece, it was only formally recognized by American psychiatry in 1987.[58]

(105) Expect your stalker to ascribe all sorts of attributes to you that you never even thought, much less intended: that you dearly love this person in return, that it is your true desire to be together forever, and that others are interfering with that possibility, et cetera.[59] (For instance, years later Chuck wrote, "Your feelings for me were roughed up but they haven't changed any." *Oh, yeah. Uh-huh.*)

(106) Stalkers take no responsibility for their actions. Their typical psychological defenses include denial ("I never threatened you! *When did I ever threaten you?*"), minimization ("I was just kidding! You *know* I was just kidding!"), rationalization ("You deserved it!"), and projection of blame upon the victim ("You wanted it. Admit it. You wanted it!").[60]

(107) Expect the link between you and your community to be damaged. Traumatic events call into question a victim's basic trust and belief regarding family, friendships, community, and society at large. A feeling of disconnection from others is normal.[61] ("The greatest loss is what dies within us while we live." Norman Cousins) Seeking safety, protection, and trust, is of primary importance in the immediate period after a stalking experience.

(108) Traumatic events often cause a crisis of faith.[62] It is not unusual for victims to reconsider their belief systems, or lose them entirely. Such experiences make one question the very existence of a kind and just society, a kind and just world, and a kind and just God.[63] Expect a change in your attitude. You may find that you'll greatly alter your understanding of spirituality, religion, or God, by actively seeking spiritual growth for the first time, or through developing a deeper existing faith, or by shattering your long-held beliefs completely.

(109) Keep in mind that being relentlessly pursued with letters, gifts, phone calls, and surveillance, doesn't prove someone's love. The fact that a stalker is persistent doesn't mean you're special in any way whatsoever. It simply means he/she is disturbed.[64] (I once presented at a Stalking Convention with a panel of people who were currently being stalked. One woman, a TV reporter from another state, gave the distinct impression that she felt above and apart from the rest of the panel—think: lovable/better/unique—because she had *several* stalkers at once. However, her television station fielded the letters and phone calls, so she didn't actually have to *deal* with any troubling behavior.) Trust me, having one stalker, or more, is nothing to take pride in.

(110) Close to half of all stalkers appear at their victim's place of employment.[65] (My friend's stalker showed up twice at her worksite, in disguise. She is convinced that the only thing that saved her was a coworker who unexpectedly arrived, and could have described him to the police.)

Chapter Five Endnotes:
PREDATOR ON THE PROWL

1. Doreen Orion, *I Know You Really Love Me: A Psychiatrist's Account of Stalking and Obsessive Love* (New York: Dell, 1997), 74-75. The author is a psychiatrist, and she also asked the same questions of herself, as do most victims.
2. Judith Lewis Herman, *Trauma and Recovery: The Aftermath of Violence—From Domestic Abuse to Political Terror* (New York: Basic Books, 1992), 51-52.
3. ibid, 95.
4. ibid, 54-56.
5. La Vonne Skalias & Barbara Davis, *Stalked: A True Story* (New York: St. Martin's Paperbacks, 1994), 174. La Vonne and I were guests on the Gordon Elliot Show together, taped in New York. She had the same reactions with her colleagues, resulting from her rape and mutilation.
6. Sting, "Every Breath You Take," *Synchroncity*, The Police, A & M Records, 1983, CS-3735.
7. Herman, *bid*, 95.
8. Melita Schaum & Karen Parrish, *Stalked: Breaking the Silence on the Crime of Stalking in America* (New York: Pocket Books, 1995), 115-118.
9. Herman, ibid, 69.
10. *Ibid*, 28.
11. *Ibid*, 72.
12. Dawn Bradley Berry, *The Domestic Violence Sourcebook: Fourth Edition* (Los Angeles: Lowell House, 2000), 4.
13. Schaum & Parrish, *Ibid*, 138.
14. *Ibid*, 139.

15. J. Reid Meloy (ed), *The Psychology of Stalking: Clinical and Forensic Perspectives* (San Diego: Academic Press, 1998), Chapter 2: The Legal Perspective on Stalking, by Rhonda Saunders, 25-49. This chapter is a great overview of stalking laws. Rhonda Saunders and I also met in New York, when we were guests on a national TV show together.

16. Berry, *Ibid*, 5-6.

17. ibid, 4-5.

18. *National Violence Against Women* (NVAW) *Survey*, sponsored jointly by the National Institute of Justice (NIJ) and the Centers for Disease Control and Prevention (CDC), through a grant to the Center for Policy Research. (Denver, CO: Center for Policy Research, 1998), Exhibit 1.

19. Robert L. Snow, *Stopping a Stalker: A Cop's Guide to Making the System Work for You* (New York: Plenum Trade, 1998), ix.

20. Schaum & Parrish, *Ibid*, 3.

21. ibid, 54.

22. Sue Horton, "Secret Admirer: Stalking As a Hate Crime," *L.A. Weekly*, 18-24 September 1992.

23. Schaum & Parrish, ibid, 109.

24. Jeffrey Toobin, "Stalking in L.A.," *The New Yorker*, 24 February & 3 March 1997, 73.

25. Gavin De Becker, *The Gift of Fear: Survival Signals That Protect Us From Violence* (Boston: Little, Brown, 1997), Chapter 11: I Was Trying to Let Him Down Easy, 194-209.

26. ibid, 123-124.

27. ibid, 167.

28. ibid, 123.

29. ibid, 127.

30. ibid, Chapter 8: Persistence, Persistence, 119-140.

31. Sam Horn. *Tongue Fu! How to Deflect, Disarm, and Defuse Any Verbal Conflict* (New York: St. Martin's Griffin, 1996), 3.

32. ibid.
33. De Becker, ibid, 203.
34. ibid, 203-205.
35. ibid, 3-41.
36. Herman, ibid, 69.
37. Deepak Chopra & David Simon, *Grow Younger, Live Longer: Ten Steps to Reverse Aging* (New York: Harmony Books, 2001), 188.
38. John Barnhill & R.K. Rosen, R.K., *Why Am I Still So Afraid? Understanding Post-Traumatic Stress Disorder* (New York: Dell, 1999), 72.
39. Schaum & Parrish, *Ibid*, 104.
40. Orion, ibid, 153 & 314, citing M. Zona, K. Sharma, & J. Lane, "A Comparative Study of Erotomanic and Obsessional Subjects in a Forensic Sample," *Journal of Forensic Sciences*, JFSCA 38 (1993): 894-903.
41. Snow, ibid, 7.
42. Schaum & Parrish, ibid, 117.
43. ibid, 104.
44. ibid, 117.
45. ibid, 122.
46. Barbara Hoberman Levine, *Your Body Believes Every Word You Say: The Language of the Body/Mind Connection* (Fairfield, CT: Aslan Publishing, 1991), 49.
47. Sherry Meinberg, *Be the Boss of Your Brain: Take Control of Your Life* (Minden, NV: Ripple Effect,1999), 51-65.
48. Deepak Chopra, *Ageless Body, Timeless Mind: The Quantum Alternative to Growing Old* (New York: Harmony Books, 1993), 24.
49. Levine, *ibid*, 34.
50. Schaum & Parrish, *ibid*, 108.
51. Paul Johnsen, "When Creeps Come Calling," *Law Enforcement Quarterly*, February–April 1993, 9; Karen S. Morin, "The Phenomenon of Stalking: Do Existing State Statutes Provide

Adequate Protection?" *San Diego Justice Journal*, 1:23 (1993): 127-128. Both articles cite Dr. Michael A. Zona and his colleagues.

52. American Psychiatric Association, Diagnostic and Statistical Manual of Mental Disorders (DSM-IV-TR), 4th ed., rev. (Washington, D.C.: American Psychiatric Association, 2000), 324-328; Orion, ibid, 69-109; Snow, ibid, 21 & 57.

53. Orion, ibid, 60 & 112.

54. De Becker, ibid, Chapter 8, 119-140.

55. Orion, ibid, 74, as well as novelists and scripts writers.

56. ibid.

57. ibid, 75.

58. ibid, 108.

59. Snow, ibid, 21; Orion, ibid, 73.

60. Meloy, ibid, 9; Berry, ibid, 245.

61. Herman, ibid, 52.

62. ibid, 54-56.

63. Barnhill & Rosen, ibid, 91.

64. De Becker, ibid, 196.

65. ibid, 153.

Love is a fire. But whether it is going to
warm your hearth or burn down your house,
you can never tell.
—Joan Crawford

Chapter 6:

FOR THE SAKE OF CONVENIENCE

The huge apartment building that I eventually moved into was brand new, and beautifully furnished. It had everything: swimming pool, jacuzzi, sauna, barbeque, shuffle board, gym, and a recreation room. Although I knew I'd never have reason to use any of these extras, I loved the idea of it all, as well as the fact that many individuals had filled the units in record time, so I felt better: safety in numbers.

The Ping-Pong table was situated right outside my entry way, so I met a lot of young adults. Since all of the front entrances were actually overly large sliding glass doors, I could see everyone who played, and vice versa. Gradually I was able to recognize the other tenants enough to wave. One fine looking young man, Jerry, and his brothers, often played there, so I saw them as I came and went. We nodded in acknowledgement of each other's existence, with occassional greetings, but we didn't exchange any chit-chat.

I was craving a wee bit of good old-fashioned fun, but had forgotten what the word meant, and didn't know quite how to frolick. My inner child never got to come out and play. I'd never learned how to just relax and have a good time. Weekends had not meant anything special to me in years, but now Friday and Saturday nights came as a welcome change. On some weekends, there were roaming parties, moving from one apartment to the next, so I met many other individuals who lived there, as well as their friends. Heretofore, I had avoided parties as if they were python pits, but now I seemed to be changing my tune, as these experiences seemed to scatter miniature Technicolor rainbows in my head.

It wasn't exactly the swingin', carefree, footloose and fancy free bachelorette lifestyle I was living, since I just *observed*, but it was a start. It's difficult to kick established habits. I was concerned, however, that being on my own didn't rev my engine the way I always expected it would. I *hated* staying by myself at night (I still do!), frightened beyond words to sleep alone, although I never admitted it. It is a character flaw, I realize, as well as a reproach to my feminist friends, but what can I say? Early to bed and early to rise was not a part of my ritual. I wondered if I'd ever feel safe again. Further, it made me extremely nervous to realize that I didn't feel the slightest bit stirred by any of those nice, good-looking guys. I worried, thinking that my experience with Chuck had ruined me forever when it came to male-female relationships, not to mention sexual situations. I thought that any romance in my life was as dead as the passenger pigeon or the dodo bird. I desperately wanted to be normal, and fit in.

At one such impromptu get-together, like a fairy godmother's wish come true, Jerry flashed me a gigawatt smile (*Lordy, Lordy, Lordy!*), and every hormone in my body stood at full attention. "Hel-*lo*," he theatrically leered, wiggling his eyebrows. "You're new here," he added unnecessarily. I nodded noncommitally, happily noting that I needed a book to fan myself, proving that I wasn't *quite* dead in that department, yet. In an easy, friendly manner, he made it his mission to take me under his wing, and introduce me to everyone.

He was so-o-o-o good looking—a photocopy of a young Burt Reynolds—one supercharged mass of hunky masculinity. And believe me, what he lacked in stature, he more than made up for in vibrancy.

Whew! What a studmuffin! Possessing charm in abundance, with a flirtatious tone and the confidence of P.T. Barnum, he had a knack for telling funny jokes and stories. A brazen peacock, with a smart-ass attitude, everyone was just naturally drawn to him. His nicknames, Motormouth and Slick, showed that he was a fast-talker, never at a loss for words. He was upbeat, light-hearted, and FUN, which was just the opposite of Chuck. *Yes!* I enjoyed all of the conversation, circulating, mingling, and interacting with others, but called it an early evening, as usual. I wasn't into being up-close-and-personal, so soon.

The following weekend, in the late evening, I was sitting on my couch, doing schoolwork, when Jerry opened my glass door, barging right into my apartment unannounced. Despite my experience with Chuck, being a product of my environment, I was still living in the good ole days—think Mayberry, USA—where no one locked their doors in the daytime, everyone was welcome at all times without an invitation, and strangers were just potential friends. No one thought in terms of boundaries. "*Excuse* me?" I congratulated myself on the tone of my voice, and my cool, discouraging glare.

"What are you *doing,* sitting here all alone on a Friday night?!" he demanded, clearly incredulous, dismissing my frostiness. "Uh, are you writing a book or something?" he added as an afterthought, eyeing the piles of paper surrounding me with disbelief.

"I'm, um, grading homework," I stammered, my voice embarrasingly hoarse and self-conscious. When he responded with a tsk-tsk, aren't-you-just-the-cutest-thing look, my heart did a little happy dance, and my smile was strictly spontaneous. I was lonlier for company than I realized. *Oh the heck with it,* I thought, *It's not as if I don't* know *him,* unconscious of the fact that I knew him only artificially. Relaxing into the moment, I gave up all pretense of outrage. It seemed the expedient thing to do at the time, and I felt my spirits lift like a helium balloon.

"Well, *no one* should be alone on a Friday night," he continued, shaking his head at the lunacy of it all. "Come on," he pleaded, "Come with me." Explaining that he was just walking a couple of blocks down to the Rusty Rooster, and that he'd love to accompany me, he assured me that if I didn't like the atmosphere, he'd walk me right back home. "I think you'll *really* like it," he coaxed. "Please come," he added. "*Please.*"

His offer held the promise of being diverting, and so, our first date began. The Rusty Rooster on Lakewood Boulevard was *the* local place to be in those days. It was a huge nightclub, with dozens, upon dozens, upon dozens of tables placed around a large dance floor, with a raised stage for live entertainment. The place was packed sardine-like, standing room only, with everyone obviously having a super fine time.

Just as we were being seated, the band concluded with a climactic fanfare, and left the stage for its break. It didn't occur to me to wonder how we got a table, when the bulk of the patronage was going without. The crowd suddenly started chanting, "We want *Jer-ry!* We want *Jer-ry!*" Everyone began wildly clapping, and stomping their feet in cadence. I turned around in an effort to see who this fabulously popular fellow was, but could not spot no one getting up. Disappointed, I turned back to the table, and found the seat next to me empty. My first thought being, *Geez, he's left me already?* I looked up in time to see my date casually making his way across the dance floor, and climbing onto the stage, while the crowd went bananas. Gawking like a schoolgirl, I watched as Jerry delivered stand-up comedy off the top of his head, zinging one-liners left and right in response to the audience. He then launched into a couple of show tunes, and ended his routine by wielding a giant-sized pair of drumsticks on the drumset and cymbals. Va-va-voom! The room erupted into loud shouts, whistles, and thundering applause.

I was stunned. And impressed. What talent! Now *here* was a guy who knew how to laugh, joke, and enjoy life: Mr. Personality Plus, with a cock-of-the-walk attitude. And he had seemed to have hundreds of friends and admirers. My heart squeezed at seeing such happy, light-hearted, unrestrained joy. Wow! Now this was what I was looking for! I was starry-eyed, already deep into mindless devotion and hero-worship mode. (As we gain experience in life, we find, much to our chagrin, that one of the major mistakes of youth is to be impressed with all the wrong people, and all the wrong things, for all the wrong reasons.) Talk about going ga-ga. I was ripe for the picking.

"Welcome to my world," he said with an infectious laugh and a slightly wicked twinkle, as his arm gestured around the room in a dramatic flourish. Wink, wink. Believe me, it was hard to hold on to rational thought, as my heart was beating a triple-time tempo in my chest. Everything he said had a slightly flirtatious edge to it, and I was swept off my feet from all the attention.

I latched onto him like Super Glue—being totally out of my element, and feeling a bit self-conscious—sticking by his side, flattered and grateful for his interest. While holding his hand as he dragged me through the crowd, or brushing up against him in the press of people, as he lightly cupped my elbow and shoulder, or placed a guiding hand in the small of my back, I was pleasantly unbalanced by his nearness. Later, when he casually wrapped his arm around my shoulder and hugged me to his side, I felt as if I'd received an electric shock. Yowsers! What a jolt! I was "All Shook Up," with heat radiating, and sparks shooting every whichaway. My immediate reaction was so strong, I was flummoxed. It was a measure of my emotional state that I didn't stiffen in discomfort, or recoil violently, at the unaccustomed touch.

Dancing together, with the music slow and torchy, I surprisingly noted that there was serious mutual magnetism generating here—as a crop of goose bumps arose out of nowhere—but I was actually *thrilled* that my pulse fluttered, and that I was experiencing all the bells, whistles, and special effects. I saw this as a *good* sign, having agonized that I'd never find *anyone* attractive again. It was all I could do to keep my emotions in check. And a *major* positive side effect to all this attention was that it helped to get Chuck off my mind for awhile. So, like a berry in a blender, I was a goner.

As we began dating in earnest, Jerry showed me an entire culture far removed from anything I'd ever known. I was purely and simply bowled over. Wide-eyed with wonder, curiosity overwhelmed my judgment again, as I watched how yet *another* segment of society lived. Attracted to the glitter and glitz, I allowed myself to become seduced by the sparkling distractions. "Bright Lights, Big City" played in the background of my mind. This was the Night Life of club owners and managers, bartenders and waitresses, band members, singers, and entertainers, as well as all of those who frequented bars, clubs, and after-hours joints; anyone who thrived in a dark, smoky, neon lit atmosphere. *Fas-ci-na-ting!* This promise of vast and unexpected entertainment— with a slight touch of sleaze—simply took my breath away. Although my upbringing termed this environment disreputable, it was intriguing, nontheless. I was far from home. It was eyebrow-raising time, as I finally understood the meaning behind the 1919 lyrics, "How You Gonna Keep 'Em Down on the Farm (After They've Seen Paree?)"

Ooh-la-la.

Wherever we went club-hopping to local sites like the Go Room, or into L.A. to the more famous clubs like the Cinnamon Cinder and Whiskey A-Go-Go, the obligatory conga line entourage of tipsy revelers in tow made the joints hoppin', happ'nin' places with a wide-open rowdy atmosphere. It took some time before I realized that this incrowd was a mardi gras unto themselves—addicted to overstimulation—with a kind of "Hail, Hail, The Gang's All Here" attitude. The atmosphere was highly infectious. They partied hearty wherever the parade took them, being anything but creatures of habit. I dubbed them all: Night Gypsies.

To be honest though, I knew I was far too serious for this crowd. They weren't into books, philosophy, causes, or planning for the future. They were into continual partying, alcohol, drugs, and living according to whim. But they were thoroughly enjoying themselves, and I needed a good dose of *that*, even if it was secondhand. Since my whole life seemed to be an act of delayed gratification, I was awestruck. This group seemed so *alive* with music, movement, and merriment, and operated at such a razzmatazz pace, it seemed no one could *ever* be bored. I became a full-time people watcher. An added bonus being that no one person cared a *fig* that I was a divorcée!

As before, being the proverbial stranger in a strange land, I'd quickly distinguished myself because: (1) I only drank Pepsi (OK, so I've got a monkey on my back. I'm a caffeine junkie. Everyone has their demons!). I can't abide the smell, color, or taste of liquor, and I don't care for coffee, tea, or water, either. I'm very limited in my libations. (2) I never smoked, because I'd known from a very early age that my parents would disinherit me if I ever did, so I never acquired the taste or the habit. (3) I simply have no use for drugs. Having suffered from epilepsy as a youth, taking twenty-one pills a day to control seizures for half my life, drugs held no special appeal for me. Plus, I'm far too squeamish for needles. And in any case, (4) I'm not into losing control, nor am I into (5) sleeping around (remember my prudish background?), even though it *was* the sixties. In addition, (6) I have always had an inconvenient moral streak running through me, with an overactive conscience. I have an inner drill sergeant: the psychological equivalent of the Gestapo or KGB. Indeed. As a teen, other parents would not let their daughters go to particular events, unless they were reassured that *I* was going to be there, also. I was always seen as more mature: the responsible, reliable, dependable one of the group.

So, even though I was considered a definite *oddity, nerd, straight-arrow, squeaky clean,* or *goody-goody* by this crowd's standards, everyone accepted me. Because of Jerry. I felt like I had just fallen off the rhubarb truck, fluttering my eyes in exaggerated wide-eyed innocence. Indeed. One person described me as "so touchingly square," that it was apparent that they were ogling me—a prim and proper, straight postured, ankles together, hands folded, respectable young woman—as much as I was eyeing them. I tried not to gape. (Picture the scene in *Dirty Dancing*, where Jennifer Grey is holding a watermelon, while staring at Patrick Swayze amid the gyrating party crowd.) Deciding that I ought to deep-six some of my traditional ideas, I was determined to ignore the precepts on which I'd been raised (when in Rome, and all that). Although it was a bit like driving my car with the brakes on, I was at least trying to overcome my sexually paralyzed puritan stance.

Now, I'm heavily into research, and have been known to spend years on a subject until I'm satisfied with the results. As such, I always had a good time watching the goings-on, even though I sometimes felt like an anthropologist living in a primitive society. Something akin to Margaret Mead, if not Dian Fossey or Jane Goodall. Besides, observing is always easier than participating. Once again, I was living vicariously. *Wheee!* I went with the rush and the thrill, leaving my uncomfortable feelings behind. I recognized that my whole frame of reference was different from theirs, but I could use the diversion, I rationalized, as I continued down my walk on the wild side. Step by step. I watched with the awed fascination of a child at the circus—oohing and ahhing—and tried to take in as much as possible. At first blush, it seemed to be all glamour and class. *Wrong.*

Of course it was just a matter of time before I tripped over my own curiosity and excitement. My personal Jiminy Cricket seemed to have long since left the building. For instance, at one after-hours party, everyone was just sitting around on the floor, quietly chatting, when some musicians started playing an impromptu version of "The Stripper," the smash hit bump-and-grind, made famous by David Rose. And just as spontaneously, a voluptuous, *gorgeous* young woman gracefully arose and began, what can only be termed, a hootchie-kootchie dance. Her sensuous burlesque routine—with hips oscillating every whichaway as she jiggled, and swiveled, and shimmied around the room, flamboyantly removing her clothing, piece by piece—had everyone voyeuristically swaying to the beat, while enthusiastically whistling, roaring their approval, and cheering her on.

Now I had taken classical ballet lessons for fifteen years, and had never seen *anything* like that! Talk about steamy! Geez! I was shocked, astounded, amazed, and absolutely riveted. Sugar and spice and everything nice was nowhere to be seen. Which gave me another chance to act morally superior with a holier-than-thou attitude, while being titillated at the same time, somewhat like a dowager Duchess in a cathouse. I had to remind myself to close my mouth, so people wouldn't think I was a tourist. So much for living up to my own high ideals. I didn't say or do anything, while watching such goings on, playing it hyper-cool. Trying to act sophisticated and blasé about such electric decadence, I just sat there, neurons atingle. My flaming face may have ruined the effect, however. (Sing along with Three Dog Night: "Mama Told Me Not To Come.") Clearly, I wasn't in Kansas anymore.

Underneath all the dazzling elegance and the seemingly normal, however, was a mixture of haves, have-nots, and wannabes, as well as loads of loonies and riffraff. There were assorted cranks, cutups, and sleazebags, weirdos, rogues, rascals, and refugees, screw offs, foul ups, deadbeats, and flakes, bimbos, hustlers, pimps, prostitutes, wayward husbands, and drag queens, along with a motley cross section of major and minor criminals, and the occasional undercover cop: an off-the-wall cast of characters that would rival any TV show, with a lot of raw locker-room language thrown in for good measure. It later became certain that many of these individuals made different selections from the cafeteria of addictions, having experimented with one too many chemicals. The truly dedicated druggies appeared to have IQs lower than a snake's belly, with all the reasoning ability of tsetse flies, but I found it a spellbinding experience, nonetheless.

This pack of merry madcaps were mostly residents of the three-minute culture, showing huge attention span deficits. They expressed boisterous enthusiasm, and yattered on with the high spirits of the hugely entertained, yet they all seemed to be anesthetizing themselves from life, numbing themselves one day at a time, in one form or another. They were drunk, juiced, wasted, trashed, out-of-control, polluted, ripped, sauced, soused, hammered, amped, wired, or blasted, totally tripped out, and more stoned than a quarry. Truly a bacchanalia!

With all the scruples of alley cats, they gave off wanton vibrations, happily straying into encounters at every turn: a carnal carnival. Most appeared to have a bent moral compass, and a highly elastic sense of ethics, with all the convictions of carrots. They seemingly lived by the rules that govern piranhas: everyone was fair game. In addition, this was a very sexist crowd, with a *might makes right* philosophy. We were not even *close* to Mr. Rogers' neighborhood. Interesting in the extreme, these people appeared to think one thing, say a second, and do a third. Clearly, they didn't have it all together. But then, neither did I. All of which gave me a major adrenaline rush: I was stoked on *situational* stimulants. I get high on information, so I was plainly in a state of wild excitement, although *still* feeling a stitch out of place.

My usual response was *Ye gods, do people really* do *that sort of thing?* I generally stared, repelled and yet fascinated, by the serial depravity unfolding right in front of me—change partners and boogie—something akin to watching snake charmers. I could certainly identify with Mary Richards in *The Mary Tyler Moore Show*, when she said, "I'm an experienced woman; I've been around…Well, all right, I might not've been around, but I've been…nearby." Close but no cigar.

Jerry was a dapper devil, a walking fashionplate and a trendsetter, having the envied position as the Beau Brummel of the set. (To quote ZZ Top, "Every girl crazy 'bout a Sharp Dressed Man.") He was not only on the cutting edge of fad lingo, but was acknowledged as a living encyclopedia on contemporary jazz, as well. Anytime we walked into any nightspot, here, there, thither and yon, no place in particular, everyone raised their glasses at Jerry in a kind of Hail, Caesar! salute, either shouting or mouthing his name (like Norm in *Cheers*). He seemed to be their leader of choice, putting me in mind of The Pied Piper. Wherever we went was *the* place to be. I was merrily swept along with the crowd, like a cork. It was obvious that he had leverage, and some heavy local connections. He knew people from all walks of life, with varying degrees of influence. It was all very heady, as I seemed to be seen in a reflected glory position, creating a nice little stir wherever we went. (Sing along with Ramsey Lewis, "I'm in with the 'in' crowd...") Gee whiz.

Being such an excellent dancer, Jerry was always winning contests. Women *loved* to dance with him, and total strangers were forever asking him to dance. (Remember John Travolta's movie *Michael*, in which he played a sort of scruffy, disheveled angel? Can you see the scene where all the women in the bar automatically gravitate toward him, as if being pulled by an invisible conveyor belt? Now *that* was the same kind of bees-to-nectar magnetic quality Jerry had, something akin to a massive pheromone gas attack. Cue: "Simply Irresistible.") Sometimes I felt like I had to stand in line just to talk with him.

And, if all that weren't enough, husbands and boyfriends would approach our table, to plead with him to dance with *their* partners. Such men would apologize to me for the intrusion, and Jerry would seemingly dance with others more often than he danced with me.

When I would be sitting it out, waiting for his dance to be over, it did not escape my attention that when other men would approach the table and ask me to dance, once they found out who I was with, they would quickly take a giant step backward. I just thought it was a matter of respect, and not overprotection and territorial rights in action. *How could I know that I was already considered off limits to anyone else?* I guess it was a matter of finders keepers, or first dibs, or squatter's rights. Misreading their reactions, I began to think that Jerry could leap tall buildings in a single bound.

At night, when Jerry would take off his jacket, he'd find dozens of slips of papers, with women's names and phone numbers in his pockets. He was so indifferent to them, tossing them in the trash without further ado, that it never crossed my mind that I might need to be concerned about this at some time in the future. So much for connecting-the-dots.

Needless to say, he was quite a ladies' man. All those women wanted Jerry, and he wanted *me*. What an ego trip! He went out of his way to be attentive, and show how much I meant to him, making me feel like HOT STUFF. Sizzle, sizzle. (And being so emotionally starved, I just lapped it all up.) We had absolutely nothing in common, other than our mutual admiration society, but that fact was conveniently placed on the backburner of my mind—where it simmered away—as Jerry's grins never ceased to flip-flop my heart, and turn my brain to Silly Putty. I was simply too besotted to notice.

We were constant companions, truly inseparable. Whenever I was around Jerry, my good sense seemed to be conspicuously absent. It was like my brain went on permanent vacation until it was too late. And so, after a whirlwind courtship of a whole six-and-a-half weeks, without a flutter of apprehension, we got married. (And the dish ran away with the spoon.) It wasn't one of my brighter decisions. Jerry was slick all right, a "Smooth Operator." He sucked me right in. Talk about taking candy from a baby. We married with more optimism than insight, and didn't have the proverbial snowball's chance.

In my defense, however, it wasn't as if I hadn't considered the obvious; *obvious* being the operative word here. Wanting to profit from my mistakes, I paid heed to the popular saying, "Unless we learn from our history, we're doomed to repeat it." I felt that I had learned *something* about choosing a partner. So I was looking for someone who was diametrically *opposite* from my first husband. In my mind, I compared Chuck to Jerry, and there was no contest between the two; the former was a cold fish, while the latter was a hot tamale.

CHUCK / JERRY
older / my age
tall at 6'2" / shorter at 5'11"
slender / muscular physique
average appearance / overly handsome
colorless / colorful
still / energetic, perpetual motion
quiet, remote, low profile / loud, outgoing, center-of-attention
rarely spoke / brash, motormouth
boring / outrageous, flamboyant
rare, low-wattage smile / constant, broad smiles
humorless / always laughing or joking around
mediocre mind / quick, razor sharp wit
no personality / great personality
a loner, friendless / tons of friends
no impact on others / a leader
slow on the uptake / instant clever response
no good times / life of a constant party
horrendous sex / fantastic sex
no music / continual music
no interests / passion for jazz, boxing, billiards, etc.
no talents / sang, danced, standup comic
lived with mom / divorced parents in other counties
saw siblings daily / siblings lived in faraway
old-fashioned / up-to-date fads, fashion, and music
living in past / living in the moment
tightly contained / free-wheeling
utter lack of spontaneity / spontaneous in the extreme
never went anyplace / always on the go
quit his job, no ambition / supervised 12 bars and nightclubs

It looked good to me! *What's not to like?* Jerry appeared to be a new and improved version. I couldn't see *any* way in which these two guys were the same. I thought I was being selective. However, I was still concerned with superficial considerations, never getting to the real meat of the issue. Again, I saw the package, not the contents, the frame and not the picture. I was looking at nothing of substance, failing to ask the more important questions regarding deep-seated values, dreams, and goals. I didn't factor in the *inner* being, nor did I see alcohol and drugs looming high on the horizon. Neither did I recognize that both Chuck and Jerry had a pretty cavalier attitude toward the truth. ("Boy, was that a wrong mistake." Yogi Berra). I was in a great expectations mode.

My thinking was that out of a virtual smorgasborg of women, Jerry picked *me!* And I was deeply flattered. My reasoning was that not only did he obviously *love* me, but by marrying Jerry, I'd be getting rid of Chuck in the process, *forever:* a sort of two-for-the-price-of-one deal. So there I was, simply confusing ego, sex, and convenience, with true love. Swell. It was a dumb idea, that was clearly destined to fail; another huge mistake that had the potential for misfortune written all over it, in flashing neon.

Again, I hadn't taken the time to *really* get to know my new partner. Nor he, me, apparently, as he didn't know me from a hole in the ground. (Sing along with The Who, "Who Are You?") But how bad could it be, right? Yet again, I was blinded by the outer wrapping, and was far too trusting. Proving, once more, that we revisit our most crucial issues again and again, in different contexts, from different angles, and at different stages of our lives.

To show that opposites attract, let me just say that on our honeymoon night, he proudly escorted me to a boxing Title Fight in Las Vegas. Our wedding photograph is of the two of us sitting at a table with the nationally known winner and his wife. Now I ask you, is this where the average gal wants to be on her honeymoon? I'm sorry, but it just wasn't *me. How primitive,* I fumed to myself. (It turned out that

Jerry had a photographic memory when it came to pugilistic stats, a more extreme version of the average guy with his baseball cards.) This did not bode well. It became abundantly clear that I was operating at a hopeless information deficit again.

Watching two grown men beat each other's brains out, is not what I call entertainment. It always bothered me that individual boxers got more attention, support, and praise from society than all of the Nobel Prize winners put together.[1] Nor did it set the proper tone for our nuptials. It appeared that he used this example as a marriage manual; a guide as to how to resolve any kind of conflict. It turned out that Jerry had a profound anger-management problem when things didn't go his way, and maintained a fairly primal approach to life's irritations, obstacles, and people in general. I began to have doubts: *Could lightning actually strike twice in the same place?* The whole situation had an extraordinary this-isn't-happening aura about it. So here I had jumped right out of the frying pan and into the fire. What are the odds? *What is the matter with me?* I pondered in earnest, as I could practically hear the bell sounding: *Ding! Round Two.*

Given my history, closeness wasn't something that came naturally to me. I had no idea that intimacy issues would zoom to the forefront of my life, as a direct result of my previous sexual violence and stalking experiences. I thought all of that was over and behind me. It didn't seem possible that such victims are at high risk of forming intense and unstable relationships, based on the contradictory feelings of fear and need. I was blithely unaware that I would fluctuate between the extremes of closeness and distance: anxious clinging and withdrawal, grasping and isolation. Terrified of abandonment on one hand and of domination on the other, I oscillated between abject submissiveness and furious rebellion.[2] Nor did I know, as later research would show, that revictimization was a pattern; that many victims left their abusers only to be ensnared in another form of abusive relationship. I was a far piece from being all right. I was in big, big trouble.

I felt like the greenest sort of rube for believing this marriage could work. I should have known it was too good to be true. I'm sure on some level, I *had* known, but, fool that I was, I went for it anyway. *Sucker must be my middle name,* I chastised myself.

I had ulterior motives, and my unrealistic expectations had blinded me. I saw Jerry as my refuge, my Prince Charming. In my preconceived mindset, I expected him to *rescue* me, to *save* me from my stalker. I thought that simply by marrying Jerry, I would be freed forever from Chuck's machinations; that I would never have to think about him, or worry about him ever again, as that dismal chapter in my life would finally be closed. And Jerry and I would party on—laughing and singing and carefree—for the rest of our days. I was ready to "Let the Good Times Roll." I mention this ridiculous reasoning merely to illustrate my compulsive need for the fantasy that clearly consumed me. This was a serious lapse in judgment.

Oh, my. When worlds collide. Instant trouble in paradise: The light at the end of the long, dark tunnel was simply another steam locomotive chugging straight at me. Once again my life had degenerated into something less than perfect. I thought we had a good thing going. And then, wham. Although we shared an intense physical attraction (after all, he was a dynamite kisser, and great in the sack, unlike you-know-who), suffice it to say that life with Jerry was not the tons of fun I imagined it would be. Storm clouds gathered with alarming speed. Our marriage was as wrong as acid rain. This was not what I had expected. In the extreme. But then, to be fair, living with *me* on a twenty-four/seven basis was not what *he* expected either. We disagreed on everything. Our basic attitudes and outlook on life were at loggerheads, and we had yawning differences in social outlook and responsibility. In addition, our schedules interfered—I worked days, and he worked nights—providing an added wet-blanket effect. Nor was he particularly funny, without a full audience to play to. I felt emotionally dissatisfied, incomplete, and unfulfilled, not to mention discontented and irritable. It became abundantly clear that we were not singing from the same hymnal. And it hurt.

Oddly, whereas *no one* ever visited when I was married to Chuck, people were *constantly* dropping by to see Jerry, uninvited and unannounced, coming and going at all hours. Grand Central Station. We were rarely alone, continually entertaining, being forever animated and distracted. All this anxious activity, accompanied by an aural assault of constant, throbbing music, played at a volume loud enough to make normal ears bleed, was too much of a good thing. There was never an uninterrupted time in which to process my thoughts and experiences, nor a quiet space for relaxation and reflection. So much for tranquillity. In addition, I already had trouble counting sheep. And, since I was the only one who needed to get up with the chickens, I was *always* sleep deprived. I never awakened in the morning feeling refreshed and revitalized. My life became a blur of sound and action, on fast forward, as relentless as a Gatling gun. I was so overstimulated, in a state beyond frazzled, that I couldn't think straight. The din that daily assaulted my ears, and the constant go-go-go atmosphere, was all very wearing. *How was it possible to both crave and abhore silence at the same time?* Conflicted, I longed for a daily dose of mellow. *(Me?)* The only upside to our union was that we *looked great* as a couple. Now *there's* a good reason to be together.

And adding insult to injury, Chuck's intrusiveness did not abate, as I had expected. I added one and one, and got three. His continued interference in my life definitely affected my new marriage. Whenever I mentioned his latest contact, Jerry would withdraw, becoming emotionally distant. I understood that he wanted to play the mucho-macho protective role, but since all Jerry heard were my complaints, and he never actually *saw* Chuck, he couldn't really *do* anything about the situation. This was tough on his ego. Jerry was a banty rooster-type character, that required *action*. So he felt somewhat less of a man—powerless, helpless, and impotent—due to Chuck's continuous contact, and his own ineffectiveness. In time, Jerry began to question whether Chuck might be simply a figment of my imagination, which, of course, didn't sit well with me. At all. Chuck was a definite drain on our lives.

Eventually the bloom fell off the rose completely, and the thorns presented themselves in an unending line. Our marriage quickly became adversarial. Jerry wanted what he wanted, when, where, and how he wanted it. *Sorry! Been there, done that, bought the T-shirt.* I refused to kowtow to his every whim and whine—to which he was accustomed—so our relationship derailed soon enough. Jerry was definitely used to having his needs accomodated. Plus, I found his insane jealousy excessively unattractive. (Suddenly he's into *ownership?* Suddenly he's *possessive? Where had all this suspicion come from?*) My heart broke into a zillion pieces, upon finding that my hero had feet of Play-Doh.

We could no longer engage in polite exchange. We disagreed on almost everything, constantly bickering and squabbling, unable to tunnel through the phony baloney and have a decent conversation. I was forever rising to the bait, and working myself into a lather. Arguing was a way of avoiding deeper issues, and became our *only* form of communication. Obviously, I was taking Phyllis Diller's advice to heart: "Don't go to bed mad. Stay up and fight." This of course, brought out the angry, aggressive part of me, that I'd been repressing throughout my first marriage. My tightly maintained view of myself as an easygoing, genuinely nice person of only goodwill and good cheer, had been punctured. I finally acknowledged that my inner self was not all sweetness and light. *Thanks for showing me my shortcomings, Jerry!* It wasn't comfortable accepting this self-knowledge. Indeed, my pride preferred to ignore this truth, displacing it on him, refusing to acknowledge my own dark side. It never occurred to me that I might be living my life in reaction to those years in which I had no control.

Our hostile, hurtful, and defiant words ensured intense and limited conversations. ("Words can destroy. What we call each other ultimately becomes what we think of each other, and it matters." Jeanne

Kirkpatrick). I was at a distinct disadvantage, as swearing wasn't my forte, and under pressure, my command of the English language would suddenly vanish. When he'd call me vile names, I'd respond with, "It takes one to know one." Talk about amateur hour.

My limited anger vocabulary, of the "Goodness Gracious," "Oh, dear me," and "gosh darn it all" variety, just wasn't cutting it. All I was left with were the juvenile sayings from my youth: "Ah, put a cork in it!" "Go fly a kite!" "Take a long walk on a short pier!" or "Go to hell, Jerry. Go directly to hell. Do not pass Go. Do not collect two hundred dollars..." and so on. Very mature. *Cad, cur,* and *bounder* just didn't carry the emotional impact I longed to deliver, as he was less than devastated by my insults. I could never think of a withering rejoinder until long after the fact. My lame responses left something to be desired, as all they did was encourage ill-natured laughter in response. Trading insults with the likes of me was clearly painful to him. Me, too.

Obviously, I had mistaken momentum for progress. I was fixated on my theory that Jerry and I truly loved each other, and was loath to let this nonsense go. I couldn't see that I didn't love Jerry for who he was, but who I *thought* him to be. And vice versa. It became abundantly clear that he didn't give a rip what I thought, preferring me to just *quietly* sit in the background, like an ornament or piece of art—a perfect, meek and submissive Barbie—representing simply another notch on the ole brag belt. *I don't think so.* There was no way I was giving up my identity again. I am not a parrot! I am not an echo! I am not a rubber stamp! Cloning just isn't my bag. *I refuse to go through life as the second seat on a bicycle built for two.*

Our bad situation could only get worse, as we were too mired in our opposing positions to even consider a change for the better. We couldn't agree to disagree about anything, and just let it go. Unable to coexist in a halfway peaceful manner, I couldn't resist tugging on Superman's cape. Who would have believed, before Jerry strode into my life, that I could have been so *reactive?* The lyrics to Ira and George Gershwin's

"Let's Call the Whole Thing Off" ("You say po-ta-to, and I say po-tah-to") exactly matched our situation: total knee-jerk behavior. He was on a continual joyride, while I was stomping on the brakes, continually raining on his parade. It seemed that I was always in a constant sputter, stiff-spined and rigid with disapproval, forever gearing up for a tirade: Lectures R Us. Calm and reasoned we were not.

His temper was a danger zone, erupting as predicatably as Old Faithful, while I countered with a combativeness that was worlds removed from my upbringing (think: Warrior Princess). We were not good for each other. It seemed I was always bracing myself for the coming confrontation, not knowing when he'd go rogue on me again. It was extremely unnerving to watch charming, hilarious Jerry morph into King Kong at a moment's notice (he seemed to be two different people, a Jekyll and Hyde[3] existence).

Ours was an ongoing, *destructive*, relationship: Punch and Judy time. Years of sublimating my emotions went up in smoke. Normally as aggressive as a hamster, I started swinging in response. *Way to go, champ.* Who knew that I could slide down the slippery slope to a caveman mentality so quickly? So much for being *civilized*. We could've used a referee, as Jerry continued to pound away like a jackhammer. (Sonny and Cher's hit song of the late sixties, "The Beat Goes On," came to have a whole different meaning for me).

Ours became a full-contact, no holds barred arrangement. Although I always got the worst of our knock-down-drag-outs, I delivered some pretty good licks myself, and always went down fighting. (Our marriage was suggestive of *Prizzi's Honor*. The scene in which Kathleen Turner and Jack Nicholson—married mob hit men—suddenly turn on each other, says it all. She shoots at the same time he throws. His aim is better, and she gets a knife in the neck for her efforts.) At least I was in defensive mode now. My background music became Koko Taylor's "I Can Love You Like a Woman (Or Fight You Like a Man"). Feeling double-crossed, I thought he should have come with a truth-in-advertising disclaimer. So much for domestic tranquillity.

In darker, distant moods, considering me a cosmic killjoy, Jerry withdrew into his own pursuits. He eventually resorted to dealing with our problems by taking off for several days at a time, with no phone calls, and no apologies or excuses about where he had been. There was no pinning him down on the particulars of who, what, where, why, or how. (Altogether now, sing "Respect," or almost anything else by Aretha Franklin). So, needless to say, I was a tad cranky. Our after-the-fact conversations went something like: "I hate to say it, but you owe me an explanation," to which he'd respond, "Sure, you're right, of course, uh-huh, OK." Period. That was the extent of it. He didn't deny anything, he just never *told* me anything, which lent a kind of *Where's Waldo?* flavor to the situation. Well, tough petunias, I didn't care. I-did-not-care. No way, unh-unh. Not me.

Nor, it turned out, did he have a full-time job anymore. I went to see him at his workplace, one afternoon, only to be told that he hadn't worked there in almost four weeks! So, I was back to being the major breadwinner. It was not a happy situation. There were moments when I fervently wished that I smoked, drank, did drugs, or slept around, so I could relieve my pent-up emotions. In fact, what little period we spent together was so fraught with trauma drama, I failed to realize that Chuck hadn't been around the periphery for some good length of time.

At length, I became tired of the daily contact with the area's lowest life-forms, knee-deep with the dregs of society. Upon learning indepth about this substratum, I found out more than I really wanted to know. It had a dark, seamy underbelly, governed more by jungle appetites than by reasoned enlightenment: a lifestyle that would have thought Sodom and Gomorrah just a tad too conservative. I had already dug up enough dirt to fill Crater Lake to the brim. Even though my ears were flapping like Dumbo, it became hard keeping up with the Scandal of the Day. My imagination was taxed to the max, as this group appeared to leave no vice untouched, constantly wheeling and dealing, perennially plotting nefarious schemes and shady shenanigans. The endless whispering gave me the impression that something scuzzy and underhanded was going on behind the scenes, although I never knew exactly what. For the most part, they were all happy-go-lucky hedonists—perpetual juveniles— never able to let an appetite go unsatisfied for long, with an enormous affinity for excess. Self-control, discipline, and loyalty, were nowhere to be found, putting me in mind of my third grade class experiment, in which the crickets turned cannibalistic when overpopulated.

I realized that I'd been hanging around the wrong crowd for far too long. I went from finding their way of life fascinating, to seeing it to be as distorted as a fun house mirror. It was demoralizing. I was beginning to understand that the people with which we surround ourselves, are not only those whom we find interesting, but those who help to shape us. We tend to become like those with whom we associate. Birds of a feather, and all that. Oh, boy. Tired of this Tilt-A-Whirl world, I was getting really intolerant of liars, fools, freaks, blowhards, and drama queens. I could no longer abide the raucous lifestyle. I didn't want to be shaped by any of them. I had overdosed on living vicariously. My comfort level was at low ebb.

Adrift, deep in Never-Never Land, I was lost on someone else's Pleasure Island, with no yellow-brick road, bread crumbs, or decoder ring to guide me home. I seemed to be searching for peace, but was addicted to conflict. Lacking a genie, the Blue Fairy, or Pixie Dust, I didn't know quite how to gracefully extricate myself. The ox was in the ditch big time. And then, of course, pride reared its ugly head, confusing the issue (*Pride goeth before a fall*). And, let's get real here, this was my husband's chosen lifestyle, as well as his career. It's not as if I didn't know about his work *before* I married him. How could I now expect him to quit, get a day job, and a whole host of new friends? After all, these people had become his extended kin, long before I met him. (The music in my mind leaned toward sad violins.)

Jerry had been a throwaway kid, whose family life was less than conventional. Dealing with the wrath of alcoholic parents, he often slept under their trailer to avoid beatings. Years later, his brothers said that he was used as a punching bag or a football on a daily basis, which resulted in Jerry running away from Utah, and being on his own at the tender age of twelve. As such, he had worked hard to surround himself with a semblance of family: friends and acquaintances who, at least, gave lip service to such a concept, and who provided a sense of belonging and emotional security. Without an early nurturing influence, he had never seen examples of real, live, functional, loving relationships.

So I always felt sorry for him, and maintained a soft-spot for his situation. I was way beyond Pollyanna. I was also on a guilt trip because he said he never had a Christmas or a birthday party, or anything else to speak of, when he was growing up.[4] It was obvious to me that his short upbringing lacked a lot of the things that I had always taken for granted. Our first Christmas together, I bought him a trainload of gifts, putting myself into major hock, and he complained that he thought he'd get *more* presents. Later, he loudly joked to others about how he'd duped me. Feeling like a first class fool, I couldn't believe his insensitivity! I'd always reacted with sappy emotionalism, focusing on the *promise*, the *potential*, not the actuality. Plus, I always bent over backwards to avoid hurting his feelings, never even considering my own.

Even though his violence was getting more pronounced with each episode, I kept hoping and wishing and praying that things would improve. I *believed* his tears, his pleading, his pledges to be a better husband, and his promises never to hit me again. I *wanted* to believe him. I convinced myself that that was the *last* time he would physically abuse me. What I couldn't get over, though, was the fact that after he'd beaten me to a pulp, and then apologized, he'd expect me to happily engage in sex immediately thereafter.[5] As you may well guess, I wasn't in a frolicking mood. He failed to understand why I would object, because this was his way of making everything all right. I simply couldn't and wouldn't, which only compounded the problem. I surmised that this was his early parental role-modeling in action. A batterer who intersperses abuse with loving acts, flowers, and gifts, uses the most powerful technique for convincing a partner to stay. Intermittent reinforcement is the foundation upon which Las Vegas is built, and the resulting behavior is the hardest to stop.[6] As such, the good times clearly overshadowed the bad times in my mind, and like Jean Harris, I traded humiliation for attention. (Bring on the Philharmonic).

It was a manic-depressive existence with no happy medium: up, down, up, down. This was not a smoothly curving sine line, but a jagged zigzag. The best times were ninth-heaven high, and the worst were somewhere below sewer level. Of course, the worse the bad times got, the better the good times *seemed* in contrast.[7] I was into denial. Big Time. I ignored my situation, because, with my eternally optimistic viewpoint, I'd tell myself that things would get better soon, and I would stay so busy that I didn't have time to think about it. Mostly, I lied to myself that things weren't as bad as they really were. I now stand amazed at my seemingly inexhaustible capacity for self-deception.

Around this time I instinctively knew that I must get some humor in my life. I needed a Grim Reality break. It was a necessity. I recognized that a little bit was better than nothing, and if I couldn't get my laughs in the normal way, I could rely on prepackaged TV laugh tracks. As a result, I faithfully watched *F Troop* each week, starring Larry Storch, Ken Berry, and Forrest Tucker. For some reason, watching this ridiculous sit-com took me totally out of my world for half an hour, making it easier to face the coming days. That mindless series simply helped me to keep on keepin' on. It is curious in the extreme, however, since I've always abhorred slapstick comedy, in any form whatsoever. I was taking care of myself in the only way I knew how.

Even so, I simply couldn't resist the emotional dependency, and clung to Jerry, even though he was endangering my life. I just didn't recognize it as such. My pendulum would swing from intense attachment to terrified withdrawal: from grasping to recoiling, from loyalty and devotion to disappointment, wrath, and scorn, and back again. I was in a state of chaos, hopelessly entangled, my energy depleted. He appeared to be my drug of choice. How weird is that?

My thinking was neither smart nor productive. I'd lost my perspective on everything. (*If I only had a brain...*) I was so mixed up. I couldn't figure out if I was kind, loving, generous, and supportive, or a foolish masochist, a dreamer, and a doormat. Talk about topsy-turvy emotions! But no stroke of brilliance, nor sudden burst of understanding came to me, and I continued on in my rut, waffling back and forth between worry and avoidance.

In the movies of my youth, I had always seen *women* throw things during an argument, although I never actually saw anyone do so, for real. So it was most disconcerting to see Jerry coming at me with hammer and tongs, throwing everything in sight. Talk about an in-your-face approach. It was perplexing to me, though, since it ruined his tough and manly-man image. For instance, during one argument, he picked up my jewelry box and heaved it at my head with such force that it tore a huge hole clear through our closet door, leaving wood splinters, the broken box, and my destroyed jewelry scattered all over the floor. If it had connected as intended, I might not be telling this tale. Luckily, I instinctively ducked, and it just missed my head by a fraction of an inch. Jerry couldn't, or wouldn't, curb his impulsive behavior. I countered by leaving messages with my lipstick, scrawled across the mirrors, so he wouldn't be able to avoid seeing them. So much for my determination to be the grown-up in our situation.

I couldn't simply belt out "It Was Just One Of Those Things," and let it all go. I wouldn't admit that our relationship was simply a matter of opposites attracting, but not enduring. Being an overachiever, I never saw myself as a quitter. Giving up simply wasn't in my mindset, and failure wasn't my bag. I was determined to *fix* the problem. It seemed that my self-image was more important to me than my physical self.

Weaning myself from this most cherished attitude, with which I so deeply identified, required an objectivity I simply didn't possess while in its thrall. I just never thought about it in those terms. In addition, most women were taught from childhood that "Love conquers all," and that we were responsible for nurturing and holding the family together.[8] The inside of my head was in complete disarray.

Although he was usually on my blacklist, every now and then, once in a blue moon, when I'd see him do something nice for an elder, or show some concern for a child, or pat a lost pet, or help a down-and-outer in some fashion, I'd get confused. Whenever I'd see him do *one* tender, loving, caring thing, I'd start thinking about how basically *good* he was inside, which always tugged at my heartstrings. Any time I'd observe a sudden, out-of-character sensitivity, gentleness, or generosity (although he only gave away *my* things), or remember a wonderful thing he'd done way back when, I'd focus on how much he'd overcome—given his background—and how much I was rooting for him to succeed in life. Talk about a cream puff! It was something akin to the unconditional love you have for your children, which is not contingent upon their I.Q.s, earning good grades, making the team, being popular, or getting into Stanford. You might not always like what they do, or the choices they make, but you love them regardless. A deep desire to offer Jerry help, support, and understanding, always caught me by surprise. Either I was being a surrogate mother, or I had the soul of a social worker.

Intermittently, I'd decide to leave, but I felt trapped.[9] Again, placing Jerry's needs miles before my own, I'd note that the timing wasn't good for *him*: he was sick, or he'd just lost another job, or his mother was in the hospital, or his best friend was in trouble, or he was down on his luck for one reason or another. Something equally unpleasant was always going on, it seemed, and I didn't want to *add* to his burdens. It just never seemed to be the right time.[10] (Years later, this was dubbed the "compassion trap" by Margaret Adams.[11]) So, I failed to act.

It became obvious that I saw villains as totally one-sided, one-dimensional creatures, diabolical Snidely Whiplash or Boris and Natasha types, without any redeeming qualities whatsoever. I expected the bad guys to look, talk, and act like criminals. I guess I wanted my villains to walk about, wearing long, twirly mustaches and capes, or sandwich boards advertising the fact. At the very least, they should don black cowboy hats. I didn't have the sense the Good Lord gave a goose. It took me a very long time to come to the conclusion that Attila the Hun and Henry the Eighth must have also had their moments.

Always putting my needs lowest on the totem pole, I never considered what *I* deserved, or that I should be looking out for myself. Unable to say no, all my energy and efforts were channeled into making others comfortable. *Why did I think everyone else should come first?* The training I'd received in my formative years went to the bone. My instinctive urge was always to apologize, placate, run interference, and quiet things down. I was programmed to display deferential behavior: to be a pleaser and a nurturer, to create emotional and physical comfort for others; to be the *responsible* one.

"What was in this marriage for Jerry?" you ask. Not only did my presence lend him a dash of respectability, but he got the chance to live at the absolute tip-top peak of his immaturity. He'd chosen me well. I turned out to be an enabler, a rescuer, a caretaker. I scolded and threatened him, but essentially put up with his childish behavior.[12] "What was in this marriage for me?" you may wonder. The only thing I could see was that I had a handsome husband, and I wasn't seen as threatening to other women anymore. It somehow wasn't enough.

At long last, I realized that my understanding and forgiving nature just wasn't cutting it. I needed to dilute or soften my overabundant empathy and overdeveloped compassion, and rise above my social and psychological conditioning. Disgust for my own soggy sentimentality, and my unmerited concern for Jerry—who had done his utmost best to make my life miserable—finally reached my consciousness, and I reluctantly admitted that my fiddle-dee-dee approach to life was not working. Some changes needed to be made.

It all became just too much for me, and after significant soul searching—while ignoring my usual justifications, rationalizations, and fix-it attitude—I made the *big decision* to get my life off hold, and leave. I had overdosed on nonsense. Making up my mind too late, however, I found that I was pregnant. So my plans abruptly changed, and I focused on the new addition to our family, with joy and hope in my heart. After a truce of a couple of weeks, once the excitement of a new baby had run its course, Jerry and I resumed our fighting. After all, it was a reflex action, a conditioned response, by now.

An emotional mess, I was unraveling around the edges, clinging to what remained of my sanity, like a life preserver. With all my systems on overload, I had no one to talk to again, girlfriend-to-girlfriend, as all of my new chums owed their allegiance to Jerry. It wasn't going well, physically, either. Months later, while we were driving down the freeway, I started having severe pains. Unfortunately, all of the cars had come to a screeching halt, due to an accident further up the road, and we seemed to be stuck in a giant parking lot. By the time we were able to exit, and drive to the hospital, I was in poor shape. Shortly after entering and getting settled in a bed, I had a miscarriage: a boy.

I needed to face and handle my grief, but our schedules resumed their frenzied pace, as if nothing untoward had happened. I had neither the time, nor opportunity, to really look at my life, take stock of my experiences, examine my goals, and come to grips with my miscarriage. My distress and emptiness was overwhelming.

Serious funk. My emotions took even more of a swan dive: the "Rock-a-Bye Baby" blues got to me. Severe postpartum depression[13] took a stranglehold on my life, and wouldn't let go. PPD isn't new, and isn't rare. Although the condition had been observed before the days of Hippocrates, *I* never heard about it. In 1965, it wasn't discussed, nor did the American Psychiatric Association include the condition in the

Diagnostic and Statistical Manual of Mental Disorders until 1994.[14] Studies show that an unsupportive husband and a bad marital relationship, coupled with a history of depression are common in PPD sufferers. Some of the symptoms listed are: insomnia, mood swings, anxiety, fear of losing control, a general feeling of being overwhelmed, feeling disconnected from everyone you love, desperately wanting to be mothered, fatigue, and repetitive, disturbing thoughts that can't be reasoned away.[15] Since many of these were symptoms I was already experiencing with PTSD, my out-of-whack hormones seemed to be issuing me a double-dose of everything.

In addition, my profound feelings of *failure* were just too much for me to deal with anymore. It was my own fault, but knowing that didn't help. My self-esteem was under the floorboards. I continually berated myself as ten kinds of a fool, and seriously questioned my intelligence. *I have a big brain and opposable thumbs,* I reasoned, *so why can't I deal with this?* I felt as dumb as dirt. My existence was pure hell, and I was just tired of the whole freakin' mess. It's not as if I could wave a magic wand and make everything go away, or hop a ride on a passing magic carpet, and leave it all behind. I just couldn't snap out of it. As I slowly surveyed the train wreck of my life, realizing that the future held no relief for me, I crashed and burned.

Logic, deductive reasoning, and hard work never cleared all of the messy emotions out of my head. I had thought it all out, literally hundreds of times, but my emotions always overrode my logic. I was beyond cognitive thought. Way beyond. I just couldn't find a trail out of my muddle. I had lost the ability to recognize any other options. I didn't realize that the longer Post Traumatic Stress Disorder drags on, one's coping skills become further eroded, and it becomes increasingly difficult to think accurately about the situation. Thoughts of suicide had taken up a very assertive residence at the front of my mind. All I wanted was to dematerialize into the ether, to simply vanish from the screen. Death appeared to be cozy, comforting, and inviting.

I seemed to be losing my marbles. I longed for the deep sleep of Sleeping Beauty, or at least Rip Van Winkle. Each morning began with Chicken Little shrieking that the sky was falling. A funeral dirge played loudly in the background of my mind—a constant presence—engendering thoughts of getting my affairs in order: making out a will and listing burial suggestions. But even *that* took too much effort. I was too exhausted to even write a note. I thought long and hard about such an act, not realizing that I had ever even *considered* this action beforehand, since it was so alien to the way in which I was raised. I was in serious meltdown mode.

My life appeared to be an open wound that couldn't be stanched. Stranded on the corner of Nowhere and Forever, thoroughly disgusted with the direction it had taken, I decided that I was in a no-win situation, and that living was pointless. Feeling that no one would really *miss* me anyway, I saw suicide as the only way to go: my escape hatch, my ticket out. Making the decision to end my agony was a last-ditch effort to be in *control:* the when, how, and where of my death.

So, I bought two bottles of sleeping pills. That Sunday night, I started swallowing the pills (sing: "Suicide is Painless," the M.A.S.H. theme song). It was a rough row to hoe, as I kept gagging. But I persevered anyway, with visions of permanent sleep on my mind: my very own poppy field. I was so tired, but determined to keep at it. I was finally closing the door on chaos, sinking into a deep, deep sleep, with the lyrics "Ashes, ashes, all fall down," circling happily in my mind. Ah, nestled all snug-like in Baby Bear's bed: Ju-u-u-st right!

Oh, great. Just great. For once in our married life, Jerry came home *early* that evening. What timing. Talk about synchronicity! Yelling obcenities the minute he charged through the door, as per usual—his fury was always disproportionate to the crime—I was so *thrilled* that I wouldn't have to hear it anymore, or deal with it ever again, that it did-n't even bother me. It must have been apparent that something was up, since I wasn't responding with my usual verve. Shortly thereafter, he found the empty bottles and packaging in the trash, and went balistic. Throwing me over his shoulder, while holding me in place, he raced out to our car, shoved me onto the seat, and roared off to the emergency hospital.

While my stomach was being pumped, Jerry stood at the end of the gurney, holding onto my feet, with tears coursing down his cheeks. I was enraged. I didn't want him even *touching* me. I considered his crying to be of the crocodile variety. *All for show*, I thought, *all for show*. But I couldn't say anything, what with the tube running down my throat. This is *not* a pleasant experience, and I wouldn't recommend it to anyone. I was trying not to be overwhelmed by the absurdity of it all: I wasn't even a *success* at suicide. *Oh, this was a great idea!* I fumed. *I am such a genius*. Talk about a downer!

When I was out of danger, the doctor commenced nonstop sermonizing. He provided a lengthy lecture about trying to kill myself: saying that what I had just done was a *felony* (Who knew?), but that he wasn't going to inform the police, due to the fact that I was a *teacher*, and should *know* better, blah blah blah. I was told to stay in bed all day Monday, and take the prescribed medication with hot tea. Not.

Needless to say, with my students being first, last, and always uppermost on my mind, I went to work on Monday. In reality, I was unwilling to take downtime for myself. I didn't know how to relax, and I knew that a whole day alone would give me too much time to think: to ponder my suicide attempt, consider my future, and acknowledge the hole in my heart. It was not a smart move. By the end of the day, I couldn't hear or understand what anyone was saying, and the handwriting on the chalkboard looked like a baby's scribbles. I felt like I was slowly moving underwater. Just as the class was dismissed for the day, I put my head down on my desk, and couldn't raise it again. It took me a long time to feel well enough to drive home. I didn't consider it the least bit strange that I was willing to *never* teach again—by committing suicide—but couldn't give up *one* day to recuperate. Hm-m-m. My old avoidance routine was thoroughly engaged.

Of course, things actually *deteriorated* from that point, but suicide was certainly off the board for now and for evermore. Let it be known, however, that I was doing my darndest to be cheerful about this unexpected development. I continually turned the problem around in my mind, up and down, this way and that, manipulating it in the manner of a Rubik's Cube, always ending up with mismatched sides. I confess that I was totally miserable, but paralyzed about what to do. I saw the piano falling, but couldn't find a way to dodge it. At peak frustration level, I wanted to grab Jerry by the shirt collar and shake some sense into him, while shouting *"Listen Up!"* But I realized that it would be wasted motion. I had reverted to hanging on for dear life, Tarzan-like, no matter what the cost. I would simply grit my teeth, clutch the rope, and hold on ever more tightly. It was an excruciatingly painful period. I *knew*, beyond a shadow of a doubt, that I should get a divorce, but the public embarrassment of a *second* failure, was too much to endure at this fragile and sensitive time in my life. It simply took too much effort. I was tired beyond belief. Instead, I became skilled in dirty looks, and developed an awe-inspiring expertise at eye-rolling, slamming doors, and childish sulks.

Chapter 6:

PERSONAL APPLICATIONS

When involved in a relationship, check out these warning signs for potential danger:

(111) As a traumatized victim, you are particularly vulnerable to revictimization. Research shows that you could repeatedly attract further incidents of victimization and similar patterns of stormy, unstable, unsatisfactory relationships,[16] since you may repeat certain self-destructive games, scripts, and emotional patterns. Experts label this tendency: captivity to the past, repetition compulsion, tape loops, neurotic obsessions, unconscious subpersonalities, engrams, archetypes, and phantoms from yesteryear that may preprogram your daily life.[17] Everyone tends to choose *familiar* relationships, and people who have suffered long-term physical or sexual abuse tend to unconsciously choose lovers who recreate the abusive situation.[18] Examine and deal with the dynamics behind your problems. Seek opportunities for understanding and acceptance.

(112) Don't fall in love with a person's *potential*.[19] Focusing on one's possibilities carries your imagination to how things *might* be, or *could* be, and away from how they actually are now.[20] Remember the old comedy routine of Flip Wilson's Geraldine: "Honey, what you see is what you get!" Reality rules. Enjoy your partner as *is*. Leave the rehabilitation to the professionals.

(113) Don't fall in lust: being in love from the neck down, confusing love and sex. The two aren't necessarily the same thing. Know the difference between sexual electricity and commitment.[21] Just because someone makes you feel good, doesn't automatically mean you were

meant to be together. It may be difficult, but make an effort to separate the two in your mind. You're *not* turning into a Hard-hearted Hannah by looking out for yourself. (Sing along with Tina Turner: "What's Love Got To Do With It?"). Being a good lover does not guarantee that he/she is a good person,[22] or the partner who is right for you. As story-tellers and authors have shown throughout history, chemistry is important in a relationship, but so are other things. A strong physical attraction isn't love, doesn't guarantee love, and may even prevent a healthy, growing love.[23] Consider the princess and the frog tale: Experts maintain that even though you may feel a tingle whenever you see a frog, you don't have to jump into the pond with it.[24]

(114) A batterer or stalker will initially operate at a whirlwind pace, rushing you into quick decisions, and pressuring you for premature involvement and commitment: exclusivity, an instant engagement, moving in together, or marriage. Keep your options open.

(115) Banish the song "Someday My Prince Will Come" from your Top 40. Consider that your Prince Charming may very well morph into the Prince of Darkness.

(116) Do not expect your boyfriend, husband, or significant other to be your knight in shining armor, ready to slay your dragons, or to be your personal Boy Scout, playing protector to your bird-with-a-broken-wing role. Do not expect him/her to be your substitute parent, to smooth the way for you when the going gets rough, or your guide to freedom. Do not expect another to rescue you or to be your avenging hero. Do not surrender your personal power. You must—first, last, and always—be responsible for your own safety.

(117) Does this person try to ingratiate him/herself through *unsolicited* help or promises? Or by manipulating a forced togetherness? This is how Office Romeos begin their pursuit: heed warnings from coworkers.[25]

(118) Does he/she seem allergic to criticism? Is this person irresponsible? Unreliable? Do his/her words and deeds match?

(119) Can this person take "no" for an answer? Or does he/she discount the word? If disregarded, know that it is a control issue.[26] Refusing to hear "no" is a clear sign of trouble in any context.[27] Stalkers are persistent in not taking "no" for an answer and wearing their victims down. It is said by some that "Men who cannot let go choose women who cannot say no".[28] Say "no," and say it like you mean it![29] Experts maintain that you must *never* relent on this issue. If you do, it sets the stage for future control.

(120) Does this person display storm trooper tactics? Does he/she resort to shouting, bullying, and physical abuse as a way of handling conflict?

(121) Is it difficult for this person to tolerate frustration or control impulses? Do minor inconveniences cascade into major catastrophes? Does he/she break things, throw things, or resort to vandalism? Do you detect an increase in abusive behavior toward inanimate objects?

(122) Is this person unreasonably jealous? Does the jealousy extend to your family, friends, coworkers, and pets? Understand that extreme pathological jealousy is a warning sign that he/she will be unwilling to accept an *end* to your relationship, and should be seen as a significant indicator of potential homicidality.[30]

(123) Words can be used as weapons. Is this person verbally rude and abusive, directing daily snubs, ugly insults, and disrespectful put-downs your way? Are you wounded by cruel, insensitive, or disparaging comments—from ego-destroying criticism, sarcasm, public and private humiliation, hurtful nicknames, or harsh and offensive words that belittle or slander?[31] Verbal abuse is not only toxic, but cummulative as well. Understand that the inner injuries caused by words can create more permanent affects than physical trauma,[32] and take far longer to heal. ("Sticks and stones can break my bones but words can break my heart." Robert Fulghum) Does he/she persist in irritating and/or demeaning teasing? Does he/she chronically let you down? Does this

person purposely embarrass you or undermine you in front of others? Does he/she ever threaten to disclose your secrets?

(124) Check for entitlement attitudes. Does this person act as an absolute monarch, ruling by divine right (king of the castle, lord of the manner, master of his/her domain, male privilege, his/her way or the highway)? This attitude—the belief that males are in charge in a master/servant relationship—is often openly and outwardly bigoted, and may be directed toward people of other races, religions, political beliefs, and sexual orientation.[33] Is this attitude used as justification for unsuitable conduct? Does he/she hold stereotypical ideas of the roles of men and women, displaying macho attitudes and beliefs?[34] Batterers won't allow their women or their partners to have any independence. If they had an existence of their own, the batterers would not feel in control. Having a self-image problem, they fear they're not *real* men if they aren't in charge.[35]

(125) Experts tell us that the first time of physical violence between partners generally begins after the third month, or during the first pregnancy. Pregnant women are especially at risk, as more than one-third are abused: 34 percent, according to the Journal of the American Medical Association.[36] And according to the March of Dimes, battering during pregnancy is the leading cause of birth defects and infant mortality.[37]

(126) After a beating, batterers will often make the effort to apologize, utilizing expressions of love, affection, and terms of endearment, along with the whole hearts and flowers routine. They often shed copious tears, with guarantees of it never happening again, while appealing to the victim's loyalty and compassion.[38] At the time, they may even *believe* their own words, until the next time they decide to lose their tempers.[39] This makes it easy for a partner or spouse—especially one with children and no other income—to *want* to believe such assurances. (Unfortunately, a batterer's promises have a short-term lifespan, generally wilting before the flowers do.[40] Make no mistake: you are

choosing to believe this person. Know the difference between trust and stupidity.[41] Experts agree that you must refuse to enable an abuser. Don't accept his/her apologies. Instead, say something like,"You may believe your pledge right now, but words are cheap. Actions are what counts. The only way to prove that you mean what you say, is to *never, ever,* let it happen again, no matter what. Let me be perfectly clear: I will not put up with a repeat performance." Later, If another session of abuse takes place, you'll know that your partner's word is not credible, and such behavior can't be considered an *isolated* event. Realize that the situation will not improve. Domestic violence begins with relatively minor incidents, and escalates in both frequency and brutality over time.[42] Make the decision to leave. Take the *option* to get out. Don't be persuaded to return.

(127) Experts agree that finding something funny, *anything* amusing under painful conditions, is good. ("If you can laugh at it, you can live with it." Erma Bombeck) Laughter causes positive physiological changes in your body, rallying your body's natural defenses against stress, pain, and disease. If you can laugh even while you feel terrible, there's hope. Work to rediscover laughter and joy. It doesn't matter what you laugh at.[43] Although my troubles began long before the advent of VCRs, you better believe that I would make good use of that tool now, in the effort to see and hear many other funny sitcoms, humorous movies, cartoons, or comic monologues. Hilarious books are now published, even on serious subjects, as are joke books, and those written by comedians. Make use of them all. ("For me, a hearty 'belly laugh' is one of the most beautiful sounds in the world." Bennet Cerf)

(128) Research shows that attachment and identification between a batterer and a victim is the *rule*, not the exception.[44] Avoid developing empathy and emotional attachment for your abuser. You aren't responsible for making your partner's life work. He/she is. You cannot save this person from his/her own mistakes and consequences. You cannot *fix* him/her. As hard as it is, you must learn to love others for who they *are,*

not for who you want them to be, or who they could be. Suppress the affection you already feel. Shine a powerful floodlight on your life, and come to an independent view of your situation. Read a good book on codependency.[45]

(129) You need to be careful of the company with which you surround yourself. People can drain your energy, steal your time, and divert your center of strength, so you are weakened in your focus and determination.[46] Reevaluate your relationships. Are your friends and acquaintances of a like mind? Have the initial reasons for your friendships or partnership disappeared?

(130) Traumatized people often show inconsistent behavior, seesawing between the extremes of uncontrolled rage and intolerance of any kind of aggression.[47]

(131) Experts in many fields tell us that life needs to be satisfying right now, in the present.[48] Living in the past, dwelling on the good times, or living in the future, hoping things will magically get better, is a worthless endeavor, wasting the present. (Sing along with Janet Jackson's "What Have You Done For Me Lately?") Continually remind yourself: that was then, and this is now.

(132) Get your life off hold. The right time to leave your partner is when it's *the right time for you*,[49] not the other way around.

(133) Be prepared to experience some confusing reactions from those you know. Expect withdrawal or emotional distance from those close to you, when discussing current stalker behavior. Some may feel weak or helpless because they can't help you. Some feel contaminated by contact, even if it's once removed. Some just want to get out of a *potential* line of fire. Others may accuse you of exaggerating, overdramatizing, or just plain lying. And a few may feel that you are actually encouraging the stalking behavior in some way, while some suspect you are to blame for putting yourself at risk, somehow. Others may tend to downplay the events, so they won't have to *deal* with the issue. Others may distance themselves since they can't help matters, have no control

over the situation, and simply don't know what to do about it. All are forms of self-protection. The literature shows that some previously close partnerships are bound to breakup over stalking situations.[50]

(134) The grief process goes through a normal and necessary five-step process: Denial, anger, bargaining, grieving, and acceptance.[51] I found that my stalking experiences followed the same procedure, and thought that I had made a profound discovery. Years later, I read that a psychiatrist made the same observation with her own stalking experiences.[52] And further, that mental health professionals say that *all* loss goes through the same steps, and should be mourned, whether the process takes thirty seconds for a minor loss (such as losing a five dollar bill, or not receiving an expected call or letter), or takes years for a significant loss (like the loss of a job, a divorce, or a death).[53]

(135) Depression is a turning inward, when life seems cheerless, and empty, and your world no longer appears to have value and meaning.[54] The depression of stalking victims, who have endured prolonged, extreme situations, is not the same as ordinary depression. It is much more complex.[55]

(136) A March, 2001, radio commercial for the Pharmacology Research Institute of Southern California, claimed that one person out of five will have a bout of depression sometime in their lives.[56] Protracted depression is the most common finding among stalking victims, and adding insult to injury, *everything* aggravates the depression.[57] There are eight features to major depression: Sleep decrease or increase, interest decrease, guilt feelings, energy decrease, concentration decrease, appetite decrease or increase, psychomotor disturbance (such as pacing, handwringing, a slowing of thought or movement), and suicidal thinking.[58] If you have a minimum of four symptoms for two or more weeks, consult a doctor. Depression is an illness. Medication and counseling can do wonders. The condition is not only treatable, but beatable. Untreated depression can raise the risk for suicide.[59] Do not let embarassment get in the way of finding help.

(137) Every day, a person thinks approximately 50,000 different thoughts,[60] and it has been estimated that 90 percent of those thoughts are a literal repeat of the thoughts from the day before.[61] As unwanted words of fright, complaint, anger, or surrender surface in your mind, say affirmations, poems, prayers, or simply count or repeat a word or a pattern of movement, over and over, to counteract and escape such negative, stressful thoughts.[62] Deliberately break that negative thought cycle.

(138) A preoccupation with suicide—thoughts, as well as attempts— is reported in the research concerning those individuals who were involved in childhood trauma, or were abused partners, rape survivors, stalking survivors, or combat veterans. Battered women have the highest incidence of actual suicide attempts.[63] Battering contributes to one-quarter of all suicide attempts by women generally, and half of all suicide attempts by African-American women.[64] While in such a situation—with seemingly no hope for survival—thoughts of suicide represent a way in which the victim can take charge: a way to gain a semblance of control over the situation, and to retain a feeling of power. It is seen as a form of resistance, a plan of action, a *fantasy* in which the abuser loses, and an activity that preserves an inner sense of pride by taking control and actually *doing* something about the situation.[65]

(139) The most profoundly afflicted, and those with long-term situations, reported more suicidal thoughts and attempts.

(140) Oddly, both suicidal thoughts and attempts persist long after the victims are released from their situation, when it no longer serves an adaptive purpose. Well, it makes sense to me: *Who in their right mind wants to remember all that unspeakable horror?* Thoughts of suicide represent a way in which to, again, take control, and permanently *erase* the pictures in your head. However, once the specific trauma is over, suicide becomes a case of throwing the baby out with the bathwater.

(141) If you fit into one or more of the above categories, then you are at risk, and thoughts of suicide[66] are a byproduct of having been in

such a confining or terrifying situation. Don't give power to these disturbing ideas. I know, it's a little like telling yourself not to think of a purple cow. But don't feed these thoughts. Just let them drift on by, like a cloud in the sky, without agitating about them. Consider them to be mental rubbish: random thoughts flak. Don't feel shocked or guilty or embarrassed about having such unexpected ideas or considerations. The thought is not the problem, the *expression* of the thought is the problem. If such unwanted thoughts persist, broach the subject with trained professionals. Talk it out, work it out, with someone.

(142) Suicide does not represent the *only* way out, or the easy way out, it is simply *one* way out of your experience. Don't direct your unexpressed rage and hatred at yourself. Don't let your stalker win by default. Do not give your stalker the satisfaction of knowing that you *will* be together—at least in his/her mind—for all eternity. Fight that inclination with a don't-even-think-about-it resolve. Pin the fault where it belongs: on your stalker. Determine to find another way out of your experience. Accept your present circumstances as they are, but persistently take small steps to make them better. Adopt a take-the-bull-by-the-horns, pull-yourself-up-by-your-bootstraps, get-going attitude, and find a way to win the battle for your life. Do not give in.

(143) An unexpected outcome of severe, repeated stress is the mind's attempt to desensitize itself. This makes it difficult to focus on negative incidents, as the mind tries to avoid or deny painful experiences altogether. Concentration also becomes difficult, as does processing information, and memory loss becomes apparent.[67]

(144) Your thinking and perceptions are often distorted by your trauma, which affects your ability to correctly assess the situation and make sound, rational decisions.[68]

(145) And in the same vein, it is worth mentioning here that those who are chronically traumatized, run a high risk of compounding their problems, through heavy consumption of alcohol and/or street drugs. Originally used as a way to numb painful memories, control

hyperarousal, or induce sleep, prolonged abuse eventually turns into addiction. Be aware of this possible side effect. You have enough problems without adding another to your plate.

(146) Experts tell us that communication is one of the keys to happiness. If you are unable to talk things out, you are doomed from the start. Your ideas are just as important as those of your partner. Being able to express yourself, how you think and what you feel, is essential.

(147) It is suggested that you think of other people as vitamins, to supplement your own natural internal resources: family, friends, or acquaintances can give you strength, focus, and clarity, while helping to cure your depression, and lower your blood pressure.[69]

(148) Take a tip from a kitchen sign: Wishes don't do dishes, or from an old fisherman's saying: Forty thousand wishes won't fill your bucket with fishes. Any baker can tell you that recipes don't make cookies. Hopes and dreams and wishes are a waste of your time, effort, and energy. *Action* is what counts: doing, becoming, unfolding, growing, evolving. It is not enough to just stare up the steps; you must step up the stairs.[70] As in walking, so in life: step out, step forward, lengthen your stride, and make your move.[71]

(149) Make yourself a higher priority: Number One. Get to know yourself. ("Three things extremely hard: steel, diamonds, and knowing one's self." Ben Franklin) Let go of the need to care for others to the exclusion of your own wants, needs, and development. Practice self-love, self-forgiveness, self-compassion, and self-understanding. Make decisions that are in your own best interests. Consider the philosophy of Groucho Marx: "I take care of me. I am the only one I've got." Be good to yourself.

Chapter Six Endnotes:
FOR THE SAKE OF CONVENIENCE

1. Gary Null, *Gary Null's Guide to a Joyful, Healthy Life* (New York: Carroll & Graf, 2000), 361. It appears that I'm not the only one with this complaint.

2. Judith Lewis Herman, *Trauma and Recovery: The Aftermath of Violence—From Domestic Abuse to Political Terror* (New York: Basic Books, 1992), 56, 123-124.

3. Dawn Bradley Berry, *The Domestic Violence Sourcebook, Third Edition* (Los Angeles: Lowell House, 2000), 45, 245.

4. George Lardner, Jr., *The Stalking of Kristin: A Father Investigates the Murder of His Daughter* (New York: Atlantic Monthly Press, 1995), 98. The author's daughter had the same guilt feelings and reaction.

5. Berry, ibid, 36.

6. ibid, 37.

7. Gavin De Becker, *The Gift of Fear: Survival Signals That Protect Us From Violence* (Boston: Little, Brown, 1997), 177.

8. Berry, ibid, 49.

9. Sonya Friedman, *Smart Cookies Don't Crumble: A Modern Woman's Guide to Living and Loving Her Own Life* (New York: Putnam, 1985), 30-48.

10. ibid, 45.

11. ibid, 107.

12. ibid, 45.

13. Maria Osmond, Marcia Wilkie & Judith Moore, *Behind the Smile: My Journey Out of Postpartum Depression* (New York: Time/Warner, 2001).

14. Susan Kushner Resnick, *Sleepless Days: One Woman's Journey Through Postpartum Depression* (New York: St.Martin's Griffin, 2000), 9.

15. ibid, 6-10.
16. Herman, ibid, 123-124; Friedman, ibid, 163.
17. Sam Keen, *Hymns to an Unknown God: Awakening the Spirit in Everyday Life* (New York: Bantam, 1994), 23.
18. John Barnhill & R.K. Rosen, *Why Am I Still So Afraid? Understanding Post-Traumatic Stress Disorder* (New York: Dell, 1999), 64-65.
19. Friedman, ibid, 167.
20. De Becker, ibid, 182.
21. Sonya Friedman, *On a Clear Day You Can See Yourself: Turning the Life You Have Into the Life You Want* (New York: Ivy Books, 1991), 198.
22. Friedman, *Smart Cookies,* ibid, 139.
23. Melody Beattie, *Beyond Codependency: And Getting Better All the Time* (San Francisco: Hazelden,1989), 153-154.
24. ibid, 156.
25. De Becker, ibid, Chapter 4: Survival Skills, 54-75.
26. ibid, 62-65
27. ibid, 121; Robert L. Snow, *Stopping a Stalker: A Cop's Guide to Making the System Work for You* (New York: Plenum Trade, 1998), 23.
28. De Becker, ibid, 203.
29. Friedman, *Smart Cookies, Ibid,* Chapter 3: From No Power to NO! Power, 83-125.
30. Lardner, Jr.,158-159.
31. Joseph Telushkin, *Words That Hurt, Words That Heal: How to Choose Words Wisely and Well* (New York: William Morrow, 1996); For a new twist on communication, try some verbal kung fu, in Sam Horn, *Tongue Fu! How to Deflect, Disarm, and Defuse Any Verbal Conflict* (New York: St. Martin's Griffin, 1996).

32. Deepak Chopra, *Ageless Body, Timeless Mind: The Quantum Alternative to Growing Old* (New York: Harmony Books, 2000), 138; Berry, ibid, 2.

33. Scott A. Johnson, *When "I Love You" Turns Violent: Emotional and Physical Abuse in Dating Relationships* (New Jersey: New Horizon, 1993), 17.

34. Melita Schaum & Karen Parrish, *Stalked: Breaking the Silence on the Crime of Stalking in America* (New York: Pocket Books, 1995), 68.

35. Lardner, ibid, 93.

36. Dawn Bradley Berry, *The Domestic Violence Sourcebook: Fourth Edition* (Los Angeles: Lowell House, 2000), 85.

37. ibid, 8.

38. Herman, ibid, 79.

39. Lardner, Jr., ibid, 172.

40. ibid, 180.

41. Melody Beattie, *Codependent No More: How to Stop Controlling Others and Start Caring for Yourself* (San Francisco: Hazelden, 1992), 222.

42. Berry, 32.

43. Norman Cousins, *Anatomy of An Illness as Percieved by the Patient* (New York: Norton, 1979); Barbara Levine Hoberman, *Your Body Believes Everything You Say: The Language of the Body/Mind Connection* (Fairfield, CT: Aslan, 1991), 16-17; Terry Braverman, *When the Going Gets Tough, the Tough Lighten Up! How to be Happy in Spite of it All* (Los Angeles: Mental Floss Publications, 1998); Loretta LaRoche, *Life is Not a Stress Rehearsal: Bringing Yesterday's Sane Wisdom into Today's Insane World* (New York: Broadway Books, 2001); Linda Richman, *I'd Rather Laugh: How to Be Happy Even When Life Has Other Plans for You* (New York: Warner, 2001), 181-182.

44. Herman, *Ibid*, 82.

45. Melody Beattie, *Codependent No More: How to Stop Controlling Others and Start Caring for Yourself* and *Beyond Codependency: And Getting Better All the Time,* among others.

46. Joyce L. Vendral, *Look In, Look Up, Look Out! Be the Person You Were Meant to Be* (New York: Warner, 1996), 183-185.

47. Herman, ibid, 56.

48. Deepak Chopra, *Unconditional Life: Discovering the Power to Fulfill Your Dreams* (New York: Bantam, 1992), 202.

49. Friedman, ibid, 45.

50. Doreen Orion, *I Know You Really Love Me: A Psychiatrist's Account of Stalking and Obessive Love* (New York: Dell, 1997), 113.

51. Elizabeth Kubler-Ross, *On Death and Dying* (New York: MacMillan, 1969); Beattie, *Codependent,* ibid, 134-140.

52. Orion, ibid, 151-173.

53. Melody Beattie, *Co-dependent,* ibid, 134-140.

54. David Wolpe, *Making Loss Matter: Creating Meaning in Difficult Times* (New York: Riverhead Books, 1999), 127; Schaum & Parrish, 126-128; Arthur Schwartz & Ruth M. Schwartz, *Depression Theories and Treatments: Psychological, Biological, and Social Perspectives* (New York: Columbia University Press, 1993).

55. Herman, ibid, 118-122.

56. Dr. Charles Wilcox, telephone discussion with author, concerning the cited research used by the Pharmacology Research Institute (PRI) of Southern California (Newport, Los Alamitos, Northridge, and Riverside), 5 April 2002.

57. Schaum & Parrish, ibid, 126-128.

58. Gary Small, *The Memory Bible: An Innovative Strategy for Keeping Your Brain Young* (New York: Hyperion, 2002), 210.

59. ibid.

60. Deepak Chopra, *Unconditional Life,* ibid, 18.

61. Deepak Chopra, *Ageless Body, Timeless Mind,* ibid, 319.

62. Carolyn Scott Kortge, *The Spirited Walker* (San Francisco: Harper, 1998), 173-174.
63. Herman, ibid, 95
64. Berry, ibid, 8.
65. Herman, ibid, 85.
66. John Donnelly, *Suicide: Right or Wrong?* 2nd ed. (New York: Prometheus Books, 1998); Emile Durkheim, *Suicide: A Study in Society* (New York: Free Press, 1979).
67. Schaum & Parrish, ibid, 123.
68. Barnhill & Rosen, ibid, 83.
69. Loretta LaRoche, ibid, 219.
70. Dan Millman, *The Life You Were Born to Live: A Guide to Finding Your Life Purpose* (Tiburon, CA: H.J. Kramer, 1993), citing Vance Havner, 390.
71. Kortge, ibid, 9.

There can't be a crisis next week.
My schedule is already full.
—Henry Kissinger

Chapter 7:

NOT ALL SCARS ARE EXTERNAL

I had switched schools, and due to our changing financial condition (a reverse Midas-touch), we moved around a lot; which I decided, were reasons enough for Chuck to have been out of the picture for quite some time. I didn't have time to give Chuck much thought, however, as I had become pregnant again. (*How had that happened? I was on the Pill!*) Sometimes life just sucked.

There is no bottom to my well of stupidity, I constantly berated myself, as my hourly headache reappeared, and I indulged myself in an orgy of self-doubt. *What a moron, a total idiot, a complete loss!* This latest mistake seemed like a brand-new personal best in the screw-up department. I gained *sixty* pounds with this pregnancy, and had a severe case of toxemia (I no longer had observable ankles), with other assorted problems. I was extremely uncomfortable.

Even though Jerry had managed twelve bars and nightclubs, when I first met him, that spiraled down to intermittent substitute bartending within two years, due to his addictive nature, and the resulting eratic attention to his jobs. And if that weren't enough, he went from posh surroundings to raunchy joints; truly bottom-of-the-barrel dives. Even so, he could still rabble-rouse even the most quiet of drinkers, turning boring into exciting, when the spirit moved him (Think: Tom Cruise in *Cocktail*).

Because of the money situation, I had only two maternity blouses and one maternity skirt to wear. I did not look or feel my best: fat and dowdy. My glamour quotient was approximately zilch. I was hardly at my most sparkling: so much for being vain, fashionable, and fastidious.

And, of course, there was a bevy of beauties waiting in line for Jerry's attentions. Which wasn't the best ego boost for me.

You can imagine my reaction when the district attorney called, asking if I would consider being a surprise witness against Charles at an upcoming trial. (*Aha!* So *that's* why he hadn't been hanging around for awhile. Since he couldn't find me, he found *other* victims to bother.) Of course, I fairly jumped at the chance, hoping that this would be the last time that I would ever have to deal with Chuck. *Dream on.*

So now, at long last, Jerry *believed* all my off-the-wall stories. Having a common enemy, we were at peace for the duration of the trial. He escorted me to court, held my hand, consoled me, and sat with me through the ordeal. During the trial, he basked in his role of the *good guy*, the protector of *his* woman, and so forth.

When I met with the district attorney, there was another woman—a few years older than me—in his office. She turned out to be Chuck's first wife (*wife?*). Once I absorbed that shock, she informed me that she had a child (*child?!*) by him. Apparently, she was so afraid of Charles, that as soon as her testimony was over, her father—*a policeman!*—was to whisk her away to some other town, where she was living in hiding. Good grief. If her *father*, who was trained to deal with such matters, was afraid of what Chuck might do, what recourse did *I* have? My thoughts were reeling, as another epic headache began.

My knowledge of the law and court proceedure is next to nil, limited to television alone. So I was shocked to find that when she gave her testimony, I had to wait outside the courtroom, so I have no idea what she had to say. All witnesses were to wait outside until called upon to testify.

The court wouldn't let us hear what the others said, in case it might sway *our* testimony. So we sat around, cooling our heels, waiting our turn. This arrangement left me with an incomplete feeling.

When I finally entered the large courtroom, the atmosphere had a muted electricty, with the sense of things about to happen. Suddenly the center of attention, I was unprepared for such concentrated focus, and stunned by the full audience. One whole side of the area had well-dressed teenagers seated therein. I couldn't figure out who all those young people were, or why they were there, because I knew that Chuck didn't have any friends. I doubted that he could have made *that* many aquaintances since my departure. It was a puzzle, to say the least. Later, it was explained that three high school classes had come to see our local jury system in action. I was so embarrassed. And nervous. It was bad enough to have to speak in front of friends, relatives, and adult strangers; I certainly didn't feel comfortable telling my tale in front of *students*.

Although the more sordid details have been judiciously edited, suffice it to say that Chuck had been keeping himself busy by terrorizing *other* women. He was originally arrested and charged with kidnapping, aggravated assault, rape, and the attempted murder of *five* women on separate occasions. However, the DA felt he had a better chance of conviction by focusing on the last victim. Her ordeal was more than just a carbon copy of the other women: it showed how his pattern had escalated into over-the-top violence. She had been: (1) plucked off a street corner, and, (2) taken to his house, (3) where he beat her, (4) stabbed her *twenty-seven* times with a knife, (5) took a beer bottle, and upon smashing it in half, gouged out her stomach, and, (6) *then* he raped her. Vicious: from the number and ferocity of the stab wounds inflicted, Chuck's appetite for violence had far surpassed the crime of rape alone, proving himself to be one extremely dangerous, demented individual.

Since the so-called spousal privilege law (a wife can't testify against her husband) was in effect, I was only allowed to talk about experiences that happened before or after our marriage, not *during*. What a crock! I wasn't allowed to say anything that was derogatory about him. And further, yes or no answers just don't cut it, leaving any reason, logic, and motivation unsaid. Talk about the letter of the law versus the spirit of the law! And now, all these decades later, it is *still* being argued whether all of the states should adopt Spousal Privilege Exception Statutes. This is simply beyond my comprehension. I didn't *refuse* to testify against my ex-husband, I was informed—in no uncertain terms—that I *couldn't* testify against him in any way that mattered, because it was considered to be priviledged communication in a protected relationship. I was not planning to discuss *statements* that Chuck made to me, but incidents and facts. The only person being protected was the guilty party. I *still* don't understand. Where is consideration for the victim? Where are the victim's rights?

The lawyer asked me how long I had been married to Charles, and my response was, "Almost three years." But he wouldn't allow me to say *why* I was married for that length of time. Chuck's threats against my entire family never made it into the trial. After giving me a contemptuous once-over look, the lawyer remarked that Charles couldn't be as bad as I tried to make him out to be, if I stayed with him *that* long. I was *steaming*, but all I could do was fidget and squirm. So much for telling the truth, the *whole* truth, and nothing but the truth.

The lawyer summed up my questioning by concluding that it was *my* fault that Chuck went around kidnapping and raping other women, because I had had the audicity to *divorce* him. If we had remained married, he announced with ill-disguised hostility, the women of the city would have been safe (conveniently sidestepping the matter of what might have happened to *me*). *Can you believe it?* Talk about displacement! Yet again, a lawyer is criticizing a victim for instigating the violence, blaming the prey, not the predator, judging the injured, not the perpetrator. And, of course, I was not allowed to respond on the stand. It was an unfair and unnerving experience.

Why didn't the D.A. try to rectify the situation? Why didn't he ask me further questions? Why didn't he clarify my testimony on redirect? Did he think he already had a solid guilty verdict? I felt I was not given a fair opportunity to state my case, and viewed this experience as an obvious miscarriage of justice, which did not engender further faith in the criminal court. Why didn't I have the right to waive spousal priviledge? Again, I felt used and abused by the system. It was an excruciatingly painful experience.

I went back to sit in the courtroom, to something less than a standing ovation, in not what could have been called a charming frame of mind. With every eye in the place staring at me, I literally felt waves of disapproval aimed in my direction. To make matters worse, the only available seating was right behind the defense table. Not good. Of course, Chuck and Jerry took an instant dislike to each other, behaving like my eight-year-old students in a tug-of-war contest. So inbetween Chuck whispering vile things to me, he and Jerry were exchanging hard looks. (Cue: "The Good, the Bad, and the Ugly.")

I was shaken to the core upon seeing my parents in the courtroom. My mother testified to the fact that Chuck had kidnapped *her* one evening, when she was in her nightgown and robe. He lured her out to his car, to speak with her privately about *me*, shoved her in, and roared away. She talked a-mile-a-minute, always having had quite a way with fast and furious words, and he eventually brought her back to the house, and let her go. Chuck didn't want to deal with her nonstop yacking; it just wasn't worth the effort. He had always been fascinated with a mother-daughter ménage à trois, having told me, on several occasions, of one such experience he had had. Never in my wildest imagination would I have thought that he might be *hinting* that my mother and I should indulge in such behavior. Oh, gross! It makes me sick to even think about it. Good grief! Of course, Mother was *mortified*, not just by experiencing the situation in the first place, but by having to relive it, and *talk* about it in open court. She obviously wanted to disappear into the ether, and I felt guilty for bringing this added negative experience into my parents' lives. (It was such an uncomfortable situation that my parents never once mentioned this court experience. We all acted as if it never happened.)

During the lull, as Mother left the stand, Chuck glared back at me once again, hissing that he was going to kill me for all the lies that I told on the stand. (*What?* I wasn't able to say *anything* damaging, more's the pity. *What was he talking about?!*) Upon hearing the threat, Jerry heatedly leaped over the little guard rail, and the two of them grabbed each other, becoming involved in a noisy no surrender, no retreat battle. It would have deteriorated into a full blown dog fight in the middle of open court, if the baliff and others hadn't quickly intervened, to the tune of the judge's gavel banging away. "Order! Order!"

Good grief. How very male of you, I stewed. This display was about territorial rights, all over again. Guys and their raging macho-driven turf wars were really getting on my nerves. *What is this? my classroom? the playground?!* I was humiliated. None of this nonsense was helping matters. Both sorely needed adult supervision, and I longed to send them to opposite corners for a time out, in dunce caps, no less. Instead, I recited a ditty to myself, by Lewis Carroll:

> Tweedledee and Tweedledum
> Agreed to have a battle,
> 'Cause Tweedledum said Tweedledee
> Had spoiled his nice new rattle.

I suddenly had an epiphany of sorts, as the tumblers of recognition turned, clicking into place, recognizing that these two guys represented flip-sides of the same coin. It was similar to that of trying on two different styles of shoes. Clearly, neither of them fit, both being too tight and constricting. Discounting their obviously opposite personality and physical traits, I now couldn't see much difference between the two: Chuck was sexually abusive, Jerry was physically abusive, and both were emotionally abusive. Birds of a feather, and all that. ("It's deja vu all over again." Yogi Berra.)

My embarrassment did not end there. Oh, no. By the time the two were pulled apart, *I* was ordered out of the courtroom for causing a disturbance. (*Me?* Surely you jest. *Chuck* threatened me! *Jerry* started the fight. *What did I do?* I watched the spectacle in frozen disbelief and astonishment, along with everyone else!) I sputtered and spewed, but no articulate words came forth. My loss of dignity was complete. Stunned, I couldn't even think what to do as a symbolic gesture, just to keep myself from a major meltdown. (Sing along with Albert King: "If it wasn't for bad luck, I'd have no luck at all.") My life seemed reduced to a *Three Stooges* routine. It made me feel like retching.

Discredited and accused, I was mad at the system again, confused by the scope and power of the lies wielded against me. *Why were men always ascribing thoughts, motivations, and deeds to me, that didn't apply at all? Why was I always getting blamed for their conduct? When did self-responsibility go out of style?* Talk about riled up! The whole experience left me with a general sense of ick, ugh, and yuck, as there was nothing I could do but glower and grit my teeth.

At the close of the trial, Chuck was finally sentenced to the Atascadero State Hospital, where he would spend the next seventeen years of his life. Thank God. Chuck definitely needed a check up from the neck up. I had to exercise the utmost self-discipline not to jump up and down like a pogo stick, yelling, "So long, farewell, auf Wiedersehen, hasta la vista, goodbye and good riddance!" *And that's that,* I said to myself, while mentally dusting my hands of the situation.

I felt conflicted. I was feeling such empathy for the women he had terrorized, but I couldn't help feeling lucky that it hadn't happened to *me*. As the steel door slammed shut behind Chuck, I felt that it also closed on that part of my life. I was thoroughly grateful. In my mind I could hear a train leaving the station, chugging off in the opposite direction, as I listened to its long, mournful sound, getting dimmer and dimmer. I finally felt safe from Chuck's clutches.

Jerry and I had approximately two weeks of a marital truce during the trial, but our union remained a one-way ticket to disappointment. After the big reconciliation scene was over, and my worries about Chuck were gone, Jerry and I were back to square one, squabbling continuously. Nothing had really changed in our situation.

After J.J. was born—of course, Jerry was nowhere to be found during the Big Event—everything was on autopilot, as I was in a near-catatonic state of exhaustion. (Where was Popeye and his spinach when I needed them?) I could do little other than care for our newborn son. There was no Snap, Crackle, or Pop in our lives anymore. Jerry and I continued to be trains passing in the night, avoiding each other as much as possible. Our lovesong was in its final stanza. The theme music for this period in my life was clearly,"The Thrill is Gone." It became evident that what little had held us together had quickly eroded and completely disappeared. I felt smack dab in the middle of nowhere again. *What to do? What to do?*

Because my parents didn't approve of Jerry, or our lifestyle, they never came to visit. The one and only time that my mother came over, she noticed that J.J.'s soft spot was slightly higher than it should have been. When she pointed it out, I panicked, and immediately flew like Mary Poppins out to the car, to whisk him to the hospital. Unfortunately, my car had been stolen.

So, for more than one reason, it was a good thing that Mother had come to visit, since she drove us to the closest hospital. The doctors thought it such an emergency that they cleared the operating room—as well as their personal schedules—to take care of the problem. But, because I was still on maternity leave, my insurance had yet to kick back in (this was 1966, and things were different then). They would not admit J.J. because I had no current hospital coverage, and Jerry had none. Without enough cash to foot the bill, we were forced to find another hospital. Mother drove us.

Turned away elsewhere, we were finally sent to a hospital in another city, many miles from our home, that handled the indigent. I couldn't believe it! I would begin teaching again in two weeks, when the new school year began, but no hospital wanted to wait for a couple of weeks for payment. With the hospital so far away, and no car to drive us back and forth, it was very difficult to find a way to *visit* our son. Inbetween time, I had to deal with the police concerning the car theft, as well as to find a way to obtain another car, while gearing up for teaching again. Nothing is easy. Finally, the problem was taken care of, and J.J. was released from the hospital.

We had a total of *three* cars stolen during that period, among other varied and sundry experiences. I wanted time to ponder the significance of these events, but things were always in turmoil. Continually caught up in crisis and chaos, my attention was often distracted, obscured, or lost in other matters, and I failed to notice many things. Persistent suspicion tapped at the backdoor of my mind, but I ignored it, as my mind kept bumbling along on about one cylinder.

Surviving for the most part on my meager salary, we were one step from starvation, living on peanut butter and jelly sandwiches. I lost so much weight, I was literally skin and bones. My ribs, pelvic bones, and shoulder blades stuck out, giving me a terminally thin look. At my new school, teachers who'd never laid eyes on me before, called me Skinny Minnie, Beanpole, Bony Maroni, Toothpick, and Twiggy. This was not the response to which I was accustomed.

I lacked a suspicious nature. When our babysitter—an older grandmotherly type—intimated that Jerry was having an affair, I made excuses for his behavior. Besides being embarrassed, I was simply unable to deal with *one more* negative thing in my life. I was just so *tired* all of the time, plumb worn to a frazzle, like a sled dog on the last day of the Iditarrod race. So I went through mind-boggling acrobatics to avoid the truth, ignoring her input, taking the classic ostrich approach to my problems. As per usual.

One afternoon, a so-called friend and I were having such a good time, playing with a Oui-Ja board, at her house. Unexpectedly, the board spelled out that this woman was having an affair with Jerry. *No. Surely not.* I started laughing, but heard her catch her breath and hold it. (Talk about an *aha* moment!) When I looked up, the blood had drained from her face, as she stood up on wobbly, unsteady legs, knocking her chair over in the process. She backed across the room, holding her hand to her mouth. Her stricken expression and demeanor told me more than I wanted to know. The raised hair on my arms and the prickling up my spine—from my tailbone to the base of my skull—confirmed the message. Alarm bells, flashing lights, and loudspeakers went off in my head, as I tore outta there in a heartbeat. *Take a wild guess here, Ace.*

I had been denying what my subconscious, my intuition, and my babysitter, had told me from the start. (I am reminded of a quote by Diane Sawyer, "I think the one lesson I have learned is that there is no substitute for paying attention." I had not yet learned that lesson.) It took me some time, but finally, Jerry's casual affairs—heavy on the *s*— became so obvious that I could no longer ignore the situation. So much for being true-blue. His attempt at monogamy fell short of the mark. Way short. Way. *His name should have been Georgie Porgie*, I fumed. Such self-deception spelled IDIOT in my mind: neon-flashing, in huge, bold, colorful uppercase letters. I pondered the vast difference between trust and stupidity, as "Your Cheatin' Heart" ricocheted wildly around in my head. "This is the last straw!" I yelled."This marriage is so-o-o-o over!" There was nothing left to salvage.

Still, I was shocked right down to my shoes. Now *why*, when Jerry had such an impressive rep as a swinging dick, was I so crushed, shattered, enraged, and devastated to find out it was true? Why did I think he would be big on commitment, simply because *I* was in the picture? *Hel-lo!* It was just tough to acknowledge that, like the old saying, I'd been treated like a dictionary: useful when Jerry needed me, but any one would do. The betrayal was overwhelming. The hurt was incredible. It was hard coming to terms with the fact that I had been only the flavor of the week, as "Chain of Fools" blasted away on my inner stereo. I swear Jerry had stampeding infidelities out the wazoo. Remembering all those pockets full of phone numbers, my suspicious mind concluded that if all the women he'd known in the biblical sense got together, an arena the size of Staples would be needed. In my rich imagination, he had populated half of Southern California.

Believe me, I had a raft of emotions I'd give anything to deny. Although I briefly considered a *Have Gun, Will Travel* approach to revenge, I knew it was not for me. I was ashamed of even *thinking* that. I could never instruct someone to inflict pain upon another, as it would have resulted in a degree of guilt that would have been unbearable. *I am not handling this well*, I observed. And although a bullwhip, a cattle prod, and Lorena Bobbitt's method of justice held a certain appeal, I knew that our love or companionship had gone with the wind a long time ago. In any case, I had no energy to follow through with any revenge plans. Lucky for him. Needless to say, this episode took the last layer of shine from our relationship.

Skidding into the parking lot, and charging into the apartment much earlier than expected, I found a red-eyed Jerry sitting at the kitchen table behind a humongous mound of marijuana. We both froze, bug-eyed and slack-jawed. In that split second, that seemed to last for aeons, everything came together in a moment of perfect clarity. It became obvious that I had married a flim-flam artist: a small-time, dime-bag Tango king, who obviously had been sampling his wares. And that my so-called *friend*, was keeping me occupied, so Jerry could do his thing. Ohmygod! Lost in a time-blur, the events of our short life together ran through my mind like a slide show on speed. No wonder he could talk a blue-streak. No wonder he was always so energetic. No wonder he had so many friends! *Well, duh.* Everything instantly made sense: the mood swings, the paranoia, the escalating violence, the odd hours, the whispered conversations, the numerous telephone calls, the loss of his jobs, his sudden irregular disappearances. It felt like the tectonic plates were shifting beneath me.

"How could you have placed me in this situation?!" I raged. All I could think of was my third grade class: I constantly ranted to my students the equivalent of "Just Say No!" only to find that my very own husband—the father of my newborn—was a dealer! How could this have happened? *How could I not have known?* I was obviously looking out for *other* characteristics. Jerry's sparkling personality and talents provided perfect misdirection.

Adding these two new major jolts to my already overloaded system, sent my blood pressure soaring. His lies had multiplied like stray cats—his nose should have been three-feet long by now—helping me solidify plans for getting out of Dodge. I had enjoyed about as much of this marriage as I could stand, and was finally looking at the corrosive problem head on, facing down the reality of my situation. I *had* to get out of this relationship, but I didn't want a major showdown right then and there, when he was clearly out-to-lunch.

I mentally selected a multitude of ways to leave (sing: "Fifty Ways to Leave Your Lover"), disgarding them left and right, because they all required money. Of which I had none. Chewing over my dilemma, it became exceedingly clear that I had to bide my time, because I had nowhere else to go: my Estimated Time of Departure being as soon as I got my next paycheck (I was paid once a month). I didn't have a helluva lot of choice. What a miserable option.

Feeling manipulated, misused, and angry beyond the pale, I began surreptitiously packing. Catching me in the act, however, things escalated, as I had feared. "No *fuckin'* way!" Jerry shouted, falling back on the overused F-word in an effort to rattle my resolve, as well as demonstrate his conviction. It was the old Dog in the Manger argument, all over again. Hostility radiated off of him in waves. His chest rose and fell with his heavy breathing, as he charged at me. The fight that ensued was not pretty. The crowning experience—the sprinkles on the cupcake of this marriage—followed, and his killer instinct took over, as he went for the jugular. And choked me out. I nearly bought the farm right then and there, and was unconscious for so long, he thought I *was* dead, which would have made him *literally* a ladykiller. At length, I awoke in a heap on the bathroom floor, to the tune of Jerry loudly sobbing in the living room. An ice cream truck drove by, providing us with a momentary soundtrack: a seriously scratched recording, with a refrain that sounded like "Oh Happy Day."

"Oh, God, it just keeps getting better and better," I moaned. So much for happily-ever-after endings. Once again, I felt screwed, blued, and tattooed. That experience—showing how far his aggression had escalated—made it imperative that I leave and file for divorce, forthwith: no ifs, ands, or buts about it. No more hemming and hawing, no more lollygagging around, money or no. ("You have brains in your head, you have feet in your shoes, you can steer yourself any direction you choose." Dr. Seuss) I'd enjoyed as much of Jerry's scintillating company as I could stand, finally admitting that the kind of life we'd been living would not be the best of role models for a young child: Ozzie and Harriet we were not. We would never be a *Leave It to Beaver* family.

Our parting was not amicable.

Jerry's choking episode made such an indelible impression upon me that I no longer felt comfortable wearing choker necklaces, turtleneck sweaters, or scarfs tied around my neck, just as earlier side effects to Chuck's behavior had eliminated silver jewelry, sleeveless blouses, and long hair. I didn't want to remember any of this.

Happily, once all of this nonsense was over, I realized that having a baby was a blessing in disguise. Rearing a son enriched my life in ways I'd never dreamed possible. I turned into a new person overnight, totally absorbed, and fiercely protective, of this new addition to my family. My father's exasperated response to my second divorce, however, was, "Now that you have a *child*, no man will *ever* want to marry you!" Like I needed a husband to be whole and complete. To which I replied, "Don't worry about it, Dad. We're a package deal." ("A woman without a man is like a fish without a bicycle." Gloria Steinem) And that was that. Subject closed. End of discussion.

As Oscar Wilde once pointed out, "When the gods choose to punish us, they merely answer our prayers." This was certainly true in my case. I wanted a less than conventional life, I wanted to avoid routine, and I got it. I wanted to venture down unnamed, unmarked paths, I wanted a life with some excitement and adventure, and I got it. I wanted Chuck, and I got him. Then I wanted Jerry, and I got him. But none of my wishes turned out to be what I expected.

Our union turned out to be a hopeless misalliance: *no surprise there.* Let's just say that he overpromised and underdelivered. He was not the white knight I thought him to be. Sir Galahad, he was not. In addition to other obvious reasons, Jerry was definitely *unsuited* for a life that included a stalker always on the periphery. (Little did I know that Jerry was in the beginning stages of becoming a stalker himself). He did not have time for such inconveniences and worries, or ego-deflating experiences. Nor did he fancy sharing my attention with our son, J.J. Suffice it to say that my life with Jerry was no afternoon walk in the park.

It turned out, over the course of years, that Jerry was addicted to the chase. His main skill was *getting* married, not *being* married. Seeing with the benefit of hindsight, it became obvious that Jerry never knew what to do with a wife, once he got her. So, he went with his strong suit, and married another, and another, and so forth. Jerry's idea of a trophy wife was a professional woman with a good enough income to keep him in the style to which he had become accustomed. All of his wives were captivated by his initial charm and winning personality, not seeing his addictive, dark side, until it was too late. Unfortunately, with each succeeding wife, his domestic violence and stalking behavior increased, along with his addictions. He married a nurse after me. And while I was simply eyeing my walls to see which one to climb, he was shooting bullet holes in theirs. Thank God I missed out on that! The stories his later wives told were truly frightening. I was thankful that I dealt with his behavior only in the beginning stages.

His last wife turned the tables on him, however, giving him a dose of what he had been dishing out for so many years. (He told of once having a long, vivid dream about woodpeckers. When he awoke from his drunken stupor, he found his wife whaling on him with the stiletto heel of her shoe. For a week thereafter, he sported dozens of small, perfectly round scabs all over his face.) She threatened him so convincingly, that he was afraid to go to sleep whenever they were in the house together. He was absolutely convinced that she would kill him. I sincerely hoped that that experience caused him to remember and acknowledge the harm he'd done to others.

When Jerry died years later, I flew to Las Vegas to give his eulogy, since no one else felt up to it. Dealing with death is an incredibly difficult process, no matter *who* the deceased is, or what type of relationship you had. It is a time to remember the good, and begin to come to terms with the rest. It had taken me years to understand that funerals are meant to bring closure to the living, by providing a way to confront and accept the physical loss of a person. In addition, funerals give those gathered together a chance to properly grieve collectively, while starting the healing process individually. They also give pause to reflect on one's own existence, and consider how to move forward. It is a place to ponder the larger questions of life, and the impact the deceased had upon those attending. Death demands respect, not only for the deceased but for the mourners, as well, and I wanted the chance to bring a *positive* experience to everyone involved. Every single person in attendance privately thanked me for doing so, afterward. It was definitely worth the effort. None of his mourners flew into show-stopping paroxysms of grief. The gentle tears of two of his ex-wives tended to be for what *might* have been, for the undeveloped *potential,* for the monumental waste of his talents, personality, and relationships. (Chemical dependence has such ravaging cummulative effects.) His younger children, who didn't have a close relationship with him—and saw only his redeeming qualities—truly grieved. No friends were in attendance, as he no longer had any.

His family was not quite sure if he had been married *eight* times or more. "Pick a number, *any* number, and it's liable to be more right than wrong," was overheard at the funeral. (For fifteen years after our divorce, I worried that our son might end up meeting and dating an unknown half-sister. Guess what. It happened when J.J. was in high school. But that's another story. Don't get me started!)

So, back to my saga. Not too many weeks after our split, when J.J. was around six months old, he returned to the hospital. With a private room, and private nurses, he had a two-week stay, due to an inner ear problem. The ear infection was eating through the bone, which could then enter his brain. The doctors were afraid that not only was he going to lose his hearing, but part of his brain function, as well, not to mention that the incision would horribly disfigure him. *Oh my God!* Kaiser specialists discussed his case all around the state, and a couple of doctors flew in. Using an entirely new method, J.J. had a successful operation: with no scars, no hearing loss, and with no loss of brain function, whatsoever. *Would wonders never cease?*

The day J.J. was supposed to be released from the hospital, however, his temperature rose slightly, just *one* degree, but enough to make the decision to keep him another night, where the staff could keep an eye on his condition. Just in case.

I had been so looking forward to taking J.J. home with me, and was feeling mighty down about this unexpected turn of events. But, at the same time, I was happy that the doctors were being so thorough. It turned out to be another blessing in disguise, because I had an accident on the freeway while driving home from the hospital. It involved a boat that wasn't properly tied down, and had simply been placed in the back of a cavernous moving van. Traveling at a high rate of speed, the boat suddenly became airborne. It flew out the open back doors, floating along for awhile, before bouncing down the freeway. Upon hitting the center divider, it arched through the air, and landed on my car first, before launching itself onto other vehicles, causing some problems behind me. About a dozen cars and trucks ended up along the side of the freeway with me, waiting for the police. No telling *what* might have happened to J.J., if he had been lying on the front seat (no child car-seat laws were in effect back then). Synchronicity in action again! The next day, I was able to take him home, safe and sound. For which I am eternally grateful.

Just as I was getting on my feet, financially, with child support required, but *never* forthcoming, Jerry's second ex-wife hit me with *her* hospital bills. (I always thought that I was the second wife, but it turned out that I was number three). Since Jerry had no insurance, and because he was paid under the table, his wages couldn't be attached. So *I* was targeted to pay. It was explained that, because I was a teacher, I would lose my job if I didn't pay them, since I was *responsible* for Jerry's bills while we were married. But he and I were divorced when her hospitalization occurred, so I still don't understand that reasoning. And, because I didn't have the time or money or wherewithal to contest that in court, I paid. *Do I have the word 'Gullible' tattooed across my forehead?* To this day it doesn't seem fair. Geez! So, I was back to working three jobs ("Heigh-ho!"): full-time teaching days, full-time hostessing nights at a fashionable restaurant, and I became the manager of a large apartment building. I was never one to just lie around and eat bonbons, but this was ridiculous. I was going crazy with my schedule, but I was being responsible. Nose to the grindstone, and all that: story of my life. None of which left a whole heck of a lot of time for butterfly kisses and Velcro hugs with J.J.

Now that I anticipated Chuck being out of my physical life for a period of years, Jerry started *his* harassment. He frequently threatened to cause me trouble in my educational career, if I didn't return to him. "I'm going to call your boss, and tell him that you drink, smoke, do drugs, and *screw around with every man in sight!*"

Even though I was concerned that Jerry might make trouble for me, I just laughed at him. "Just who do you think they're going to believe? *You*—an obvious ne'er-do-well and malcontent? Or *me*, someone they *know*, who has an *excellent* teaching record?" My derisive laughter convinced him that I wasn't worried about his threats, and after several other extortion attempts he changed his tactics.

He then began to bother me at my night job. (*Double, double, toil and trouble!*). Jerry's harassment caused scenes on the restaurant premises, and tied up the business phone, putting *that* job in jeopardy. Finally, my boss had a major private face-to-face discussion with him. I don't know what was said, but it did the trick, and Jerry eventually moved on to romance—and disappoint—his *next* wife-to-be.

I seemed to be living inside an Excedrin ad. My relationship with men was not the most mature corner of my personality, and what went on between Chuck and Jerry and me, was certainly not a paradigm of mental health. I felt *slimed!* Deciding that I had beans for brains, I began to see the disturbing pattern of my life as one step forward, five steps backward, and thirteen steps upsidedown with a slide sideways. I felt trapped inside an Escher drawing, always dancing on the edge, surrounded by the litter of my life. *Another fine mess,* I thought absently. So, now my existence was even more complicated: a baby to care for (this was *not* my area of expertise), and *two* ex-husbands to deal with: not a happy predicament. My life seemed to be one long game of Pick-Up Sticks, and was turning out to be as poetic as a garbage truck.

My glory days are obviously in front of me, I mused, as I'm not into rosy revisionist history. Believe me, I'm not someone whose finest hours are spent slo-o-o-wly strolling down memory lane, nor am I one for flipping through vast musty, dusty snapshots, having thrown all my old photographs away for that very reason. I refuse to mentally view even sanitized reruns of *This Is Your Life*. The words *catastrophe, calamity,* and *disaster* don't even come close to describing my personal male associations. I'm simply not into reliving the highpoints of my misspent years; a "Sentimental Journey" is not my style. In fact, I couldn't wait for most of my life to become a distant, smoggy recollection.

Yet, if there was anything I'd learned from my past it was that the more attracted I was to a guy, the more trouble I seemed to get myself into, which was proof that I didn't understand men. At all. I appeared to be blinded by the light, not unlike all those insects—moths, June bugs, and mosquitoes—that are forever bashing their brains out, seemingly drawn to destruction by their own desires. No longer trusting my judgment, I second-guessed everything now. Self-doubt ruled. *I am clearly relationship challenged,* I admonished myself, acknowledging that I have more baggage than LAX could deal with. Since both of my marriages were clearly laced with conflict—during which I lost my independence, self-control, and self-esteem—I made a solemn vow, shaking my fist at heaven in the manner of Scarlett O'Hara, "As God is my witness, I'll never get married again!"

Chapter 7:

PERSONAL APPLICATIONS

Consider these facts and safety measures when dealing with a stalker:

(150) Alas, in order to prevent any prejudicial information in the courtroom that might legitimately taint the defendents, they seem to be tried in a vacuum.[1] (I once testified against two gang members in court. I had seen them, off and on, for years, as they had grown up in our larger neighborhood area. When they became teenagers, the two had joined separate gangs: a Latino gang and a Skinhead gang, each sporting the official gang-affiliated style and attitude. Both got high together one afternoon, and as an obviously spur of the moment decision, burglarized my neighbor's house. Since I was home sick that day, I observed the deed as it was happening, giving the police a play-by-play account, until they arrived on the scene. A long story: the crux of the matter was that by the time the trial began, one individual had cut his hair, while the other had grown his hair out, and both wore clean, pressed, acceptable clothing, and displayed proper public behavior. The change was remarkable. Both looked like normal, average, everyday, clean-cut high school students, clearly incapable of the crime I had witnessed. Lest the real world intrude in court, witnesses are often hampered with answering only "yes" or "no" questions, leaving the bulk of what they witnessed unsaid. Even so, I was able to dispel the folly of appearances. The two were convicted.)

(151) According to several credible sources, including a special Justice Department report, a gender bias is often shown by judges, who blame females for instigating or causing problems.[2]

(152) Odd mental gymnastics enable erotomanics to see themselves as pursued, and sometimes even persecuted, by their stalkees.[3]

(153) A verbal death threat, delivered during an argument or stressful situation, is the *least* likely to be carried out. It is only a statement of intention, given in the heat of the moment.[4] Do not retaliate. Don't get caught up in his/her desire for confrontation. Counterthreats only make things worse.[5]

(154) Revenge fantasies of imaginary retaliation are normal responses to stalking experiences, abusive treatment, and feelings of helplessness. It is normal for you to be angry, and it is understandable that you want to achieve justice. You may feel that you have the right to get rid of this person.[6] (Think: "Goodbye Earl," by the Dixie Chicks.) The desire for revenge represents a way to vent your pent-up rage in safety,[7] lessoning the tension, while giving you a sense of power, without you actually doing something criminal in the process. Daydreams and fantasies are acceptable substitutes for action.[8] Eventually, you'll come to terms with the impossibility of getting even, and let go of the need to avenge yourself. ("He who fights with monsters might take care lest he thereby become a monster." Friedrich Wilhelm Nietzche)

(155) Don't be revolted by any personal revenge thoughts that pop up out of the blue, causing you to judge yourself harshly. Experts agree that feelings of rage and revenge fantasies are perfectly normal responses to abusive treatment,[9] so why expect yourself to be above it all? A whopping 65 percent of victims *admitted* to entertaining aggressive thoughts toward their stalkers,[10] so the actual rate is likely much higher. Let go of blame, and shame, and have some compassion for yourself. You may be forced to surrender who you always thought you were (which is not for the fainthearted!), and suspend some of your most precious beliefs about yourself. Relinquish your former self-image and move on.

It's a hard fact to swallow, but we all have the ability to do what any other person is capable of. We have a shared humanness. Each person is capable of doing kind, loving, and noble deeds, as well as cruel, hateful, and despicable things. ("I am capable of what every other human is capable of." Maya Angelou) History shows that humans have a complex mixture of halos and pitchforks, good and evil. ("I am as bad as the worst, but thank God, I am as good as the best." Walt Whitman) Anything can happen to anyone. Specialists show that we carry both the monster and the witch[11] inside, and they must be faced, and worked with, if we are to grow, unfold, and develop to our highest potential.[12] View yourself with honesty, humor, and flexibility, because, unfortunately—as many have pointed out—there is a little Hitler in all of us.[13] Circumstances are key.

This was exceedingly hard for me to comprehend, much less, accept. I worked it around in my mind over the years, as a tongue worries a loose tooth. I chastised myself, having always thought myself to be a better person than one who would wish harm to another. It took me a long time to face this about myself, and come to terms with my own dark side: to acknowledge and integrate my shadow into my Self,[14] and to live a more conscious, and expanded life. ("I now rejoice whenever I see another portion of the dark side of myself. I know that it means that I am ready to let go of something that has been hindering my life...so I can heal it and move on." Louise Hay) Be honest about your own thoughts, without being judgmental or critical. Look for new aspects of yourself that you've denied, devalued, repressed, or disowned.[15] Shed old interpretations. Embrace your opposites. Love yourself in spite of your perceived flaws.

(156) Realize that actual revenge will not bring the relief you desire. You will suffer even more severe disturbances if you actually take matters into your own hands, and attempt vigilante justice. If you try to even the score, there is no way for you to return to normal. Payback doesn't work, and will only bind you more firmly to the one you despise. Understand that *nothing* can ever compensate for the damage done to you.[16] (Consider the quote from Jane Ace: "Time wounds all

heels.") Let it go. Get past it. Rise above it. Move on. Know that simply *surviving* is the best revenge of all. Then make the oft quoted saying, "Living well is the best revenge," your personal motto. I have it embroidered on a pillow that I see daily.

(157) When trauma exists for an extended period of time, your coping skills become eroded. As a result, it becomes increasingly difficult to think accurately about your situation.[17]

(158) Once the pattern is set for beating the mother, the children will come next. Sear that into your brain. Fifty to 70 percent of men who abuse their female partners also physically abuse children in the home, and 25 to 33 percent sexually abuse them as well.[18]

(159) Between 70 and 87 percent of children in homes where their mother is beaten witness the violence. Parental role models are of crucial importance. When children see a father repeatedly delivering blows, and see the mother accepting the blows, without leaving the relationship, the son and the daughter will likely continue the cycle of domestic abuse when they are grown. After all , if it is a regular experience, they become conditioned to it, seeing it as normal or acceptable behavior.[19] Experts show that more than three million children directly witness acts of domestic abuse each year.[20]

(160) When it becomes imperative that you get out of your situation, take precautions to do so safely. Leave immediately, money or no money. If you can't stay with family or friends, there are now shelters that will help you. Get yourself to a safe place, check your local Yellow Pages, and start calling. Several years after I left the situation, Jerry's current wife also found it mandatory to leave him in a mad rush, as his behavior escalated drastically. She came to my house—a safe haven—with her two children, and spent the afternoon calling. All of the local shelters were full, the only available place being forty-some miles away. She gladly took that opportunity. As late as 1970, there were no shelters. Today there are several thousand service programs, and over thirteen

hundred shelters. However, up to 60 percent of those in need are turned away, for lack of room.[21]

(161) Research shows that the most dangerous time for a battered woman is when she leaves a relationship.[22] It is estimated that 73 percent of emergency room visits, and up to 75 percent of domestic violence calls to the police, occur *after* separation.[23] Women are more likely to be killed while trying to leave, or shortly after successfully separating from a battering relationship. That's considered to be the flashpoint; the most dangerous time. (Years later, I read a Lethality Guide[24] and found that Jerry displayed ten high-risk factors out of a possible fifteen. Egads! *Who knew?*) Experts agree that the majority of husbands, boyfriends, or significant others who kill their former partners, stalk them beforehand, and far from the "crime of passion" that it is so often called, killing one's partner is a *decision*, not a loss of control.[25] It is estimated that victims who leave a battering relationship have a 75 percent higher chance of being killed by their partners,[26] and that 90 percent of all women killed by their ex-husbands or boyfriends had been stalked.[27]

(162) It is reported that 74 percent of abused women who work outside the home are harassed by their abusers on the job, either in person or by telephone, or both.[28]

(163) Although stalkers don't give up easily, research shows that some will abandon their original victim, if the stalkee can't readily be traced, or the prey proves to be too difficult to pursue. They are apt to transfer the fixation, and redirect their efforts at a more vulnerable target.[29] In most cases, they have to attach themselves to another victim, before detaching completely from the current one.[30] But, they always have the option to return to the first victim whenever the opportunity presents itself, as did Chuck. Experts agree that over half of the stalkers in America have been involved in prior incidents of stalking,[31] and occasionally in large numbers.[32] Interestingly, research shows that it isn't uncommon for stalkers to seek out relationships with women who resemble their former victims.

Chapter Seven Endnotes:
NOT ALL SCARS ARE EXTERNAL

1. George Lardner, Jr., *The Stalking of Kristin: A Father Investigates the Murder of His Daughter* (New York: Atlantic Monthly Press, 1995, 120.
2. ibid, 261.
3. Doreen Orion, *I Know You Really Love Me: A Psychiatrist's Account of Stalking and Obsessive Love* (New York: Dell, 1997), 40.
4. Gavin De Becker, *The Gift of Fear: Survival Signals That Protect Us From Violence* (Boston: Little, Brown, 1997), Chapter 7, Promise to Kill, 103-118.
5. ibid, 169.
6. John Barnhill & R.K. Rosen, *Why Am I Still So Afraid? Understanding Post-Traumatic Stress Disorder* (New York: Dell, 1999), 78.
7. Judith Lewis Herman, *Trauma and Recovery: The Aftermath of Violence—From Domestic Abuse to Political Terror* (New York: Basic Books, 1992), 189.
8. ibid.
9. ibid, 104.
10. Orion, ibid, 164-165, citing Pathe, M. & Mullen, P., "A Study of the Impact of Stalkers and Their Victims," *British Journal of Psychiatry*, in press.
11. Jon Kabat-Zinn, *Wherever You Go, There You Are* (New York: Hyperion, 1994), 82.
12. ibid, 83-84.
13. Elisabeth Kubler-Ross, *The Wheel of Life: A Memoir of Living and Dying* (New York: Scribner, 1997), 80; The great Indian sage Khrisnamurti also said that we all have a Hitler within us, according

to Elizabeth Stratton, *Touching Spirit: A Journey of Healing and Personal Resurrection* (New York: Simon & Schuster, 1996), 124.

14. Debbie Ford, *The Dark Side of the Light Chasers* (New York: Riverhead Books, 1998).

15. Dan Millman, *Everyday Enlightenment: The Twelve Gatewaysto Personal Growth* (New York: Warner Books, 1998), Chapter 10: Illuminate Your Shadow, 237-255.

16. Herman, ibid, 189.

17. Barnhill & Rosen, ibid, 33.

18. Dawn Bradley Berry, *The Domestic Violence Sourcebook:Fourth Edition* (Los Angeles: Lowell House, 2000), 9.

19. De Becker, ibid, 179.

20. Berry, ibid, 10.

21. ibid.

22. J.R. Meloy, (ed.), *The Psychology of Stalking: Clinical and Forensic Perspectives* (San Diego: Academic Press, 1998).

23. Berry, ibid, 7.

24. Meloy, ibid, Table 2, 146.

25. De Becker, ibid, 183.

26. Melita Schaum & Karen Parrish, *Stalked: Breaking the Silence on the Crime of Stalking in America* (New York: Pocket Books,1995), 56; De Becker, ibid, 184.

27. Orion, ibid, 185, citing Ed Royce, "Keynote Address," (lecture presented at the Fifth Annual Threat Management Unit Concerence, Los Angeles, CA, August 1995).

28. Berry, ibid, 9.

29. Schaum & Parrish, ibid, 65.

30. De Becker, ibid, 203.

31. Robert L. Snow, *Stopping a Stalker: A Cop's Guide to Making the System Work for You* (New York: Plenum Trade, 1998), 115.

32. ibid, 113-114.

"I don't want to know the odds!"
—Han Solo, in *Star Wars*

Chapter 8:

ANTICIPATORY TERROR

Talk about a rough patch. I was dismayed, bewildered, and once again dissatisfied with my lot in life. I wanted to emerge from the smoldering ashes of my divorces as a phoenix. But I still seemed to be living a TV movie of the week, slogging through the swamp. The next few years were an emotional bungee jump of false moves, dead ends, and working my way out of the maze. It made me old before my time. I began entertaining major pity parties, until it occurred to me that if Mick Jagger could get up every morning and face the day, so could I. *How could I feel any more jaded than he?* So I gathered my energies and courage, squared my mental shoulders, and refastened my seatbelt for yet another bumpy ride. It didn't take a shrink, a genius, or a psychic to deduce that I had an addiction to colossal mistakes—hot water seemed to be my natural element—and I always seemed to be jumping into the deep end of the pool. Which gave me something else to obsess over, as I went about the daily business of raising my son.

Although I wasn't singing "Life is Just a Bowl of Cherries," things slowly settled down, and I found a way to reconstruct my Humpty Dumpty life. As lonely as a lighthouse, I still resisted dating. So, there I was, minding my own business, stumbling, fumbling, and bumbling along just fine, moonlighting at Bob's Big Boy restaurant, when Wayne came into my life by sitting at my station. (Whoa. Be still my heart.) Oh, no. No, no, no, no, *no*. Not another handsome guy! Absolutely not. My radar went up immediately, and I was on full alert, my defense shields rising.

But his broad shoulders and towering stature gave every appearance of strength. I tried to control myself, and act nonchalant. I do not thrive on complications, nor am I happy with emotional messes. I had already proven that I was not the most reliable judge in the world (think: clueless kitten). With my trust factor seriously jeopardized, I couldn't rely on my own assessments when it came to men, since I seemed to have a knack for choosing those who were unsuitable for me. With my self-image and self-confidence shattered, I refused to let my heart get cleat-stomped into the ground again. Twice burned, and all that. Terrified to risk, I determined to simply wait for the fascination to pass. Uh-huh. I was not in a major rush to blindly throw myself off the edge of a cliff into an another emotional abyss. I grimly reminded myself that if I didn't watch my step now, I'd more than likely land in something equally unpalatable. I didn't think I could handle a repeat performance of either Chuck or Jerry (Talk about Three Blind Mice!). I vowed to become more discriminating in the future, since I clearly engaged in unbalanced relationships, by attracting troubled men: abusive, addicted, and sexually compulsive.

I waffled. *Get a grip!* I instructed myself firmly, as I watched Wayne coming into the restaurant on a nightly basis. I reminded myself that I had made a pledge, a pact, and that I didn't want another pocketful of regrets. ("Do you have the patience to wait till your mud settles and the water is clear?" asked Lao-tzu. Apparently not.) Stern lectures to myself, full of valid arguments, went by the wayside. My promise to myself was falling on my own deaf ears. How was that possible? *What was the matter with me?* Things change, what can I say? There seemed to be an underlying biological imperative operating here, as I was exhibiting a sizable need for specific male companionship. So Wayne and I began dating.

Like a fairy tale in which it always takes three times to get it right, four years later, when my son was close to five years old, I married for the third and last time. After all, I told myself, J.J. was ready to begin kindergarten, and needed an official father. Hope triumphed over experience, once again! *How is it that I'm still a cockeyed optimist?* And, trust me, the word "obey" was not in our wedding vows. It was a tough decision to make, and we deliberated long and hard about the subject. Wayne and I finally decided to go for it, fortified with new strength and understanding, along with the childish urge to knock-on-wood, and cross our fingers, toes, eyes, arms, and legs. Luckily, after all of the normal ups and downs of raising a family, while working, and pursuing wildly different outside interests—in addition to experiencing stressful intermittent stalking behavior—we've celebrated thirty-two years of marriage, so this union proved to be successful. The third time was the charm for us!

Although Chuck was incarcerated for a period of seventeen years in the Atascadero State Hospital for the Criminally Insane, he was gone, but not forgotten. He continued to send mail intermittently, and even called me on the telephone once, neither of which was supposed to happen. I never could figure out how he managed to do that, nor was I able to find the correct person to complain to about the situation. I was reduced to simply stacking his incoming letters with the others, tying them together with a black ribbon, and giving directions to Wayne that they were to be delivered to the police, in case of my *accidental* death.

If Chuck had been rehabilitated during his time in Atascadero, I had truly missed the transformation. I was in a state of constant waiting, never knowing when his next contact would be. Upon his release, Chuck called me on a nightly basis, usually between two and four in the morning, causing yet another sleep disturbance. He said he called at such odd hours, because he had learned to play an instrument while incarcerated for all those years, and was now working in a club in Las Vegas. I was profoundly thankful that there were so many miles between us; at least a four-hour drive. I felt obligated to answer my phone, because my father was ill, living by himself, and I worried that he might need assistance. Neither the police nor GTE wanted to hear my protests. Each said that the problem belonged to the other, continually bouncing me back and forth across town, from one department to the other. Neither wanted to deal with my complaint. (All of which put me in mind of Lily Tomlin's Ernestine: "We don't care. We don't have to. We're the phone company.")

Then I started receiving phone calls in the afternoon, from about three to four o'clock, one right after the other, at the rate of fifteen to twenty each day. But these calls had a totally different *feel* to them. Not only was the timing off, but the breathing sounded different, somehow. Finally, after my continued complaints, with great reluctance, GTE placed a trace on the line.

It was determined that the afternoon calls were from a former friend of my son's, both of whom were enrolled in middle school at the time. *What are the odds?* Apparently, the two had had a parting of the ways, and the rejected boy wanted to make his displeasure known. GTE representatives visited the boy's home, and spoke to his parents, emphasizing that a phone is not a *toy*. It was forcefully disclosed that should the boy continue to use the phone in such an illegal manner, it would be permanently removed from the family dwelling. They also revealed how lucky the boy was to be so young, because otherwise, he could have been prosecuted for my *night* phone experiences. It worked, because we never heard from that youngster again. In addition, Chuck was finally confronted about *his* unwanted late night phone calls, and was told that he would be prosecuted if the harassment continued. These calls, too, stopped abruptly.

Sometime thereafter, he was returned to San Quentin a rather heavy-duty prison—although I never found out the reason why. No one seems to know. Chuck says that he was sent away on "trumped up" charges, from which the accusing woman eventually recanted her testimony.

Since he always lied about everything else, how could I believe him? But it *is* a puzzle; What's the big secret?

I was just so *tired* of his interest. So, in my infinite wisdom, I decided to sabotage my appearance in an effort to make myself into an Ugly Duckling. This, I decided, was the perfect way to ward off any further involvement. Unlike Joan Rivers ("I've had my face revised from time to time. Darwin would be happy to know that my face is in a constant state of evolution."), I wasn't into facelifts, liposuction, or silicone augmentation; just the opposite. I worked at becoming a Plain Jane. First, I cut my fingernails short. Eeek! Then, because some thought my best physical asset was my dancer's legs, I covered them up by wearing pants outfits forever after: no more dresses or skirts for me. After all, I reasoned, if Marlene Dietrich and Katharine Hepburn could wear pants, why couldn't I? I wiped out an *extensive* wardrobe in one fell swoop.

I then became a serious eater of anything warm, sweet, and fluffy: cakes, pies, and bakery goods became my staples, and I quickly became known as the Doughnut Queen. No more fresh fruits, yogurt, or juice for me. No more vitamins or minerals. Workouts, dancing, and sports were no longer a part of my lifestyle. If it was good for me, I wanted *nothing* to do with with it. Healthy eating was out. Sugar, fat, and caffeine was in. Ah, the comfort of junk food.

I love the quote from Erma Bombeck: "I got to thinking one day about all those women on the *Titanic* who had passed up dessert at dinner that fateful night in an effort to 'cut back.' From then on, I've tried to be a little more flexible." My sentiments exactly. And, being an avid believer in the therapeutic qualities of chocolate, I packed the pounds on, guilt-free, until my hourglass figure was completely whacked out of shape, lo-o-o-ng past its prime. Talk about a turnabout! I didn't like being pregnant, because I thought others would think I was FAT. To give you some indication of my physical change, an older J.J. once looked at earlier photos of me, and with a shocked expression on his face, demanded, "Mom! What *happened*?!" When my body was *beyond*

Rubenesque, actually, I suppose, as big as a barn door might be a more accurate description, although gargantuan also comes to mind, I was finally able to *relax*. I was convinced that Chuck would see that I no longer looked the same, and would lose whatever the appeal or fascination was. An added plus was that others no longer automatically gave me the quick once-over. I no longer worried about strangers following me home—which had happened more than once—or unwanted eyes tracking up and down my body.

Even so, my deteriorated roly-poly condition—with this extra sixty-pounds that I still lug around on thunder thighs—did *nothing* to deter Chuck's continued obsession. Nor does the fact that all these years later, my face is full of discolorations, age spots, and crow's feet. Taking the position that a lived-in face is a sign of character, I see my wrinkles as badges of honor: battle decorations. *I earned them!* The long auburn hair of my youth remains short and red, with a touch of gray now peeking out at the temples. Instead of a stylish wardrobe with ultra high heels, I now wear snuggly, thick, *oversized* sweats and tennis shoes. My clothes are roomy, accomodating, and comfortable! The point being that I look about as *different* as one can be from the original version, turning from youthful, fresh, and wholesome, into old, faded, and tough. (The theme song for this period of my life is clearly,"The Old Gray Mare, She Ain't What She Used to Be.") But, it appears that none of this mattered one whit. In his letters, Chuck has continually called me "pretty girl," and "young lady," stating that after forty-two years, I've never changed. Ri-i-i-ght.

What I didn't realize was that the *real* me wasn't actually being seen or heard:[1] I was merely the screen upon which Chuck projected his needs, and his *idea* of what I was, and what I looked like. Even when I was under surveillance, he wasn't actually seeing me in my fatty flesh, but a *fantasy* creature in his head. If I had recognized this fact years earlier, I could have saved myself a lot of grief. So this plan—a form of self-defense and self-preservation—to disguise myself, and make myself less attractive, all came to naught. It was one of those cases in which I won the battle, but lost the war. It was definitely not one of my better decisions. Although research shows that *other* stalking and rape victims had come to this same ill-conceived solution, making themselves unattractive, and subconsciously hiding their sexuality,[2] believe me, it was not a consolation. So now I have the unpleasant task of trying to *undo* all those years of unhealthy neglect. Oh, woe is me.

It is so true that health, beauty, and energy are wasted on the young. Over my lifetime, I've been of perfect size, shape, and weight, I've been skeletal, and I've been fat; and I have to say that I've learned to live comfortably with my extra pounds. I felt more balanced, able to ward off blows, while less likely to be knocked down. I had the satisfaction of knowing that no one would ever again crush me in a Kodiak hug. If push came to shove, I'd be able to deliver punches with more staying power. I had the confidence to accept my own physique, and came to love my full-figured body, every overstuffed, comfy inch of it. ("A woman may develop wrinkles and cellulite, lose her waistline, her bustline, her ability to bear a child, even her sense of humor, but none of that implies a loss of sexuality, her femininity..." Barbara Gordon) Oddly, I liked myself much better as a larger-than-life woman, than when I used to obsess over every little ounce, and perceived flaw, and imperfection.

It took years for me to realize that the way you perceive your body is a *learned* concept. Beauty standards are both historical and geographical. Beauty is in the eye of your culture. Knowing this, I stood firm against our cultural and advertising messages that conspire against obesity. However, I finally came to realize that all of this extra weight is simply not healthy. So, my weight loss—if or when—will be natural, gradual, and for matters of health and longevity alone. Self-love is a wonderful thing.

Meanwhile, finally released from prison again, Chuck was somehow able to go into partnership with his nephew, obtaining a local liquor license. How is this possible? First, how could he come up with that kind of money? Secondly, felons aren't supposed to fraternize with other criminals, nor are they supposed to be around guns. He later wrote that his sister provided the startup money, so that answered one question. While working at Studd's Liquor, there was a robbery shootout at the store, that Chuck dearly loved to write about in his letters, although he always exaggerated or rearranged the facts, adding numerous details that never happened.

During this period of time, his obsession with me entered another dormant stage, with only a few random phone calls, and actually ceased for a good long while. With the length of this latest remission, I got my hopes up, once again, that it was really and truly over. No such luck.

Everytime I thought my life was finally in apple-pie order, Chuck would always come out of left field to upset my applecart. So, after this period of relative silence, out of the blue, a woman called, saying that her husband was a friend of Chuck's. *Uh-oh.* Instantly, a pit the size of a Florida sinkhole, opened in my stomach. She explained that she was asked to call me, to see if I would like to meet Chuck, and have dinner with him some evening. Caught completely off-guard, a frisson of alarm skittered up my spine, my synapses screaming danger as a thousand thoughts clamored for my attention. Adrenaline instantly flooded my system as my heart began pounding, and a sudden onset of the shakes took hold, while every neural fiber was immediately on red alert. Chuck *still* had the power to twist me into a mass of knots. The right side of my brain was shouting, *How can this be? That all happened decades ago. Get over it!* At the same time, the left side of my brain was digging into research: Scientists say that every year 98 percent of my body's atoms and molecules are replaced, and within three years, none of the same atoms are in my body.[3] H-m-m-m. And neurologists say that each time I have a thought or a feeling, it chemically etches a neural pathway in my brain.[4] So the fear grooves in my brain must be *extremely* deep.

In as controlled a voice as possible, I carefully explained to the woman that a meeting would *never* be possible, since I was happily married, with a family. And promptly hung up, knowing with a certainty that it was starting all over again. I had convinced myself that it was all over and done with, and was caught off-guard by Chuck's sudden reappearance in my life. I determined never to let hope rule my thoughts again. Weak-kneed just thinking about it, I was working on taking deep breaths, trying to come to grips with this latest development.

And that's how it goes. Stalking is a cyclical experience. You think it's finally gone forever, and suddenly, it's "Hey there, long time no see, did you miss me?" And so began another round of harassment and obsessive behavior. Chuck refused to recognize that not only are Wayne and I still married, but within our family, we have four grown children, and nine grandchildren. Chuck's subsequent letters merely stated that my "boyfriends better hit the road now," because he was coming back, and so on. His letters were long, with tiny, cramped handwriting on legal-sized paper, six-to-ten pages each: garbled, inappropriate, and graphic. His subtle-as-a-sledgehammer message, "You haven't seen the last of me," ensured that I'd be thinking of him, allowing him to live rent-free in my head. His writing became more ominous, alternating between charming, and threatening behavior, the good ole sandwich approach. "When I went to prison, I had getting you back on my mind. And one other thing. Revenge…" The metaphorical daisy picking of "he loves me, he loves me not" tone of his letters was ensuring both fear and anger, as well as some outright laughter.

Chuck kept suggesting that we meet in a public park, but that if I felt uneasy or the least bit uncomfortable—suspecting ulterior motives of any kind—we could meet in a *church*. Oh sure. Like *that*, along with a restraining order, would help protect me. Let's get real, here! He's about as trustworthy as Iraq. His fantasy was so transparent: he'd like to blow me to Kingdom Come in a religious building, of one kind or another, staging one hell of a grand-exit spectacle. Talk about a Bad Boy self-image. This was shaping up to be Trouble with a capital T.

I had been under constant surveillance for weeks, before I finally figured out that Chuck was *not* in Nevada. He sent letters to his sister, who promptly mailed them to me from Las Vegas or Henderson, so they would have an out-of-state postmark. So, all those phone calls came from only three-miles away. Chuck was on my block constantly, even bringing his grown nephews along for the ride. So much so, that the neighbors began complaining about "a stranger" being parked in the cul-de-sac early in the morning, and late at night. Unfortunately, the information never trickled down to me! It was later determined that Chuck actually placed many of the gifts—mostly bottles of *Charlie* perfume—on my front porch. He used packaging materials from other states, such as Arkansas and Oklahoma, spending a great deal of time carefully glueing other postmarks and postage in the appropriate places. From reading the various postmarks, I couldn't figure out why or how he was doing all of that traveling. Duh.

It finally became apparent that the packages that were left on my front doorstep in the mornings, were delivered way too early to have been placed there legitimately. It also became clear that Chuck was attempting to peer in our windows at night, when Wayne pointed out our trampled flower beds in the morning. Then, just to make sure, he began flooding those areas with water each night, and footprints would greet us as the sun rose. I didn't want to believe it, but this was proof positive. Chuck's stalking behavior became increasingly frequent and severe, finally escalating to shadowing my car again.

Intermittently, over all those years, my family had heard my complaints about Chuck following me and harassing me. But since there was nothing anyone could do about it, and they were never around to deal with it personally, they actually didn't have a *clue* as to what it was like, or how it felt. Eventually, however, Chuck became curious about my husband, and followed Wayne's truck, totally *freaking* him out.

Wayne couldn't *believe* that it was happening to *him*. And, overreacting, he mentioned it again, and again, and again, getting angrier with each telling. He would have dearly loved to squash the little red car with his big 4x4 truck, providing Chuck with an instant sunroof. But, alas, Wayne had no such opportunity, which left him feeling furious, unfulfilled, and impotent, with no way in which to vent his frustration. *Welcome to my universe.*

That really got on my *one* last good nerve. Here I had put up with this type of surveillance behavior off and on for decades, and Wayne was followed for a *few* minutes, on *one* day, and he came *unglued!* Give me a break. So again, instead of focusing all of my anger at Chuck, I'm thinking about how my husband is handling the experience. Good grief. It is safe to say that my response to this situation left something to be desired. The positive side affect to this experience, however, was that Wayne's anger was finally mobilized, and he was now *completely* involved, using the words "us," and "we," as in "*we* are being stalked," when explaining the details to others. So, we finally became a united front.[5]

Which just goes to show that no one can relate to the emotional stress of *prolonged* exposure, until they are in a similar situation. The adrenalin rush as you go into a state of alert, the persistent expectation of danger, and the constant state of vigilance, all takes an enormous toll on the victim. But I wouldn't wish that on anyone.

Chapter 8:

PERSONAL APPLICATIONS

Consider these facts and safety measures when dealing with a stalker:

(164) A stalker will intermittently drift through your life like a dangerous virus. Like domestic violence,[6] stalking follows a repetative cycle. It waxes and wanes, and even has periods of full remission,[7] becoming increasingly frequent and severe. There are three stages in the cycle: a long Tension Building Phase, an Explosive or Acutely Violent Phase, followed immediately with the Hearts and Flowers Phase.[8] The cycle often tapers off and ceases for months at a time, only to resurface unpredictably into a fresh series of events. During the lull or dormant stage, however, the victim remains constantly on alert for signs of his/her stalker, never knowing if the stalking is actually over.[9] About the time the victim finally relaxes, thinking it's finally finished, the process begins again, giving them no respite.

(165) Mental health experts maintain that the recognition of your trauma, and the telling of your story, is central to your recovery process.[10]

(166) The most common of stalking behaviors, is repeated telephone calls (of the hang-up, anonymous, or harassing variety) to someone who does not welcome them.[11] The caller simply wants some kind of connection, some kind of attention. It doesn't matter whether it's positive or negative. For example, one stalker may call just to hear the victim's voice, another may call to keep tabs on the victim, a third may deliberately start an argument, while a fourth may simply want to sweet talk with the target. Of course, stalkers may originally call for one

reason, and within the course of the conversation, end up with another purpose altogether.[12]

One New York telephone company, NYNEX, reported 15,000 complaints of threatening and/or obscene phone calls *each month*. Both are integral parts of harassment by stalkers,[13] and no one knows how many go unreported. That's just *one* telephone company in one state. The estimated number in the U.S. would be astronomical. Do not speak with the stalker, thereby encouraging repeat calls. Again, this is the principle Las Vegas was built upon: intermittent reinforcement. Ignore the behavior, and eventually, it will subside.

(167) Mail from a stalker is the second most common form of contact.[14] Schizophrenics don't do well with people face-to-face, so they write long rambling letters. Believe me, I know that it's easy to get all riled up upon receiving unwanted letters, notes, and cards, expecially when they are in massive amounts, over a great length of time. Even more so, when they are disturbingly detailed, pornographic, or threatening. Take heart in the knowledge that your stalker is expending his/her time and energy in *writing*. Instead of getting freaked out, consider the fact that such corespondence can't actually hurt you. Reduce your fear and anger by simply choosing not to read them. Do yourself a favor, and have a family member pile them in a box, unopened. Keep them for your lawyer, detective, or D.A., should they ever be needed. Otherwise, don't bother with them. Unfortunately, e-mail is now becoming another way that stalkers can reach their victims. Make a copy and delete those unwanted messages.

(168) It bears repeating: No response is *always* the best policy. Appearing to do nothing at all, while seeming to ignore the harassment, is seen by the experts as the *fastest* way to end such an obsession: PROVIDE NO REINFORCEMENT WHATSOEVER. Of course, that takes patience and control.

(169) After stalkers have been incarcerated, many continue to contact their victims through mail and phone calls from prison. Each time

this happens, contact the officer in charge of your case, as well as prison officials. This will cause your stalker to lose good-time credits, which will not allow him/her an early release. The longer this person can be kept behind bars, the better.

(170) A stalker is not only jealous of any other relationships you may have, but of *perceived* relationships, as well. Nothing you can do will change understandings in this regard, because it is all a figment of his/her imagination. The stalker sees these others as standing between the two of you.

(171) Know that you will make major lifestyle changes in response to being pursued, since the stalker will invariably bring chaos into your life. The never-ending harassment and intermittent surveillance inflict enormous psychological damage and social disruption. Victims feel as if they are experiencing an unrelieved state of siege.[15] Expect intermittent disruptions. Don't let them throw you.

(172) You are responsible for your physical health, at the subtle level of thoughts, as well as the obvious level of actions.[16] You need to be in top form to deal with the stress of the situation. You need to increase your endurance, strength, and resistence. Invest in yourself and your future. Take care of your bodily needs with multivitamin and mineral supplements, exercise, and use whatever relaxation measures that work for you.

(173) While under a stalking siege, it's easy to let your interest in food slide, existing on a diet of candy and caffeinated sodas, to achieve an added adrenaline boost. Fight that temptation. Eat three well-balanced meals daily. Consciously keep your energy and endurance levels up by snacking on raisins, trail mix, bran muffins, carrot sticks, and other healthy alternatives. I know, *I know.* If you're a sugar freak like I am, this tip is hard to swallow. But you can't afford to let your physical self deteriorate. Why give your stalker yet another advantage?

(174) It is also typical to let your grooming slide. Regardless of how you feel, make the effort to take showers, brush your teeth, comb your

hair, keep your clothes clean, and so forth. The less you care about your grooming, the worse you feel about yourself. So put yourself together before you go out in public: scrubbed, presentable, and smelling good. It is important, not only for health and social reasons, but to affirm your self-image. Exert extra effort and attention in the area of self-care. Practice self-nurturing and self-love. Make it a lifetime commitment.

(175) Breathe.[17] Oxygen is your primary food, and proper breathing placates your mind. Shallow breathing appears during times of fear, anger, and stress. Such rapid inhalations pump air in and out of your throat, without getting much into your lungs, making you easily winded and fatigued. Consciously slow your breath. Steady deep breathing calms your mind, allowing you to *think*, and relaxes your muscles. Let oxygen restore your cells, as well as your focus. You don't want to be hyperventilating when your stalker is around. And remember the adage: fresh air brings about fresh ideas and a fresh point of view.

(176) Do not neglect your exercise. Medical researchers have amassed convincing evidence showing that physical exercise provides the greatest health benefit. Can you believe that by 1980 alone, the U.S. Bureau of Statistics reported over 70,000 studies that showed a positive correlation between exercise and mental performance?[18] Standard fitness guidelines recommend a minimum twenty minutes of moderately vigorous exercise three times a week.[19] Be firm in your commitment. Tolerate your discomfort. After all, if you can deal with the continual trauma of a stalker, you can deal with a little physical discomfort *of your own choosing*, in your effort to thwart him/her. Do it for yourself. Be patient and persistent, and your discomfort will soon go by the wayside. Be iron-willed about it. Just do it, with no excuses.

(177) Setting up a physical fitness program (walking, aerobics, swimming, et cetera), demonstrates that you are in charge of your life, and are willing to act on your own behalf. The hard part is acquiring the habit. As a rule, it takes three weeks to three months for the body to

adjust to the demands of a new level of exercise. Be realistic. Make your pace steady and purposeful (not exhausting). This new discipline and self-control will bring about a sense of accomplishment that will keep you moving in the right direction. Consistency counts. Experience pleasure with small, achievable, physical goals, and improve your self-esteem.

(178) Experts determine that not only does exercise get rid of your pent-up emotions and angry feelings, it is also as effective as medication for the blahs, a bad mood,[20] or depression.[21] Even walking for only five minutes a day can reduce your anxiety,[22] and lift your spirits.[23] You will survive times of turbulance better if you regularly exercise.[24]

(179) Experts agree that meeting with your stalker, even years later, is absolutely the *worst* thing you can do. It will only encourage or increase stalking behavior.

(180) Many stalking and rape victims try to change their appearance, so they will not be recognized, or to discourage further interest. They hope to achieve this by cutting, growing, or dyeing their hair, or by gaining or losing weight, or through breast reductions or augmentations, or by wearing completely different types of clothing, with their shapes camouflaged by beige or oatmeal or unflattering colors, or by wearing multi-layered, bulky, or tentlike clothes. They are simply desperate to look common and ordinary, by blending into the background, in a subconscious effort to hide their sexuality.[25] It doesn't work. Stick with what is comfortable for you. On the related front of date violence: a Minnesota teen sex survey (2001) gave almost the identical results of a South Carolina teen survey (2000), with over 83,000 public school teenagers participating in the research. The results showed that disordered eating habits resulted from date violence. The abused students tried to manipulate their bodies, in one way or another, to appear unattractive to others.[26]

Chapter Eight:
ANTICIPATORY TERROR

1. Doreen Orion, *I Know You Really Love Me: A Psychiatrist's Account of Stalking and Obsessive Love* (New York: Dell, 1997), 74.
2. Paxton Quigley, *Armed and Female* (New York: St. Martin's Paperback, 1989), 56.
3. Deepak Chopra & David Simon, *Grow Younger and Live Longer: Ten Steps to Reverse Aging* (New York: Harmony Books, 2001), 32, 225.
4. Elizabeth Stratton, *Touching Spirit: A Journey of Healing and Personal Resurrection* (New York: Simon & Schuster, 1996), 130.
5. Orion, ibid, 134. The author, a psychiatrist, had the same experience with her partner.
6. Lenore Walker, *The Battered Woman* (New York: Harper & Row, 1982). The author pioneered the landmark research regarding cycles of violence.
7. Melita Schaum & Karen Parrish, *Stalked: Breaking the Silence on the Crime of Stalking in America* (New York: Pocket Books, 1995), 62-67; Dawn Bradley Berry, *The Domestic Violence Sourcebook* (Los Angeles: Lowell House, 2000), 35-37.
8. Schaum & Parrish, ibid, 131; Elaine Landu, *Stalking* (New York: Franklin Watts, 1996), 43-45.
9. Orion, ibid, 39. The author had the same experience.
10. Judith Lewis Herman, *Trauma and Recovery: The Aftermath of Violence—From Domestic Abuse to Political Terror* (New York: Basic Books, 1992), 3-4, 175-195.
11. J. Reid Meloy (ed), *The Psychology of Stalking: Clinical and Forensic Perspectives* (San Diego: Academic Press, 1988), 288-292; also see tables 11 & 12 on 132-133.
12. Meloy, ibid, 288

13. Robert L. Snow, *Stopping a Stalker: A Cop's Guide to Making the System Work for You* (New York: Plenum, 1998), 11.

14. Gavin De Becker, *The Gift of Fear: Survival Signals That Protect Us From Violence* (Boston: Little, Brown, 1997), 133.

15. Schaum & Parrish, ibid, 220.

16. Barbara Hoberman Levine, *Your Body Believes Every Word You say: The Language of the Body/Mind Connection* (Fairfield, CT: Aslan Publishing, 1991), 35.

17. Jon Kabat-Zinn, *Full Catastrophe Living: Using the Wisdom of Your Body and Mind to Face Stress, Pain, and Illness* (New York: Delta, 1990), 47-58.

18. Carolyn Scott Kortge, *The Spirited Walker* (San Francisco: Harper, 1998), 169.

19. Deepak Chopra, *Ageless Body, Timeless Mind: The Quantum Alternative to Growing Old* (New York: Harmony Books, 1993), 128.

20. Kortge, ibid, 169.

21. Chopra, ibid, 86; Kortge, ibid.

22. Kortge, ibid.

23. ibid.

24. ibid, 170.

25. Meloy, ibid, 134; Quigley, ibid.

26. Kicklighter, Kirk, "Date Violence Reported at 5-10 Percent," *Press-Telegram*, 27 August 2001, A12.

*A restraining order is "a document
about as useful as a parasol
in a hurricane."*
—Stephen King

Chapter 9:

FALLING BETWEEN THE CRACKS

I was tired of living in a bull's eye, always dodging darts. Chuck kept intermittently coming back, dropping by for an unexpected visit, like a bad case of heartburn. Eventually, his stalking intensified in earnest. I hated to give in to paranoia, but I didn't for a minute think that many of my experiences, such as ten-inch roofing nails in my tires, were random. I struggled with the uncertainty regarding which events were related to stalking and which were not. I would coast along for a while, placing Chuck in the back corner of my mind, when he would return in some form (phone calls, cards, letters, gifts, footprints, surveillance), as unwelcome as a splash of ice cold water, bringing me back to reality. Came the dawn when every little thing of negative consequence was suddenly seen in a more sinister light: Chuck did it.

Paranoia ruled, and it was catching. When I finally came to my senses, everytime something strange happened, *others* would automatically attribute it to Chuck. I later found myself in the awkward position of taking the opposite view, showing how he *couldn't* have been the perpetrator of such and such, because of thus and so. It was not a posture I relished. For example, when our house caught on fire, many people attributed the disaster to Chuck, while I took the unpopular stance that it was the result of the Fourth of July party held on the next block, where everyone had been indiscriminantly shooting off illegal bottle-rockets from Mexico. Even when the Fire Marshall's investigation supported my interpretation of the incident, others were reluctant to take the blame off Chuck's shoulders.

"Why are you defending a jerk like Chuck?" people asked, giving me funny looks. Logic and proportion flew out the window when he was the subject under discussion. It was an odd position in which to be placed, and one which made me question my reasoning, especially considering the old adage: Just because you're paranoid, doesn't mean they aren't out to get you. (And the quote attributed to Jean Kerr, "If you can keep your head while all about you are losing theirs, it's just possible you haven't grasped the situation," also gave me pause to ponder.)

Over the years, Chuck's letters continually issued dark warnings, sandwiched between assurances of love. The latest texts, however, gave a specific date by which he stated we would meet again. He mentioned a gun, and promised that I was in for "an experience that I'd never had before and would never have again." *Like I can't read between the lines?* I decided it was high time to get the Long Beach Police Department involved. The situation warranted it.

After a particularly horrendous day at school, coupled with a head full of worries about Chuck, I drove downtown to lodge an official complaint. Now that the situation had escalated, and now that California had two new laws in effect (the Stalking Law and the Three Times and You're Out law), I knew that I could finally get the help that had eluded me for over three decades.

I was exhausted, and not thrilled to be standing twelfth in line, with my high heels hurting my feet, on top of everything else. Although each person had a different reason for being there (wanting to see someone in jail, needing to give clothes to someone in jail, needing information as to how to bail someone out of jail, et cetera), the line moved along quickly enough. Even when two men spewed four-letter words around, they were helped with a minimum of fuss and bother. Upon finally making it to the front of the line, however, all lighthearted fun and easy chitchat ceased. The clerk couldn't even muster up a courteous smile. There wasn't so much as a token civility in her tone. I was not expecting this, as I am constitutionally incapable of being anything but polite. At the very least, I felt that I deserved equal respect. How rude.

In a carefully nonconfrontational voice, I began my request. When I asked to see a detective, the clerk acted like that was the most outrageous request she'd ever heard, something akin to requesting an audience with the Pope or the Queen of England. She demanded to know why I wanted to see one. I told her that I had a long-term stalking experience on my hands, and things were working themselves into a fever pitch. She absolutely had no empathy for my situation, even going so far as to theatrically roll her eyes, and make a joke with the other office personnel within her area. They thought it funny that I would want some help with my "little" problem. I cannot tell you how amused I was. To put it kindly, she lacked a certain social grace. She then instructed me to go home and phone 911. *Oh, yeah. Uh-huh.*

I told her that the use of 911 was for immediate emergencies only, and that my situation was not *yet* an emergency. She told me to do so again. I explained that I was trying to *forestall* an emergency, and that 911 wouldn't consider my request unless something was happening *right that minute*, and I simply couldn't wait around for a catastrophe to happen. She stared at me, mute, so I continued on to say that Chuck's last threatening letter had given *a specific date and time*, which according to research, is definitely something to be mightily concerned about. She told me a third time to go home and call 911. *Fat chance.* I refused to be so easily conned.

The reluctance of the police to act was all too familiar to me. I was used to being ridiculed and dismissed by many of them. But now to have a *civilian* actively trying to dissuade me from even *approaching* the police was simply too much to bear. My blood pressure was moving into a dangerous neighborhood, and I was perilously close to losing my composure. I responded that I had made the effort to come all the way downtown to make my complaint in person, at great inconvenience, I added, and that I wanted to talk with someone in authority. I said that time was of the essence, as I held up my shopping bag full of evidence. She wasn't interested.

She countered by saying that the police were all out in the field. "Are you telling me that in this huge six-story building, there is not *one person* who can take my complaint?" I questioned. Apparently, there wasn't. She further informed me that, "An officer would have to drive all the way back to the station, and park, and walk all the way up here, just to see you." *Just?*

Why was she trying to make me feel guilty? Why was she trying to make me feel *unworthy* of police consideration? Why did she help everyone else in line without a qualm? Why had she been accomodating to those who were annoying, loud, and verbally abusive, but not to me? She had no call to speak to me in that superior tone of voice. *Does she sweet talk every middle class person this way?* I harrumphed. *Or should I consider myself special?* I too, was a public servant, having been one for my entire adult life, and knew better than to treat others in such a hostile manner. Obviously, she hadn't yet learned that it takes far less time and energy to be polite, than to calm someone who is rapidly moving from merely miffed to incensed to enraged. I couldn't fathom her reaction. *Are there that many women who cry wolf? Are there that many who file stalking complaints, only to later drop them?* I could not *believe* that I was still getting the runaround, after all these years. Same ole, same ole.

"*Oh, pul-leeeze.* You've got to be kidding," I muttered, having reached my limit with bureaucracy, while pounding my head against an inner brick wall. Even knowing that this clerk was the Keeper of the Door, there was simply no way I was going to play the good little girl and meekly turn around and go home. *I'd had it!* I finally dug in my heels, and told her in no uncertain terms, that I would not leave the station without satisfaction. It was imperative that I talk to someone about my situation, and I wasn't going until I had done so. A touch of impatience may have crept into my voice, as I explained that I wanted justice and I wanted retribution and *I wanted my day in court!* She fumed in mute disapproval, but finally relented, and said that I could take a seat.

I sat. The wait for service seemed endless—seethe, seethe—but I was determined to outwait them. After all, I reminded myself, I've waited for all these years, what's a few minutes more? Actually, I was willing to stay all night. I came prepared. I had brought along a fat, heavy, hot-off-the-presses copy of John Grisham's *The Chamber,* to read. The title seemed appropriate.

Time passed like a gallstone, as my small store of patience was rapidly depleting. Moan, groan, whine, sigh. *Forty minutes* later, the clerk motioned to the police officer guarding the front doors, to take care of me. I couldn't *believe* that she had made me wait for no good reason! After telling me that an officer would have to come "all the way back" to the station to take care of my complaint, the policeman who was standing less than five feet across from me the *entire* time was the one who would do so. I was torn: thrilled that I would get some assistance, and furious that it had taken so long. What right did this minor city functionary have to deny me the help I so desperately needed? Tired, frustrated, and pushed to the edge of teeth grinding irritation, I was on the verge of saying something I might regret, but knew it would be counterproductive. "Rats!" I groused loudly to myself, permitting a substitution for a more apt, but offensive word."Rats, rats, rats, rats, *rats!*" The situation warranted as much.

We went through the heavily locked doors, back into the bullpen. He looked serious and official. And young. With absolutely no observable warmth or humor. *Oh, boy.* So much for diluting tension and encouraging trust. It was a stance designed to make a complainant feel intimidated. He stared impassively—a sphinx—eerily silent, as I launched into my story with the forced cheerfulness of a Chatty Cathy, just for counterpoint. Trying to give a fast account of Chuck's stalking behavior in record time, was not easy, but I perservered. I kept looking for a reaction, even a slight nod of his head, or a blink of his eye, to show that he was following what I was saying. He was steeped in indifference, maintaining a verbal deep-freeze, practically yawning in my face. Ho and hum. He was not properly sympathetic.

My knee-jerk desire was to provoke a reaction out of him, but my experienced self knew better. After all, confrontations with police personnel aren't something relatively normal people take lightly, and let's face it, I was looking to *them* for help. It wasn't the time to be burning my bridges. I again held up my shopping bag full of evidence, but he wasn't interested in it, either. I felt exhausted, like a ladybug trying to make an impression on a whale. It seemed to me that he was just going through a required look-see.

Get a grip, Sherry, I said, as I gave myself a hard mental shake. First off, I wasn't crying and hysterical, as most victims are. That kind of behavior was years behind me. OK, so I could see how this might throw him off as to how a believable complainant might act. And, although he might not be a rookie, he was no seasoned officer, so this might be a different experience for him. Maybe he wasn't taught anything about stalking at the academy, since the laws were pretty recent. Maybe he was being disciplined for some odd infraction, and was made to stand by the door all day as punishment, and, was taking it out on me. (So here I was, making excuses for others again. A tough habit to break.) No matter *what* reason I could devise for his inability to deal with my story, I was still concerned that he wasn't writing anything down. Zero, zip, zilch. Not even so much as my *name*, much less, my phone number. A snail seemed hyperactive compared to him. Nothing I said seemed to catch his attention or pique his interest. I felt invisible in his eyes. What was going on? I was getting downright annoyed. *Just what does a person have to do to get some consideration around here?* I complained to myself. I wanted to suggest that he take a refresher course in dealing with the public—Interview 101—but knew it would fall on deaf ears. This sucked like a vacuum cleaner.

I pondered the fact that this added lack of concern, by both the clerk and officer, was akin to whipped cream with a cherry perched on top of the thirtysome years of inaction by the LBPD. I had definitely worked myself into one of those *Love me or hate me but don't ignore me* moods. I was getting seriously irked. I felt they both needed sensitivity training, if nothing else. The least they could do was slap a pseudo-smile across their faces. But I was afraid to complain, and thereby alienate the entire police department, since I knew I would have to rely on them in the not-too-distant future.

Totally as an aside remark, I casually mentioned a situation that had *nothing* to do with me: Chuck's reported half-interest in Studd's Liquor store, and a recent shoot-out that had gone down there, as well as the name of the LBPD detective involved in the case. The officer was galvanized into action so quickly, I was totally unprepared for his response. He hot-footed out to the records department, and shot back with a long read-out of the incident in question. I finally had his undivided attention. Of course, the detective listed on the case was recently retired, but he was working locally at a new car dealership in town (presumably in the security detail). *Now*, at long last, the young officer was interested, and wanted to take some notes. So, we started all over again. He later assured me that the proper detectives would contact me the next day. And so I left, somewhat convinced that I would finally get some action.

But I was completely flummoxed. How is it, as a responsible person and a solid citizen, a contributing member of society, who works hard, follows the law, votes, and pays taxes, that the police didn't believe *me*? Why did it take a convicted felon's record to convince anyone that *I* should be taken seriously? My life had been turned upside down, violated, and corrupted, and yet my stalker seemed to have more clout. How is it that I was deemed lower than Chuck on the foodchain? I felt doubly victimized. It was a bitter pill to swallow. I maintained this wonderful state of mind all the way home.

The next day, the Chief of Detectives of the Criminal Investigation Division called me at school, to briefly question me. After a short discussion, he told me that he had assigned my case to Detective Robbie Hill-Morrison, and that she would be handling it thereafter. So, I met with her on several occasions, and what a difference! She was courteous, interested, and professional. During the first days in which we came to know each other, a highly publicized kidnapping occurred. She found the child and caught the culprit, giving me even more faith in her abilities to help me. I was elated. Hot dog!

Detective Hill-Morrison advised me to go to the courthouse and start the restraining order proceedings, which I did, the very next afternoon. What a bureaucratic mess! That took two more days out of my work week. The frustration involved was overwhelming, and I didn't even have a problem with the language, or a passel of crying kids hanging onto my skirts, as I tried to follow the directions (thank goodness for small favors!). The last thing I did was to pay for a marshall to hand-deliver the TRO.

Several days later, on Saturday—Chuck's *chosen* date for our meeting—he drove by the house. I called 911, to no avail. It seems that no one thought it a crime to drive back and forth, up and down my *cul-de-sac*, for no good reason. The dispatcher refused to send anyone, because, once again, nothing "physical" had happened. I couldn't convince any operator that Chuck was major league BAD NEWS with a four-inch headline. He was off the rails completely, and no one cared. Both the current 1994 California Stalking Law, enhancing the ability of law enforcement to intervene and protect victims at the *earliest* time, and Penal Code Section 422, the making of a terrorist threat, were ignored. By everyone. And no one wanted to *hear* about them, either, easily dismissing the recent *People vs. Carron* ruling, that a stalker's *intent* could be considered.

When I continued to call, the switchboard began to route my 911s to various substations, in an effort to let someone *else* consider my pleas and deal with my problem. I was bounced around from pillar to post. One woman actually cut me off in midsentence, making me feel thoroughly expendable. (OK, so this was Long Beach, not Denmark: but something here *still* smelled to high heaven.) I was furious beyond words. Nor did I know to whom I could express my disgust and disapproval about the lack of service. *I am a private citizen, just like everyone else. I pay my taxes! I have a right to police protection!* I fumed to myself. The last thing I needed was another road block. So again, I couldn't totally focus on Chuck, because I was so distracted by the inaction of my police department. (I was reminded of a quote by Susan B. Anthony in an 1890 interview, in which she said, "All we can do is agitate, agitate, agitate." My sentiments exactly.) I was beginning one of the great headaches of the decade, realizing that my chances were slim to nonexistent.

A couple of hours later, after working myself into a righteous froth, I dialed 911 again, while Chuck made yet another lap of the block, presumably, working up his nerve for the grand finale. I made one final valiant stab at remaining outwardly calm. That lasted all of about two-seconds before I erupted into a fuming firestorm. I totally lost it. Emitting a bloodcurdling shriek, I yelled, "What is the *matter* with you people?!" Hypertension and stroke lurked uncomfortably close, as I continued on with my tirade."Get someone over here *now!*" I exploded in disgust as I slammed down the receiver. (As Stephanie Powers once said, "Unfortunately, sometimes people don't hear you until you scream." Heretofore, I thought that fussing and hollering and yelling in public was undignified behavior. It would have helped had I taken her words to heart earlier.) Apparently, I should have shouted in the first place, because shortly thereafter, the police appeared. Obviously, screaming, crying, and carrying on, is the *only* clue that says you really, really, *really* need help.

The first squad car arrived, and we were ecstastic. Wayne and I were in the midst of explaining the situation to the policeman, when the second cruiser arrived, with a female officer. Hope soared, only to be immediately dashed when we started our tale, yet again. Unfortunately, the policeman's position was pretty obvious. Rigidly standing with feet apart, arms tightened defensively across his chest, he gave us the non-committal bland look that is standard procedure when assessing a situation, although his body posture conveyed the message that he'd already made up his mind (as in "Go ahead. *Convince* me that I need to be here.")

After listening politely, he gave us the same old song and dance routine, and I didn't know whether to laugh, or cry, or throw up on his shoes. That was so-o-o-o not what I wanted to hear, as my anxiety barometer rose several of notches. A rousing rendition of the Stones' "19th Nervous Breakdown" played loudly in my mind. It became abundantly clear that our situation was too inconsequential to warrant any further attention. He too, was just going through the minimal motions, with an exaggerated facade of reasonableness. The female officer wasn't in accord with what her partner was saying—her body language clearly showed this—but since she was not the primary, she held her tongue. (I felt for her. *After this is all over, assuming everyone's still standing, I'm going to look her up,* I thought.) History was repeating itself, as usual. I released a long, weary sigh, and shook my head. With a heavy heart, I realized that we had pretty much exhausted our options. (*"Houston, we have a problem!"*) The situation was going nuclear, and the police were *not* helping matters, and we had no Plan B to fall back on. They were my first, last, and *only* line of defense. I had been *depending* upon the police for the final showdown, proving yet again, that false expectations can be deadly.

As the officers were getting back into their squad cars, and we were saying our halfhearted goodbyes, our neighbors across the street were jumping up and down, waving their arms, and shouting, in an effort to gain our attention. I sped across the street to talk with a couple of them, and they excitedly explained that Chuck had just driven by *again*, and raced around the corner. Since the second officer was making the U-turn in our cul-de-sac, I ran back to tell the first officer, who was just opening his car door. He refused to give chase."So where did he *go*?" he asked me, elaborately shrugging his shoulders, as if the situation was simply too much for him to understand. "Where did he go?" he repeated, like I would be privy to such information. *Geez, Mister, how would I know?* I said to myself, thinking, *It must truly be time for this guy to log off work,* as he made no effort whatsoever to disguise his grudging, foot-dragging, reluctance to help.

"I don't know *where* he went, but you can find him if you hurry!" I urged, pointing. "Chuck just went around that corner!" No such luck. The policeman climbed in his car, in full-tilt turtle mode, shutting the door with the heavy thud of finality, and headed back to his base site. Wayne and I were left standing in the middle of the street—our mouths hanging open in dumb astonishment—watching him turn in the *opposite* direction. Talk about flagrant disinterest! We were incredulous, flabbergasted, and nonplussed. *Thank you for your concern. Really.* The message was received: *It's official: we're toast.*

Patrol Officer Kerry Enright stopped her cruiser next to us."What's going on?" she asked. "What were you guys talking about?" I forced a few deep breaths and reached for a measure of calm, as I explained that our neighbors had just seen Chuck go by, as we were all walking out the front door together, adding that her partner refused to follow him. "Was that a *red* car?" she asked. The collected neighbors excitedly yelled, "YES!" all pointing and gesturing in unison.

"*I saw that car!*" she yelled, as she stepped on the gas and took off in hot pursuit. Wow! Superwoman to the rescue! I was impressed, as well as thankful. Officer Enright chased Chuck down, and cornered him in another cul-de-sac, blocking his exit with her squad car. After she radioed for her partner to come back and watch over Chuck, she brought me his driver's license, to make sure she had stopped the right guy.

"That's him all right!" I assured her, while marveling at how his dark hair had turned perfectly white over the years. She asked me if I had a restraining order against him. After I said yes, she used our phone to call downtown, to verify that it was actually on file. Receiving confirmation, she went back to arrest Chuck. When the two officers began checking out his car, they found a fully-loaded gun, with extra ammunition, giving full meaning to the word *overkill*. It was suddenly obvious to one and all that Chuck was past the talking stage.

The primary officer then returned. *Now he comes back*, I thought. *Thanks for nothing. I could be dead already!* With a sheepish expression on his face, he attempted an apology, of sorts. His parting remark being, "He'll never see the light of day again!" (OK, you tell me, should I have felt safer then?) Although we fervently wished his words were true, we had the experience to know better than to believe it. (Officer Kerry Enright is now Corporal Enright! Yahoo!)

After the squad cars turned our corner, I refused to even *look* at Chuck, I wouldn't give him the satisfaction. When all of our neighbors and the lookylous went home, Wayne and I were suddenly left in the silence. "What do we do now?" we asked each other. It was so weird. All of the urgency was gone, and the need for adrenaline had abated, so we were left in an uncomfortable position. "What do we do now?" we reiterated, shrugging at each other. It was a very strange feeling; with all of the stress and strain over, we didn't know how to act. It was so-o-o-o anticlimactic. We finally went out to dinner, in an attempt to calm down and repair our ragged nerves, while trying to make sense of the day.

Our happiness was short-lived however, as the minute we returned home our phone began ringing off the hook. With no relief in sight. Chuck's family began calling, en masse, pleading for me not to file charges. "It was all a mistake," one assured me. "He didn't mean it," said a second. "Charles would never hurt you," another maintained. (Little did they know). The older nephew said that having the gun in the car was *his* fault, and so on and so forth. Finally, in desperation, Wayne interrupted, saying that all of the phone calls were being monitored by the police. They weren't, of course, but the calls abruptly stopped.

The quote, "He'll never see the light of day again!" reverberated in my brain. Having learned the hard way not to have blind faith in what others say, I elected to follow-up on the police officer's remark. Overconfidence is dangerous, an ounce of prevention, and all that. So, I called the jail early Sunday morning. The information officer, assuming I was a relative of Chuck's, *assured* me that he could be out on bail Monday morning. The general rule being that the court lets you post bail with a 10 percent deposit. "Chuck's bail is set at ten thousand dollars," he explained, "so all your family members have to do is come up with one thousand dollars between you, and Charles will be home shortly." I couldn't even begin to make my mouth work. Filling the gap in the conversation, he kindly added, "Don't worry." *Oh, joy. Oh, rapture.*

I'd say that this turn of events was right up there in the ranks of royal screwups. I was forty kinds of furious. My heart began thudding in my chest, and my body was vibrating enough to log in on the Richter scale. I tried to ignore the tremors—uninvited, unwanted, renewed behavior—while my thinking was as circular as a Mobius strip: *Why wasn't anything easy? Why did I always have to keep jumping through hoops? Why am I not supported by my own police department? What else can go wrong?* I had a buzz like a bad neon light in my head, while Wayne and I both agitated throughout the entire day.

Early Monday morning, I called Detective Hill-Morrison, saying that my life was worth considerably more than a thousand dollars. She in turn, called the D.A., who raised the bail to a quarter of a million dollars. Knowing that Chuck's family couldn't afford one tenth of that sum, I finally was able to relax. Somewhat.

That Friday, four days later, I returned home after a rather heavy-duty week of teaching, eager to change clothes and attend my close friend-and-classroom-partner's retirement party. It was to be a joyous celebration, that all of my colleagues and I felt both happy and envious about. Wayne called me into the den, in a high state of excitement, to share the news about O.J. and Nicole Simpson. I froze where I stood, in a somewhat catatonic state for *hours*—totally missing the party event of the year!—simply staring at the prolonged slow-speed chase of the white Bronco traveling around our freeways. I was in a state of shock, disbelief, and suspended animation. I was so totally focused on the TV screen that it was hard to hear Wayne over the mantra looping endlessly in my mind: *That could've been me! That could've been me a week earlier! There but for the grace of God go I.*

Chapter 9:

PERSONAL APPLICATIONS

(181) Experts maintain that a potentially dangerous letter writer is one who (a) expresses a desire for contact, (b) mentions sharing a specific destiny or fate, (c) has a specific date, time, or place in mind, (d) mentions a weapon, (e) writes from more that one address, (f) makes religious references, (g) mentions death or suicide, (h) telephones you, and, (i) is willing and able to travel long distances to see you. Taken altogether, the unspoken message is quite clear, and indicates someone that is a definite threat.[1] (Note that although these items are actually noted for potential *celebrity* targets, they proved to be true in my case, as well.)

Of course, if the letters are written in blood, or are blood-soaked, you don't need an expert to tell you that you are dealing with an extremely disturbed individual. Likewise, inappropriate gifts (urine, feces, dead flowers, dead animals, nude photos, syringes, and the like) suggest further derangement. Have someone else take photographs of the offending material for you. Often, such items are hand-delivered, meaning that the stalker was on your property. Notify the proper authorities.

Other messages may include nasty words painted across your home, garage, fence or wall, or scratched onto your car, or semen sprayed thereon. Take pictures of everything. Now that DNA testing is available, invite the police to take several swabs of the sample, before you wash your vehicle.

(182) At some point, nearly every victim expresses a feeling of frustration by the seeming inability of police to simply listen, to recognize their problem, or to intervene. Even now, with the antistalking laws on the books, the laws are not effective if they aren't implemented. In addition, some policemen *still* need an attitude adjustment, when it comes to

stalking or battering situations. Recently, two women with several children in tow, were observed running into the police station, requesting the policeman manning the desk to call Su Casa, a well known local shelter. The young mother was crying and shaking in fear, while trying to keep her children quiet. The officer involved was clearly unenthusiastic about the situation, and unsympathetic to her plight. He grilled her, forthwith: Why did *he* have to call? Why couldn't *she* make the call herself? Or why couldn't the friend who brought her make the call? *Why* did he have to get involved at all? The young woman had the shelter number scribbled on a crumpled piece of paper, desperately trying to hand it to him, pleading with him to make the call. (When a shelter is called from police personnel, they know it's a legitimate emergency, and a representative will drive by the station and pick up those in need. Since shelter locations are strictly secret, this is one way in which to assure that the wrong people aren't requesting admittance.) You'd think that police personnel would be more understanding regarding the fear and terror that this family was obviously going through.

(183) Although the police represent your first line of defense, they can't help you if you aren't able to get past the 911 operator. (Three months into his new term, the Long Beach Police Chief Anthony Batts is in a difficult position. Tackling cutback issues, he must shrink his budget by $8.7 million. Yet, he says, "The citizens have told us that when they pick up the phone and call, they want us there. Period." He says that he doesn't want to hear excuses that include words like money, downsizing, and layoffs. He wants effective policing. I sincerely hope this will be accomplished during his administration.[2]) If you find the 911 operators, department clerks, or the police minimizing or dismissing the seriousness of your problem, you must stand your ground, speak up for yourself, and demand to speak to a higher authority. ("The greatest tragedy is indifference." The Red Cross) Make sure you receive the service and protection you deserve, as the bigger danger lies in not fighting for those rights.[3]

(184) To be fair, however, the lack of instant concern regarding stalking complaints may be that TROs are issued at more than one thousand a day in the U.S.[4]

(185) Think of going through all the bother of obtaining a restraining order as simply homework assigned by the court, to prove to the police and the judge that you are committed to the process of holding your stalker accountable.[5]

(186) It is important to be prepared when dealing with the police. Have clear documentation (a log, a diary, or a calendar) of the chronology of events. This not only ensures that you won't forget important details or dates in your story, because of stress, nervousness, the busy station, or the newness of the police experience, et cetera. It shows that you are reliable, and ready and willing to work as a team. Bring *copies* of letters, photos, tapes of telephone messages, and gifts, to back your claim.[6]

(187) Take down the name of each person you talk with, as well as their badge number, or the office to which they are assigned. Add that information to your growing documentation. Don't depend upon your memory. Keep such important papers all in the same place. (I was so rattled and disorganized, I had papers stashed all over the house, unable to find them, when needed.)

(188) If you don't think you are receiving the proper response, or feel that the police are asking rude questions about your previous relationship—the nature, extent, and duration of events—with your stalker, remain calm. Understand that they are trying to sift through the facts. They are not necessarily acting inappropriately, they are trying to determine the believability of your claims.[7]

(189) Ask if your police department has a brochure or pamphlet explaining your rights. Research the laws pertinent to your state, and the local guidelines that specify your rights.[8]

(190) You are entitled to a copy of your police report. This is a right protected under the Freedom of Information Act, passed by Congress

in 1966, and strengthened in 1974 and 1976, which allows individuals access to information held by government bodies such as law enforcement agencies. Request a copy for your own files.[9]

(191) After you have filed your original police report, your case may be handed on to a special investigator, hopefully one who is seasoned in handling stalking cases. Expect to tell your story all over again. He/she will more than likely talk to you face-to-face, as well as over the phone. Establish a good relationship with this person. It is in your best interest.

(192) If you feel that an arrest should have been made, and it wasn't, you are encouraged to contact the prosecutor directly to request that a warrant be issued.[10] You have the right to discuss the matter with the prosecutor.

(193) Restraining Orders, or "injunctions" or TRO's, are filed in a civil court. Although the language involved presents a pretty standard list of limitations ("no contact" or "stay 100 yards away," and the like), you can *request* an amendment to the list, regarding specific behavior, since every experience is unique.[11]

(194) In my particular case, when Chuck repeatedly drove past my house, after he had already placed his threats in writing, he definitely qualified for immediate arrest under the California Penal Code Section 422.[12] Unfortunately, no one knew what I was talking about. To ensure that this doesn't happen again, I suggest that you photocopy the stalking laws printed in the back of this book, and keep them handy. Place a copy in your car, purse, pocket, and suitcase, along with your TRO, to show them to those individuals who may not know about these laws, or who might be lax in supporting them, so you can *demand* to file a report, showing cause that your stalker should be arrested.

(195) You can often predict the behavior or intent of others, based on your ability to read certain signals. Most body language, facial language, and gestures, are valid worldwide, with only a few cultural differences. Nonverbal communication is mostly unconscious. Read some good

books on the subject, to help you gain meaning and perspective behind the words people use.[13]

(196) Don't expect a piece of paper, or court orders, to protect you. Someone may drop the ball, so your belief in the system, or overconfidence in the word of someone, may cause you grief. Be aware at all times.

(197) The danger a defendant poses to other individuals or the community at large should be grounds for a high bail or for denying bail altogether.[14] Throughout the nation, however, ridiculously low bail bonds are set, and assailants are still released on bond without regard for their victims' safety. This is your life! Get involved enough to suggest changes in the court-imposed conditions of bail. Afterall, the aim of the law is to protect *your* safety.[15]

Chapter 9 Endnotes:
FALLING BETWEEN THE CRACKS

1. Melita Schaum & Karen Parrish, *Stalked: Breaking the Silence on the Crime of Stalking in America* (New York: Pocket Books, 1995), 32-34, citing the data of Dr. Park Dietz, an expert on criminal pathology, and his colleagues; Doreen Orion, *I Know You Really Love Me: A Psychiatrist's Account of Stalking and Obsessive Love* (New York: Dell, 1997), 241 & 251, citing the "pre-incident indicators" of Gavin De Becker; Elaine Landau, *Stalking* (New York: Franklin Watts, 1996), 24.

2. Wendy Thomas Russell, "LBPD shifting to Patrol." *Press-Telegram*, 22 January 2003, A1.

3. Sonya Friedman. *Smart Cookies Don't Crumble: A Modern Woman's Guide to Living and Loving Her Own Life* (New York: Putnam, 1985), 227.

4. Gavin De Becker, *The Gift of Fear: Survival Signals That Protect Us From Violence* (Boston: Little, Brown,1997), 191.

5. ibid, 185.

6. Schaum & Parrish, ibid.

7. ibid, 145.

8. ibid.

9. ibid.

10. ibid, 147.

11. ibid, 156-162.

12. For a fascinating chapter on the evolution of stalking laws, read: J. Reid Meloy (ed), *The Psychology of Stalking: Clinical and Forensic Perspectives* (San Diego: Academic Press, 1998), Chapter 2: The Legal Perspective on Stalking, by Los Angeles Assistant District Attorney, Rhonda Saunders, 25-49. Rhonda Saunders and I met in New York, when we were guests on a national TV show together.

13. Desmond Morris, *Bodytalk: The Meaning of Human Gestures* (New York: Crown, 1995); De Becker, ibid, 92; Paxton Quigley, *Not An Easy Target: Self-Protection for Women* (New York: Fireside, 1995), 39; Sherry Meinberg, *Be the Boss of Your Brain: Take Control of Your Life* (Minden, NV: Ripple Effect, 1993), 72-75; Desmond Morris, Peter Collett, Peter Marsh & Marie O'Shaughnessy, *Gestures: Their Origins and Distribution* (New York: Stein and Day, 1979); Desmond Morris, *Manwatching: A Field Guide to Human Behavior* (New York: Abrams, 1977).

14. George Lander, Jr., *The Stalking of Kristin: A Father Investigates the Murder of His Daughter* (New York: Atlantic Monthly Press, 1995), 87.

15. Schaum & Parrish, ibid, 156.

While others may argue
about whether the world ends
with a bang or a whimper,
I just want to make sure
mine doesn't end with a whine.
—Barbara Gordon

Chapter 10:

COURTING DIASTER

Having already missed too many days as the school librarian, inconveniencing the entire elementary school, and with time being a factor, I hired a consultant. A former policeman, I trusted him to run interference for me, and to observe the proceedings of Chuck's arraignment. He was to let me know what happened during the proceedings, the date on which Chuck was to be sentenced, and to advise me as to having my say in court. The plan was that I would be present on the day of the penalty portion of the hearing. I had been assured by my consultant, and the detectives, that two separate days would be involved: one for the arraignment, and one for the penalty, since this was the normal procedure for courtroom scheduling.

Alas, this was not to be. In a routine hearing, processed like the slice of baloney it was, the judge sentenced Chuck to a flat four year term. I realized that under the current California law, a four-year term was the *most* he could be sentenced to, but then the judge immediately took two years off for good behavior. *Say, what*?! Of *course* he was going to be good. There are no *women* housed in the men's prison! And that was that. I had no opportunity for input. At all. I felt cut-off at the knees. Relief warred with disappointment and anger, as a ton of feelings ricocheted through me.

If you averaged out the whole of my last four decades, it simply wasn't normal. Fear always gnawed around the edges of my conscious mind. Yet, for all of the harrassment, threats, assault, serveillance, kidnapping, and stalking behavior, including a gun in the mix, this convicted felon received the equivalent of a two-year sentence. This was wrong, wrong, wrong. How is it that Chuck ended up with the same penalty as a Sonoma County man who was carrying eight grams of marijuana? Or the same penalty as that of a Long Beach gang member who let his friend out of the back seat of a squad car? How is it that a Redondo Beach man, who stole a piece of pizza, got the full brunt of the Three Strikes law? How is it that a Sacramento man, who stole two packs of cigarettes got twenty-five years to life? Or a San Francisco man who stole a new wallet and a pair of shoes got life? Or another man who stole two bicycles and a car, and is serving twenty-five years to life for *each* offense?[1] (About 85 percent of all those sentenced under the original Three Strikes laws were involved in nonviolent crimes, which was eventually revised). More recently, a lot of media attention was given to a case of Road Rage, in which a man threw a dog onto a highway, causing its death, and he received three years. A San Francisco man received three years and eight months in prison, along with a thousand dollar fine, for attacking a kitten. Yet another man in Long Beach killed a dog during a liquor store holdup, and was sentenced to twenty-eight years, his second strike also. Recently, a man received a two-year sentence for mailing talcum powder in a letter (during the Anthrax scare). And, as a last example, a local unemployed musician received a two-year jail term for a building code violation on his property: a substandard roof, weeds, peeling paint, and a lack of screens. Good grief. *Where is the equity?* My life is worth infinitely more than a slice of pizza, eight-grams of marijuana, two packs of smokes, a wallet, a pair of shoes, two bicycles, screens, paint, a roof, and a car all put together. Shouldn't my plight merit as much concern as that of an animal? What kind of a message does this send to our girls and young women?

Of his previous crimes, only the seventeen years Chuck spent in Atascadero was considered to be a strike against him, and this latest sentence would represent his second strike. To me, it is simply a question of hazardous tendencies. The news media clearly shows that animals are handled differently: when a dog bites a human—or a wild animal is simply *capable* of biting a human—they are quickly taken off the streets. Why don't we do the same with stalkers? Aren't they an obvious threat to the public? Based on my experience, and his history before and after our marriage, I'm certain that Chuck will strike again: that women are at risk. When a *pattern* is clear, when *intent* is clear, when *prior history* is clear, why give a stalker a break? After all, a person's past behavior is a good predictor of future behavior.[2] It has taken thousands of years to finally get stalking laws on the record. Why not actually use them?

Chuck's quick two-year sentence represented a win for the Assistant D.A., with little work on his part, by lumping together the Stalking law, Terrorist Threats law, and being a felon with a gun, while conveniently ignoring altogether the admissibility in court of *People v. Carron* (intent), and *People v. McClelland* (prior history). What a crock! Talk about assembly-line justice.

This outrage, this meager effort to pacify the public, simply satisfied the court. *Now* was the time to protect the citizenry, by removing this dangerous felon from his target population. Chuck had viciously assaulted a number of women, and had always skated. But, no-o-o-o, it is as if stalkers and sexual predators are on a never-ending conveyer belt: from a minimal prison stay, they are sent out into the general population where they commit more crimes, and return to prison. In, out, in, out.[3] Obviously, our laws value our wallets more than our bodies. Assault and battery are considered to be minor offenses, whereas petty theft and burglary are treated much more harshly. The justice system seems to value our computers, golf clubs, and electronic equipment more than our teeth, and shows more concern about stolen cars and drug buys than our broken bones.[4] To say that this judgment soured me on the court system is an understatement. Why wait until I'm dead and gone, to find out how the courts failed me?

Victims should not only have the right to confer with prosecutors *before* any plea-bargain is made, they should be scheduled to do so. Although I was stunned with the ruling, Detective Hill-Morrison was furious! The next morning, she stomped over to the Assistant D.A.'s office full of righteous indignation, leaned over his desk, and told him *exactly* what she thought—in no uncertain terms—about his handling of my case. This big man, feeling intimidated by the small woman who got in his face for a *legitimate* reason, tattled to his boss that the detective had no business coming into his office and *bothering* him. His boss, in turn, called her boss, and she was immediately called on the carpet for speaking her mind, and standing up for victims' rights. So much for the First Amendment. I truly felt for her, as good-ole-boy politics is still alive and well. (She has since moved on to Organized Crime Intelligence and Administrative Security!) The ridiculousness of the short sentence didn't stop there. It seems that the prisons were *overcrowded*, and in an effort to ease the housing situation, another six months were later deleted from Chuck's sentence. (Prison overcrowding is a nationwide concern. Example: Both to save money, and to cover budget deficits, the last two Los Angeles County Sheriffs granted inmates early releases.[5] News reports show that the department occasionally allows inmates to serve only *half* of their sentences. So my question is: If overcrowding is such a problem, why not use *tents*, like in Phoenix, Arizona? Let the leadership of Maricopa County Sheriff Joe Arpaio—dubbed "America's toughest sheriff"— prevail. *He* knows what's important: the protection of the public *and* the proper punishment of prisoners. Most criminal offenders leave his county, after serving their time!)

Later, adding insult to injury, the powers that be tried to chop off yet a few *more* months of Chuck's sentence. Apparently, bonus points are handed out for what is classified as good time, or work time, or taking part in programs, cutting sentences even further. To my untrained eye, it appears that criminals are simply processed as fast as possible through the system, with little or no regard for their victims.

I went ballistic, as you may well imagine, writing and calling everyone involved—individuals, noted officials, and agencies, as well as newspapers, newsletters, and magazines—in an effort to leave a paper trail, if nothing else. Relatively few bothered to respond. And, of those who did, most had no suggestions, or supplied conflicting data, at best. It took fifty-one separate letters to the powers-that-be before I received my first response regarding information on this case. Interestingly, Janet Reno, the Attorney General, and Bonnie Campbell, the Director of the Violence Against Women Office, both housed in the U.S. Department of Justice, had the *fastest* turn-around responses, bar none. I was amazed, and thankful, since I was used to being ignored and forgotten.

While waiting for some kind of reply from the prison officials, I commenced background research on my own. When the courts and police wouldn't or couldn't cooperate, I went to the local newspaper morgue, which held old files in the basement of the *Press-Telegram*, and found information regarding Chuck's 1955 incident. (Yowers! Two years before I met him, he was already into dangerous behavior.) I sent a fee to the *Los Angeles Times* for a detailed search, but it didn't have any coverage. Neither did any of the smaller surrounding city newspapers, since the event happened before most were in existence. Next I spent several hours in the Long Beach Main Library, searching through the microfiche and microfilm files (a technology that now seems to be as antiquated as telegraphs, Morse code, and messenger pigeons).

Fast-forwarding, I was looking for anything that jumped out at me, which was not an easy-on-the-eyes experience. At length, I found articles from two local defunct newspapers, *The Independent* and the *Mirror*, which basically told the same story as the *Press-Telegram*.

The crux of all three stories was that when Chuck was twenty-two, he had dated a fifteen-year-old girl a couple of times, and she refused to go out with him thereafter. (I wish I knew the details of *that* story!) One evening, several months later, he banged on the door of her house. The mother answered, and he pushed his way inside. Luckily, the young girl was not there. Unfortunately, the mother took the brunt of his tirade, and was threatened, abused, and held against her will. Her subsequent hospital stay was lengthy.

In fact, the scheduled trial had to be postponed, because she was *still* in the hospital. When the woman was finally able to be in the courtroom, she was so scared of Charles, and so traumatized by his behavior, and by what he'd put her through, she maintained she wasn't sure if he was her tormentor or not. She said that she didn't get a good look at him, because his head was covered, even though her ordeal lasted a number of hours. But she *did* recognize his voice and his build. She was too afraid to face, and finger him outright in open court, although she had apparently done so with the police. As a result, Chuck was released, with prejudice.

This doesn't mean that he was *innocent* of the crime, however, as his later brushes with the law all fit the same pattern. (Interestingly, in his last letter to me, he briefly mentioned this event, dismissing it with the words, "I was acquitted." But, as we all know, acquital and innocence are not necessarily one and the same. Chuck never said he *didn't* do it, only saying that the court lost his papers.) So I found out all these years later that he *did* have secrets, afterall. I was suddenly in need of a heavy dose of Excedrin.

In the fall of 1994, I was advised by the Department of Corrections that Charles' earliest possible release date was August 18, 1997 (although it was subject to change), and that I would be able to present my input, before he would be granted parole. However, in December 1994, I was advised by Governor Pete Wilson's Chief Deputy Legal Affairs Secretary, that Charles would not appear before a parole board; and that he would just be released, with no projected date. When I called the Department of Correction's Victim Services Program, the staffer said that Charles was in yet another prison, with a new release date.

It seemed that no one concerned with this case was dealing with the same facts and figures. I was told by one person that his previous crimes were "grandfathered," and by another that they were "too old to access on the computer." Most said that his first crime was in 1957—Egads! The year I met him!—while another said 1955 (the newly found newspaper articles confirmed this). I testified against him around 1965 or 1966. Unfortunately, I do not know the particulars of any of these events, even though I tried every way I could think of to access those records. I was told by a number of court clerks (both face-to-face and over the phone) that court records aren't kept after ten years. *Say, what?!* If so, then what is the point of the Freedom of Information Act (of 1966, revised in 1974, 1976, and 1996), if there is no information left to read? I felt like I was getting the royal runaround.

The second paragraph in the letter from the Governor's office begins with the phrase, "As you are aware…" And that's just the problem. I was *not* aware of any of the facts in this case, or in his background, because no one would give me the pertinent information, even though I was intimately involved, and *needed* said information in case of future problems. The fat files that law enforcement officials brought with them to my house, were unavailable to me. Not even a picture for my flyers!

Now my question is: When technology has intruded upon our daily lives, with our banks keeping track of our income, credit cards keeping track of our purchases, air flights, and car rentals, supermarkets tracking our eating habits, book stores and libraries tracking our reading interests, governmental agencies tracking our large cash transfers, taxes, employment, marital and family situations, driving, passports and visas, and with camera systems stationed in our stores and on our street corners,[6] where companies, or any savvy computer hacker, can view all aspects of our existence *without* our consent, why can't I get some information from my stalker's file that could actually *help* me? *Why is a convicted felon's privacy considered more important than my life?* Where does the victim fit in the system? The law appears to bend over backwards to keep prisoners' past crimes and misdemeanors a secret, while law-abiding citizens are left to dangle around in the unknown by themselves.

It's hard to fight the system when you don't even know where the playing field is. It is no wonder then that women with little education, no money, or a language and cultural barrier, choose not to deal with the police and court system in cases of stalking or domestic violence. To many observers, it appears that our system of justice provides more protection to the perpetrators of crime than to the people they clearly victimize.

Since I always seemed to be playing in a danger zone, I finally realized that I had to be responsible for my own safety. Although having survived my "little" problems in the past, I learned the hard way that in a major, grade-A crisis, I could not depend on anyone else to save me. Because the police couldn't completely protect me, and the courts wouldn't keep Chuck off the streets, it was fruitless for me to just sit around waiting for *others* to take care of me. Since my survival depended on my being able to protect myself, I needed a way to defend myself other than purely by guts and instinct alone, especially since experts tell us that an assertive response can prevent as much as 80 percent[7] of potential assaults.

In an effort to feel some control over the situation—and have confidence in my own ability to protect myself—I began to check out various nonlethal weapons, improvised weapons, and lethal weapons. ("The thing women have got to learn is that nobody gives you power. You just take it." Roseanne Barr) I studied self-protection guides and considered different types of self-defense classes. Since I was literally gun shy—they've always scared the daylights out of me—I spent time slowly browsing in gun shops, just walking up, down, and around the aisles, familiarizing myself with firearms. I not only wanted to get acquainted with this foreign element, but comfortable, as well. I didn't like feeling frightened or intimidated by something I didn't understand.

After much reading and deliberation of the pros and cons, I came to believe that a handgun is a safety tool, as necessary as a smoke alarm or a fire extinguisher. I saw it as simply a useful machine, to be used as needed, like an iron, a toaster, or a vacuum cleaner.[8] Feeling that a gun is an effective deterrent—serving as a great equalizer[9]—I elected to buy one. Believe me, this was not an easy decision. I was amazed and gratified, however, to find that many studies show that when a gun is used in self-defense, the vast majority of the time, it is never even fired. Just *showing* your gun to an attacker is often good enough to scare him/her away.[10] I wanted to be physically prepared to deter a potential problem, or to put up a major resistance, if worse came to worse.

First, however, I was determined to take the proper gun training. Having been a guest on *Paxton Quigley's Hour of Power* radio program, I found that she was presenting gun training in the local area, at the LAX Firing Range in Inglewood. So I signed up for the course, and traveled up the freeway to be a student in one of her classes. Boy, it was *nothing* like I expected! I had entered a whole new world, vastly different from that of my imagination. I was totally out of my element, where my masters and doctorate degrees did diddly for me. Everything about the situation was foreign. (I got a real feel for the stress and pressure that kindergartners and new immigrants must deal with upon entering our public schools for the first time!) I knew doughnut holes and goose eggs about this subject matter, as the vocabulary and experience were worlds removed from my background. It was totally exhausting.

We started by learning the basic rules for firearms safety. Second, we memorized the parts of a gun, so we'd all be using the same terminology. Then we handled various gun models, for size, feel, and weight, to find those with the most comfortable fit. Next, we practiced dry firing. Later, we practiced loading our gun(s) of choice, followed by practicing speed-loading. At long last, we were allowed in the shooting gallery.

The area was full of men expertly wielding all kinds of weaponry. What an intimidating experience! Guns are *heavy*, especially when holding them in both hands with extended arms, for any length of time. I used muscles I hadn't thought of in years. And the recoil was much more than anticipated. Plus, the *noise* is deafening, so much so that you are required to wear ear protectors. The gunfire on TV doesn't come close. Goggles were also required. And, even more unexpected, in all of the shoot-'em-up movies I'd seen in my lifetime, I never saw red flames coming from the barrel of a gun. But it happens. In addition, the distinct smell of cordite was overpowering. Yowsers!

We learned things that had never even occurred to me, such as: after practicing on a shooting range for a time, you need to take a shower, and immediately wash the clothes you were wearing, to get rid of the gunpowder residue. It's not good for you. *Who knew?* Nor had I any idea that gun owners had to clean their weapons after *every* session. Sheesh. (We have self-cleaning ovens, why not self-cleaning revolvers? If we can put a man on the moon…) I was not pleased with this news.

When first aiming at the targets, I was great. Load, point, shoot. Load, point, shoot. I seemed to have a natural talent. My shots were neatly clustered at the center of the torso, even flying through the bullet holes I'd already shot. After every five shots, masking tape was placed across the holes on the back of our silhouette target papers, so we'd know if we were improving or not. I was receiving tons of positive feedback for being so skillful. Lots of unexpected kudos were coming my way, because I was a consistent shot in the heart and chest area.

Then our instructor said to pretend that the bad guy was wearing a bullet-proof vest, and we had to aim for the head. I was the only one in the class that could put a mental face on my silhouette, and it unnerved me in the extreme. After all, it is one thing to wish a guy dead and gone all those years, and quite another to be the instrument of his demise. Even in an either/or situation. (I always worried about the impact on my soul.) Pointing a gun at an attacking stranger is an entirely different matter than aiming at an ex-husband, even one who has betrayed you in the extreme, and who has obvious loose screws.

Thereafter, my sighting was totally off, making a large arc around the target head. From that point on, the muzzle of my weapon automatically pulled down when I was aiming for the chest area. I was getting worse, much worse, while my fellow students were all improving. It was such a tiring, emotional, unexpectedly stressful day, I cried all of the way home.

Even so, after I had sufficient training, I was determined to buy a handgun. I felt like I needed an Uzi or an AK-47. Or possibly a rocket missile. Even a shotgun would have been a good choice for me, given that it fires a pie-wedge pattern. This would certainly have improved upon my nervousness and fear, since my wobbly aim would have a better chance of actually hitting the target. Unfortunately, it wasn't a serious consideration, since I have grandchildren, and didn't want a weapon that was so big and obvious. I needed something that could be placed out of their reach, but was easily within my grasp.

So I bought the gun with which I was the most comfortable: a Smith and Wesson 357 hammerless snubnose, with hollow point bullets, courtesy of the store clerk, and unbeknownst to me. Later, I purchased a pistol cleaning kit. With the *Rocky* theme resounding in my head, I finally felt like a contender. Now we were more evenly matched, and I was finally ready, willing, and able to defend myself.

I drove back to the police department to apply for a permit to carry a concealed weapon. Numerous clerks and officers told me that it wouldn't do me any good; that no private citizen in the City of Long Beach had *ever* received such a permit. A couple even laughed at me for even attempting such a quest. I ignored them all, asking where I could get the form, and was finally directed through the heavy locked door to the inner sanctum. A group of about twelve officers were standing in a tight clump, having an impromptu meeting of sorts, in front of the desk where I needed to be. When asked what I (a civilian!) was doing there, I told them. One officer flatly announced that it was out of the question. Another said to save my effort. Several said not to even try, because I wouldn't be granted one anyway. Yet another said that it would cost me $79.00 to file the form, just to be turned down, while others echoed that it was a waste of my time and money. "Don't bother," was heard above the din, as everyone shook their heads in unison at the foregone conclusion. In a loud voice, I explained that I needed the form regardless, and would send in the required fee. And then, if my request was denied and I didn't get the permit, I was going to *sue* the department. Everyone was seemingly struck dumb, as they stared in awe. *How dare anyone try to turn me down without reading the reasons for my needing the permit in the first place!* I fumed to myself. Eyes widened involuntarily and eyebrows arched all over, as they moved out of the way to give me passage.

I filled out the form, sent a long letter describing the stalking behavior that I had put up with for an unreasonable amount of years, and enclosed numerous newspaper articles about my plight, along with my check. The department wasn't eager to break its unwritten rule to refuse private citizens a permit to carry. Later, I received a letter stating that in order to obtain a permit, I had to take a class, to prove that I could shoot, conveniently ignoring my previous gun training. I suspect that was because it was given by—you guessed it—a woman! Paxton Quigley is internationally recognized as a personal safety authority: Morley Safer called her "the *great persuader*," Tom Brokow called her "the *self-defense guru* of 15 million women," and she was honored with the Annie Oakley Award in 2000. Paxton Quigley has given seminars and training in personal safety and handguns all over the world, and has written several books on the subject. She has been interviewed on numerous TV and radio shows, has been featured in many newspaper and magazine articles, and has hosted her own hourly radio show. In addition, she was the first female spokesperson for Smith & Wesson, as well as for Pachmayr grips. Yet, for some reason, I had to take *more* training.

So I did. I took individual lessons from Jack Solomon, a former policeman, who owns the Insight Shooting Range in Cerritos. I sent another long letter to the LBPD, detailing my training, added to the training already received through Paxton Quigley's class. And I waited.

At length, unexpectedly one afternoon, the Long Beach Deputy Chief of Police, Jerome Lance, parked in front of our house. He ceremoniously handed me my permit to carry a concealed weapon, making me the *first* private citizen in the City of Long Beach to have ever received one. He said that, because I had had to put up with so much time and red-tape to get it, the LBPD was going to make it *easier* for other stalking victims to obtain one. In addition, he informed us that the police were going to open up their private outdoor shooting range for other stalking victims, to practice their shooting skills. I felt like a trailblazer! (Jerome Lance was later promoted to Chief of Police, and has since retired, amid much admiration and respect.)

Truly, the squeaky hinge gets the oil, because to top it off, my barrage of letters to the prison officials must have worked. Finally, for one reason or another, they backtracked, and settled on a total of a one-and-a-half years incarceration out of the original four. A mere slap on the wrist. Can you *believe*?! On the other hand, it was better than the alternative of an even *shorter* stay in prison.

Even so, it was hard to keep track of Chuck's whereabouts. He was moved around for what seemed to be no apparent reason. Although he started out in a *maximum* security prison in Northern California, labeled a High Risk, Serious Offender, his elderly middle sister wrote a letter saying that Charles needed to be housed closer to her place of res-idence, so that she could visit him. (I doubt if *that* ever happened, since she was bedridden.) So he was moved to Norco California Rehab Center, a *minimum* security prison, just a hop, skip, and a jump from Long Beach. This did not ease my mind. Everytime I'd hear on the news that an inmate had walked off the grounds, and was still at large, I was immediately on the phone to ask if the AWOL was Chuck. It was not a relaxing situation, knowing that he was so close.

After serving his time, Chuck was scheduled to be released back to Lakewood, a mere three-miles from my house: less than a five-minute drive. Again, I contacted Agent Lupe Herrera, Jr., Chuck's parole agent, registering my complaint. He was instrumental in having Chuck released to a halfway house in Palmdale, a small city about 75 miles away, and I breathed a sigh of relief. Agent Herrera came to see me immediately after driving him from Norco up to Palmdale. He main-tained that I had more than just a cameo role in Chuck's fantasies, as he had talked nonstop about me during the entire trip. Worried about the conversation that had transpired, the agent was convinced that Chuck would be back. Drawing his hand to mimic a cocked pistol and shoot-ing, he asked to walk our property. He checked our outside doors, as we discussed safety precautions. The whole discussion resulted in a rather severe case of the heebie-jeebies.

Agent Herrera also said that Chuck spoke at length about the big shootout at Studd's Liquor (that he always mentioned in his letters to me). He rarely kept his facts straight about all of his bullet wounds. Chuck was so relentless about telling how many times he'd been shot, that when they got to Palmdale, Chuck's shirt was removed, and the parole agent said he didn't have a scratch on him anywhere on his torso. So although the robbery *had* happened, the specific bullet damage that Chuck raved about, had not. It was all a figment of his imagination (as if I didn't already know that!). But confirmation is always good.

After his confinement and release, while on parole in Palmdale, Chuck was advised—on several occasions—to register as a Sexual Predator. He said he would, but never bothered to do so. As a result, he was rearrested, and sent back to prison for another year. Shouting hosannas of gratitude during this time, I continued to provide safety features for my house (solid outside doors, deadbolts, motion lights, et cetera), preparing for his eventual return.

Sometime during this period, Chuck's middle-sister died, and her house was sold. So upon his release, he was paroled to Henderson, Nevada, where his youngest sister lived, and could sponsor him, and provide housing. Thinking that, (1) he lived far enough away, and (2) he lacked enough money for transportation, I felt that I needn't worry about him, and put him on the backburners of my mind, so I could totally focus on my own life as a university adjunct instructor. I was later shocked to find out—when I paid for a computer search—that not only did he *own* a car, but Chuck had access to three *other* cars at that same address. Again, my feeling of safety was an illusion.

Everything was quiet on the homefront for a number of months, until Tuesday, the 20th of February, 2001, when I received another six-page letter from Chuck. Surprisingly, this was the shortest and most normal letter I'd ever received from him. He actually recognized Wayne as my *husband*, not a boyfriend, and invited us both to dinner in Las Vegas. In my mind, there was the distinct possibility that we'd never be heard from again. All I could think of was all that sand, sand, sand, in which to bury us.

Chuck wrote that he wanted to give me a manuscript that he had written about "our 42 years together" so "we" could have "our book" published. "I'm alone now my people all passed on," he wrote, conveniently forgetting a sister, brother-in-law, and numerous nephews and nieces, saying that was the reason he had to see me in person, since there was no one left to hand the manuscript to me. He maintained that "we had something special," and that "this book has been ours 50-50 for 42 years." After mentioning the word *gun* and *killer* several times in the text, he ended with, "How many women can say they were the inspiration for an original book that took 42 years to write?" *How many would want to?* I thought.

I immediately faxed the letter to his new parole officer (Agent Herrera had also been promoted!), and to the Interstate Parole Department, because Chuck was not only violating his probation, but my restraining order as well. After all, the judge had clearly stated that he was *never* to contact me again, in any way, shape, form, or fashion.

Realizing that another cycle of stalking behavior had begun, I was more than a little nervous as I drove over to my local police substation. I wanted to appraise them in person of this recent development and to request periodic drive-bys. Now I ask you: Could I get the time of day from the clerk at the window? You guessed it: that's a big N-O! Her response to my complaint was a monument to indifference. The thing that bothered me the most was the fact that an older woman in the line next to me was complaining about someone *teasing* her dog, and *she* was getting more attention, from a clerk *and* a policeman, than I was, with my life at stake. I was taken aback, then offended, then furious all over again, because the clerk was not writing anything down. I strongly suggested that she at least record my name and phone number. My outrage was complete. Shaking, it was all I could do to steady my voice. I said, "Listen, I have a gun, and my stalker has a gun, and if you hear shots coming from that direction...," I turned, dramatically pointing the way, "the police had better get over there ASAP, because one or both of us is going to be DEAD!" Whereupon she proceeded to give me a *lecture*, ending with the words, "even if he is on your property, legally you *cannot* shoot him!"

Bet me! I responded with, "I *know* what the gun laws are. Thank you for your input!" As I abruptly swiveled on my heel to leave, irate beyond words, she belatedly called out that she'd leave a message for the shift commander. I was not a happy camper. After zooming home in a wired state, my jaw didn't start to unclench until I called the California State Parole Office and informed them of my plight. They were aghast, and immediately contacted the LBPD, to tell them of the seriousness of the problem. Periodic drive-bys commenced forthwith.

Upon receiving the faxed letter, the California State Parole Office called the Interstate Parole Office, who called the Henderson Police Department, who called a judge for a warrant. After obtaining the warrant for Chuck's immediate arrest, the HPD went to his listed address. Guess what? *He wasn't there.* (No wonder he put a return address on each page of his letter. He didn't have to worry, because it was where he was *assigned* to be, not where he was actually living.) It turned out that Chuck and his nephew were rooming together elsewhere (both felons, which is a no-no!), but he wasn't there, either. So the hunt was on.

The Interstate Parole Office called the California Parole Office, who called the LBPD. Suddenly, police drive-bys were instituted on an almost hourly basis. The biggest change was that Officer Mike Minton of the East Division was assigned to the case. In addition, two Special Enforcement and SWAT members from downtown, Officer Theo Covey, and Officer Brian Tulian, became involved. All three met with us separately, on a daily basis, and connected by phone, as well. They checked on our well-being, and relayed the latest information and news from Nevada. What a welcome change. They were courteous, concerned, and consummate professionals. Each was a perfect example of what I had always envisioned police protection, help, and service, to be. And I'm grateful for their support.

On Friday, February 23, we were informed that Chuck had been arrested. What good news! It only took four days from start to finish, while I was prepared for the long haul. Wow! Chuck was being extradited to California, where he was slated to return to Norco California Rehab Center, to complete his sentence. According to the law, he had to return to his last place of incarceration, but couldn't stay beyond his original sentence. Everyone told me that his release date would probably be July

14 (or thereabouts). Later, I received a letter explaining that August 19, 2001, was the official date of Chuck's release, which gave us a few more weeks to breath easy. For which I was thankful.

However, *nine weeks* after his arrest, an agent from the Interstate Parole Office called to inform me that Charles had been arrested on February 22, and was given a year for that infraction. (My initial response was that they must *really* be backed up in their paperwork).

In spite of my misgivings, my heart did a little happy dance, as I asked, "A year? You mean he'll get out on February 22, 2002?" Oh, joy! She said that she couldn't give an *exact* date, but that it would be a year from his arrest. "*Sometime* in late February," she affirmed. Several times.

Although wanting to believe her, I explained that I had heard differently, from several sources: August 19, 2001. She maintained that the information she gave me was correct. Our conversation became lengthy, as I continued to question her. Becoming defensive, and a tad huffy that anyone would question or contradict her, she demanded to know who gave me the misinformation in the first place. I said that members of the LBPD Special Enforcement Unit and SWAT Team, not to mention two officers from the California Parole Board. She couldn't understand why *they* were all involved with this problem, so I felt obliged to explain some of the details. She still couldn't understand their reasoning for giving me such an early release date, as we talked further.

When I told her that Chuck was only supposed to stay until his parole time would originally have been over, she quickly changed her tune. A loud intake of breath followed my explanation, as I could hear her rapidly flipping through the pages of a notebook. "I didn't *think* to look at his maximum time!" she explained, backtracking as fast as humanly possible. "It didn't *dawn* on me to check that out," she reiterated. Several times. In a short period thereafter, she apologized about a dozen times. So our whole conversation was a total and complete waste of time and energy. Not to mention confusing. What bureaucratic sloppiness! At least she graciously apologized for supplying misinformation, which is more than I can say for others.

This is another prime example of the right hand not knowing what the left hand is doing. Now I ask you: What if I had taken her information as the gospel truth? If I had not pursued my questioning, I would have been unprepared when Chuck was actually released.

Later on, a few weeks before Chuck's release, I was advised by both Officer Covey and Officer Tulian to obtain yet another restraining order. So I spent an additional day at the courthouse. Upon receiving the temporary restraining order, I sped home to write a letter to Chuck's prison counselor at Norco, requesting that she serve him with the TRO papers and have him sign them, and zoomed to the post office forthwith. When she returned the signed papers, I was required to travel back downtown and file the documents with the police department.

Three weeks after obtaining the TRO, I had to return to the courthouse, and go through the entire sequence again, in order to receive the *final* restraining order. Which I did. That same day, I rushed home to write another letter to Chuck's counselor at Norco, stressing the importance of having him served *immediately* with the new papers, as he was to be released on August 19th, and time was of the essence. I then took the letter directly to the post office, so it would be postmarked that same day (7/30/01). Sending it by certified mail, it was signed off as having been received, the very next day (7/31/01). So I was able to relax, knowing that there were 19 days left in which to have him served. Plenty of time.

You know Robert Burns' old saw about "the best-laid schemes of mice and men"? Well, guess what. She dropped the ball. Chuck wasn't served the final papers before he was released, nor was he served with a paper that the LBPD had requested. Several weeks *after* the fact, his counselor returned the TRO and my letter, with a single sentence handwritten at the bottom: "Charles…was released on August 19, 2001." Which parroted the first sentence of my letter to her. There was no

"Sorry" scribbled thereon, nor any attempt at apology. Oh, boy. So everything had been signed, sealed, sent, and unopened.

Now it was up to me to find him, and have him served. Upon calling the LBPD, I was informed that since Charles had done his time, he now had no strings attached whatsoever, so no one knew where he was. I then went to the Lakewood Sheriff's Department, to access their Megan's Law computer, to see if Chuck had signed up as a Sexual Predator in California. It was amazing to see how many sexual criminals live in our midst. Experts say that a more realistic number is four-times what the register holds, since most have not been caught, convicted, or registered, which is sobering to think about. Chuck's picture came on the screen, with the words: OUT OF STATE. So, I went home and called Henderson, Nevada.

I called on several different days, and couldn't connect with anyone who dealt with stalking or domestic violence issues. They were either on their days off, or out in the field. It was extremely frustrating, to have to speak with four or five people, before actually getting the name of the person I needed to talk with, only to be forced to leave a message. At length, two people returned my calls, leaving messages. So we were playing telephone tag. Finally I was informed that, yes indeed, Charles *was* back in Henderson, and that he *had* signed up as a sexual predator, but that they couldn't serve him. That was the Constable's duty. *Constable?*

When I finally connected with the Constable's office (a division of the court), I was told that they would serve the papers, for a fee. "Yes, I understand that," I happily agreed. But it turned out that the fee was based upon how far they had to drive to serve him. *What?* Not only didn't I know *where* Chuck lived, but I didn't know how many *miles* from the Constable's office that would be, so I couldn't compute the proper fee. And nothing could be done without the proper fee upfront. So, I was back into a holding pattern. Where I remain, waiting, until he resurfaces. Again.

Stay tuned.

Chapter 10:

PERSONAL APPLICATIONS

(198) Plea bargains are often struck without notice to the victims.[11] Make your needs and wishes known to the D.A. *before* the court proceedings take place, or you're liable to be blindsided.

(199) When juries convict stalkers, many judges mete out extremely light sentences (suspended jail sentence, probation, or a short jail or prison term), viewing stalking not as a serious crime, but simply a relationship or domestic problem.[12] Consider the following cases: The whole world watched on TV, when tennis champion Monica Seles[13] was at a German tennis tournament in 1993, as her stalker thrust a jagged-edged nine-inch boning knife into her back. She suffered sufficient physical and emotional injuries to keep her out of professional tennis for two years. When her stalker was tried for the crime, he received a *two-year suspended sentence!*[14] And closer to home: An Illinois victim was horrified to learn of her stalker's early and unsupervised release, after he had already accrued 223 technical violations of the electronic monitoring system he had been placed on, to ensure that he stay away from her.[15] And in 1994, in Pennsylvania, a thirty-two-year-old man was found guilty in court for more than 100 counts of stalking, and sexual harassment, of thirty-five women since 1990. The women were extremely fearful of his threatening and bizarre behavior. This serial stalker could have received as much as 100 years in prison, but instead, received a sentence of *one-and-a-half to three years!* He reportedly grinned at all of his victims, saying, "See you all down the road!"[16]

(200) Many prison officials and parole boards view stalkers as less of a problem than the average criminal, because they are considered to be

low-risk/low-maintenance prisoners. Displaying a normal, harmless, more wholesome demeanor than others prisoners, stalkers are eligible for work release programs, have been granted 48-hour furloughs,[17] and are candidates for early release.

(201) Nationwide, prisoners are automatically given generous early-release credits for good behavior (with no guarantee of good conduct), or for taking part in special prison rehabilitation programs (vocational training, academic education, substance abuse programs, or therapy sessions), or simply to relieve prison overcrowding, at the expense of public safety. They serve little more than one third of their sentences.[18]

(202) According to a mass of research, experts agree that short six-week programs do *nothing* to modify the behavior of disturbed, or violent inmates, or have only minimal effect, at best. With few isolated exceptions, rehabilitative efforts have shown no appreciable effect on recidivism,[19] while some critics go so far as to say that certain forms of treatment actually produce an *increase* in the rate of relapse into criminal behavior.[20] Several officers offered the opinion that they had never seen anyone released from Atascadero in any better shape than when they went in. (I can attest to that!) If so, then why are the courts and prisons in such an all-fired hurry to *release* inmates, when 94 percent of them are violent or repeat offenders?[21] What happened to the protection of society? After all, studies show that two-thirds will be rearrested. in less than three years, for serious crimes.[22] As a result, I am a strong proponent of Truth in Sentencing. If prisoners were made to complete their *entire* sentence, perhaps longer treatment programs could help. If not, it would still keep them off of our public streets.

(203) Despite Megan's Law, requiring convicted sex offenders to register, almost half of California's known sex offenders aren't registered.[23] The state has lost track of at least 33,296 sex offenders (2002 data), due to overworked police departments and budget restraints. That's 44 percent of the 76,350 who registered with the state.[24] Most agree that the best solution for stalkers and sexual offenders is to pick 'em up on the

first complaint, lock 'em up, and permanently misplace the key, because once they leave the prison population, the tendency to relapse into previous criminal behavior is almost 80 percent. Yet, when the parole boards meet, the sex offender is the most likely to be paroled, because they are often considered nonviolent.

(204) It is clear that displaying a gun is highly successful in warding off an attacker, because it equalizes the playing field, changing the odds.[25] Of the almost seventeen-million women in the U.S. who own a gun,[26] 200,000 a year use it to defend themselves against sexual assault.[27] When a woman resists a stranger rape with a gun, the probability of completion of the rape was 0.1 percent, and the probability of victim injury was 0.0 percent, compared to 31 percent and 40 percent respectively, for all stranger rapes![28] Americans use guns in self-defense about a million times a year, but only fire their weapons in 4 percent of those cases.[29] Only about 2 percent of the 200 million guns in the hands of private citizens are used to commit crimes.[30]

(205) Research shows that would-be criminals are deterred from choosing victims who *might* be carrying a hidden handgun tucked in their pocket, belt, or purse. Strong evidence from all 3,054 counties in the U.S., both rural and urban, over a span of eighteen years concludes that violent crime *drops* after states uphold concealed-weapons laws, and crimes rates continue to go down, the longer those laws are in force.[31]

(206) However, do not allow the simple ownership of a gun to give you a false sense of safety. Owning a handgun for self-protection is not for everyone. If you're prone to freeze in a crisis situation—rendering you incapable of moving or pulling the trigger—your gun can easily be taken from you, and you'll more than likely end up as a statistic. Simple common sense suggests that if you live with children, or with someone who is an alcohol or drug addict, or with someone who is violent, depressed, or suicidal, it is best not to have a gun in the house. The danger in these situations overshadows the benefit of owning a gun.[32]

(207) Tidy resolutions happen only on TV shows. Know that any-time you deal with more than one agency, the chances increase geometrically that wires will get crossed, someone will forget a deadline, or drop the ball, papers will get misfiled or lost, you will receive conflicting, confusing, or incorrect information, or you will not be notified in a timely manner. Such shortcomings and failures are commonplace.[33] My experience, added to those of untold others, pinpoints the biggest weakness in our justice system: the failure of all of those involved to communicate with each other, not to mention, the victim.[34] It is obvious to all concerned, that victims operate out in the cold and the dark, proving to be the absolute bottom of the priority barrel.[35] Prepare to be frustrated.

(208) You must be responsible for your own safety. Do not expect laws, the police, a security service, or a body guard to save you. Certainly utilize their services, but you must be proactive and watch out for yourself.[36] Remember that you are the one standing up for your rights. You are the one responsible for ensuring that law enforcement has all the accurate information pertinent to your case.[37] Experts tell us that the stalking problem belongs to the victim, not to the police, highway patrol, or sheriff's departments, not to the social workers, psychologists or psychiatrists, and not to the lawyers, judges, or courts.[38] Harsh words, but true.

Chapter 10 Endnotes:
COURTING DIASTER

1. Sherry Meinberg, "Stalked!" *Voice*, Summer 1966, 38-39.
2. Gavin De Becker, *The Gift of Fear: Survival Signals That Protect Us From Violence* (Boston: Little, Brown, 1997), Chapter 6: High-Stakes Prediction, 98-102 & 315-319.
3. George Lardner Jr., *The Stalking of Kristin: A Father Investigates the Murder of His Daughter* (New York: Atlantic Monthly Press, 1995), 4.
4. ibid, 195, 267, & 279.
5. It's a political issue. The Los Angeles Sheriff's Department and the L.A. Board of Supervisors are warring over money. Supervisor Yvonne Brathwaite Burke states: "...they will have criminals coming out of the jails [on early releases] and we have to increase the budget by $100 million." Troy Anderson, "Inmates Freed to Save Money." *Press-Telegram*, 21 June 2002, A3; Now, in 1993, the state of California is facing a nearly $35 billion budget deficit, and considering proposals to shorten the release date of elderly and nonviolent prisoners that would save hundreds of millions of dollars. Alexa H. Bluth, "Prison Inmates May Be Released." *Press-Telegram*, 24 December 2002; And, as if all that weren't enough, evidence of hair, blood, and semen samples in 6,000 unsolved L.A. County rape and murder cases have been destroyed because of limited storage space. Which means that even *more* violent perpetrators will remain on our streets, continuing to rub shoulders with the general public. The statute of limitations for the rape cases had not run out, and the crime of murder has no statute of limitations. So, I ask you: What is the point of using all that time, effort, energy, manpower and money, gathering important evidence, if neither the LAPD nor the Los Angeles County Sheriff's Department is able to use it? Who made the decision to dump such samples? And who

followed said orders to destroy perfectly good evidence? (No one is owning up to it.) Now the DNA information cannot be placed in a database for future reference. Is it just me, or does this sound not only unreasonable, but illegal, as well? How often does this sort of thing happen? (According to newspaper sources, this isn't the first time.) Who's minding the forensic science section? Again, it appears to boil down to money over justice. Paul Wilborn, "Murder, Rape Evidence Feared Destroyed." *Press-Telegram*, 3 April 2002; Now, adding insult to injury, the California Attorney General and the Los Angeles District Attorney are urging local officials to increase their spending on DNA testing. What is the point, unless policies for storing and preserving all such evidence in perpetuity, are in place? City News Service, "DNA Testing Urged in Sexual Assault Probes." *Press-Telegram*, 28 September 2002, A2.

6. Anick Jesdanun, "Are We Heading for a Surveillance Society?" *Press-Telegram*, 2 September 2002, A24.

7. Paxton Quigley, *Not an Easy Target: Paxton Quigley's Self-Protection for Women* (New York: Fireside/Simon & Schuster, 1995), 42.

8. The same sentiment was expressed in: Paxton Quigley, *Armed and Female* (New York: SMP, 1989),134.

9. ibid, 133-4; Rich Lowry, "A Woman's Best Friend?" *Press-Telegram*, 21 August 2002, A15.

10. Christina Nealson, "A Last Resort." *Voice of Reason*, Vol. 2, Issue 1, Spring/Summer 2002, 2; Quigley, ibid, *Not an Easy Target*, 152.

11. Robert L. Snow, *Stopping a Stalker: A Cop's Guide to Making the System Work for You* (New York: Plenum Trade, 1988), 174; Lardner, ibid, 230-231.

12. ibid, 168, & 174-175.

13. S.L. Price, "The Return," *Tennis*, 22-26; Joni Blackman, "Bloody Obsessions," *People*, 17 May 1993, 71.

14. Elaine Landau, *Stalking* (New York: Franklin Watts, 1996), 32-32.

15. Melita Schaum & Karen Parish, *Stalked: Breaking the Silence on the Crime of Stalking in America* (New York: Pocket Books, 1995), 162.
16. Snow, ibid, 113-114.
17. ibid, 176.
18. Lardner, ibid, 126, citing Robert James Bidinotto, "Revolving-Door Justice: Plague on America," *Reader's Digest*, February 1994, pp. 33-39.
19. Lardner, ibid, 147.
20. ibid, 300-301, citing James Q. Wilson, *Thinking About Crime* (New York: Vintage Books, 1985). Refer to Lardner's entire endnote section of Chapter 13, 307-317 for excellent references on crime statistics.
21. Lardner, ibid, 232.
22. ibid, 238.
23. Editorial, "Enforce Megan's Law." *Press-Telegram*, 12 January 2003, A14.
24. Kim Curtis, "Sexual Predators Missing." *Press-Telegram*, 8 January 2003, A15; Kim Curtis, "Sex Offender Tracking Laws Ignored." *Press-Telegram*, 31 January 2003, A5.
25. Romesh Ratnesar, "Should You Carry A Gun? A New Study Argues for Concealed Weapons." *Time*, 6 July 1998, 48.
26. Lowry, ibid, citing Second Amendment Sisters, *Firearms: TheUltimate in Feminine Protection.* Check out their website: Second Amendment Sisters.
27. ibid, citing research by Criminologist Gary Kleck.
28. U.S. Department of Justice, Bureau of Justice Statitics, "National Crime Victimization Survey" from 1996-2000. Check out related websites: Federal Bureau of Investigation; National Crime Victimization Survey; Office of Community Oriented Policing Services; Office for Victims of Crime; Sourcebook of Criminal Justice Statistics; Violence Against Women Office, et cetera.
29. Quigley, ibid, 152.

30. Lardner, ibid, 240.

31. John Lott, *More Guns, Less Crime: Understanding Crime and Gun Control Laws*, 2nd Edition, (Chicago: University of Chicago Press, 2000), 50-96.

32. Quigley, ibid.

33. Lardner, ibid, 62.

34. ibid, 252.

35. ibid, 124.

36. DeBecker, ibid, 12. Search for other website matches to find links to other instructive sources (see appendix).

37. Schaum & Parrish, ibid, 143.

38. Doreen Orion, *I Know You Really Love Me: A Psychiatrist's Account of Stalking and Obsessive Love* (New York: Dell, 1997), 224, citing Lieutenant John Lane of the Threat Management Unit (LAPD).

AFTERWORD

Stalking—psychological terrorism in the extreme—is considered to be epidemic, the fastest-growing crime in our society, and touted as the Crime of the Millennium. Research shows that one in twelve women[1] and one out of every forty-five men[2] in the USA, will be stalked in their lifetime. These findings equate to an estimated 1,006,970 women and 370,990 men that are stalked *annually* in our nation.[3] There appears to be far more stalking activity than is generally recorded, however, because about half of the victims are not reporting their stalking experiences (55 percent of females and 48 percent of males).[4]

Far from being an individual problem, for every actual stalking victim, countless others (family, friends, neighbors, coworkers, and uninvolved onlookers) are affected; no one is exempt. It is similar, in a much smaller way, to the 9/11 Twin Towers experience in New York, in which immediate bystanders, as well as distant media viewers were witnesses, and were immediately affected; everyone in the country was touched and involved, both individually and collectively.

Understand that stalking is not an irresistible impulse, or a sudden outburst of passion by a lovelorn suitor. It is premeditated.[5] Unlike random acts of violence, stalking is a crime that continues day after day, month after month, and decade after decade, leaving you with a permanent *expectation* of danger. Stressful, repetitive, and escalating in nature, it is all very wearing, both physically, emotionally, and socially. Experts place the *average* span of being on the receiving end of erotomanic stalking behavior at 125 months. Those averages will rise, no doubt, without society engaging the issue in a focused manner. After all, I'm into forty *years* of this nonsense, with no end in sight.

This is a substantial public issue that will not go away, simply because we ignore it, or hide it, or pretend it rarely happens, and then only to celebrities. In fact, research shows that 38 percent of stalking victims are ordinary citizens, 32 percent are lesser known entertainment figures, 17 percent are highly recognized celebrities, while 13 percent are former employers or coworkers.[6] Stalking is a serious social, legal, and health concern that must be recognized and addressed. Victims, as well as the public at large, must bring this matter to the forefront, as a way to raise awareness, broaden understanding, and change cultural attitudes.

As a survivor, you must refuse to be silent. Rise above any fear, shame, and stigmatization you may feel, and hold your stalker accountable. Tell your story! Others may not wish to hear such horrifying tales, but they *need* to be told, because denial and repression should have no place in this day and age. Regain your self-esteem by fighting for your rights, and in so doing, you'll be fighting for the rights of others.

Involve yourself in some kind of meaningful action, be it a social, educational, judicial, political, or religious effort. Make your voice heard. Demand justice! Work for social change in a way that is comfortable for you—through individual or group activism. Influence the political process by simply getting the word out, by talking with friends and neighbors, or writing letters. Later, you may want to participate by giving speeches, or supporting candidates who take stalking issues seriously, or by voting, lobbying, or campaigning. Actively work to strengthen stalking laws:

- Inattention to stalking crimes, and failing to deal with such deviance at the outset, encourages the escalation of such behavior, as the stalker becomes convinced that he/she can get away with such conduct.[7] Stalkers must be held accountable their very first time in court. They must be penalized by removing them from the general public. Minimum jail time should be mandatory for a first offense, especially when involving obvious assault and battery.

- Pertinent information in a stalker's file should be made available to the victim: threats, photograph, and so on.

- The judicial system seems alien and remote to the average person. Make it easier for stalking victims to deal with the court system.

- Stalking victims should be allowed permanent restraining orders.

- A stalking victim should be able to consult with the prosecutor *before* any pre-sentence recommendations are offered. If this can be arranged, then having the arraignment and sentencing on the same day is preferable.

- During a trial, a traumatized stalking victim should not be forced to face his/her stalker in court, which is tantamount to putting ones physical and emotional safety on the line. It only gives stalkers a sense of power and control, and further cements their obsession. Remember the Madonna fiasco?[8] Video taped earlier, or from another room perhaps, but never in a face-to-face situation. The only one who wins in this situation is the stalker. *Any* contact is considered positive by the stalker, and reinforces said behavior. A detective summed it up by explaining that going to court is like "going on a date" to stalkers. Stalkers get focused attention, not only by being in the same room with their target, but getting to talk about, or to, the victim. As an added bonus, they get to learn new details about the stalkees' lives,[9] and watch themselves on the TV, and read about themselves in newspapers and magazines. Do not allow stalkers to manipulate the system.

- Tougher mandatory sentencing for stalkers should be in place. Research clearly shows that short-term classes, such as anger management, victim empathy, sexual abuse, drug and alcohol addiction, and therapy don't work. Judges should never consider counseling or treatment programs in lieu of jail time; such conditions may be required in *addition* to, not instead of.

- When a stalker has completed his/her time, as well as a state-sanctioned treatment program for predators,[10] and is *still* seen by evaluators as a threat, this person's release should be blocked, until such time as he/she is no longer deemed a threat to others.

- A requirement of parole should be that the stalker participate in a court-ordered outpatient treatment program or private counseling upon release. Penalties for not attending appointments should be clear, and enforced.

- When a TRO or a restraining order is violated, or electronic monitoring is broken, no excuses, no second chances, and no negotiations should be accepted. Infractions should never be tolerated; the perpetrator should immediately return to jail.

- The courts should impose tougher penalties for repeat stalking offenders.

- Stalkers must serve their full sentences, with no time off for good behavior; and,

- There is a growing need for specialized Stalking and/or Domestic Violence Courts, because judges are still reluctant to view either as serious crimes. Statistics clearly show that when stalking or domestic violence cases are included on court dockets along with *other* crimes, they are treated as less harmful, and less worthy of the court's time. They are considered to be low-risk, low-injury cases. Permissive judges seldom gave significant sentences to those who were found guilty, resulting in mere slaps on the wrist—setting extremely low bonds, suspended jail sentences, and usually probation, or outright dismissals.[11] Specialist courts would ensure informed judicial sensitivity and expertise. They would provide an atmosphere in which the victim feels understood, supported, and protected. Such a court would hold the stalker or batterer accountable, ensuring close judicial supervision of probation. As a result, regular contact between the defendants and the sentencing judge, would be the rule, not the exception.[12] Support state bills that address this social problem.

Refuse to give in to the bullies of our society. Use your personal trauma as a way of connection to others in your community. Add your voice to those of other stalking victims, along with concerned medical personnel, mental health providers, social workers, educators, law enforcement, and religious officials. Support legislative reform and send the message that stalking will no longer be tolerated. Stand firm for your safety and quality of life.

AFTERWORD ENDNOTES

1. *National Violence Against Women* (NVAW) Survey, sponsored jointly by the National Institute of Justice (NIJ) and the Centers for Disease Control and Prevention (CDC), through a grant to the Center for Policy Research, 1998, Exhibit 1.
   Violence Against Women, 2000 M. Street NW, Suite 480, Washington, D.C. 20036. Phone:(202) 467-8700 FAX: (202) 467-8701
   E-m: SRC@ncvc.org Victim Assistance: 1-800-FYI-CALL, M-F, 8:30 AM–8:30 PM, EST
2. ibid, Exhibits 1 & 9.
3. ibid, Exhibit 2.
4. ibid, Exhibit 15.
5. George Lardner Jr., *The Stalking of Kristin: A Father Investigates the Murder of His Daughter* (New York: The Atlantic Monthly Press, 1995), 25.
6. Karen S. Morin, "The Phenomenon of Stalking: Do Existing State Statutes Provide Adequate Protection?" *San Diego Justice Journal*, 1:123 (1993): 128; Paul Johnsen, "When Creeps Come Calling," *Law Enforcement Quarterly*, February-April 1993, 9-10.
7. Lardner, ibid, 34-35; For an absolutely fascinating take on nipping crime in the bud, read: Malcolm Gladwell, *The Tipping Point: How Little Things Can Make a Big Difference* (Boston: Little, Brown, 2000), chapter 4: Bernie Goetz and the Rise and Fall of New York City Crime, 133-168.
8. Robert L. Snow, *Stopping a Stalkier: A Cop's Guide to Making the System Work for You* (New York: Plenum Trade, 1998), 79-81 & 214-215.
9. Lynda Edwards, "Trespassers of the Heart." *Details*, December 1992, 34-40.
10. Amber McDowell, "Female Sex Offenders Get Life-Changing Help," *Press-Telegram*, 4 September 2002, A18.

11. Snow, ibid, 168 & 176. Read chapter 15: The Criminal Justice System and Stalking, 165-177; Lardner, ibid, 34.
12. Darby Mangen, "California Needs Domestic Violence Courts," *Press-Telegram*, 29 September 2002, A21.

Refuse to be a victim.

The act of stalking harkens back to the instinctive predatory behavior of prehistoric man. Most likely it was a subject of early oral history, since it has been a reoccurring theme in literature since the days of ancient Greece. Only recently, however, has stalking been recognized as a crime. The first anti-stalking law in the United States was passed in California, in 1990 (and revised in 1994), with other associated stalking provisions and statutes following suit. There are now specific stalking laws in all fifty states, as well as the District of Columbia.

STALKING LAW

"Any person who willfully, maliciously, and repeatedly follows or harasses another person and who makes a credible threat with the intent to place that person in reasonable fear for his or her safety, or the safety of his or her immediate family, is guilty of the crime of stalking."

(CA Penal Code Section 646.9)

RELATED STALKING LAWS

It is a crime for any person who is convicted of stalking (felony or misdemeanor) to possess or have custody or control of a firearm.

(CA Penal Code Sections 12021 (a)(1) and (c)(1)

The victim has the right to sue the stalker for general, special, and punitive damages.

(CA Civil Code Section 1708.7)

The victim is able to obtain a civil restraining order at no cost.

(CA Code of Civil Procedure Section 527)

A stalking victim's employer has the right to obtain a restraining order.

(CA Code of Civil Procedure Section 527.8)

Stalking victims or threat victims may now request that their DMV records remain confidential.

(CA Vehicle Code Section 1808.21)

TERRORIST THREATS

"Any person who willfully threatens to commit a crime which will result in death or great bodily injury to another person, with the specific intent that the statement is to be taken as a threat, even if there is no intent of actually carrying it out, which, on its face and under the circumstances in which it is made is so unequivocal, unconditional, immediate, and specific as to convey to the person threatened a gravity of purpose and an immediate prospect of execution of the threat, and thereby causes that person reasonably to be in sustained fear for his or her own safety or for his or her immediate family's safety."

(CA Penal Code Section 422)

THE TARASOFF DECISION

This decision of the California Supreme Court states that "The protective privilege ends where public peril begins." It rules that psychiatrists, psychologists, and other health professionals are duty-bound to use reasonable care in protecting the intended victim of a client/patient's violence. This decision also gives them permission to warn the victim of a credible threat.

(Tarasoff v. Board of Regents, 1976)

FEDERAL STALKING LAWS

Violent Crime and Law Enforcement Control
Act of 1994

FBI records are now available to both civil and criminal courts for use in domestic violence and stalking cases.

(Title IV, Subtitle F, Sections 40601-40611)

The Interstate Stalking Punishment
and Prevention Act of 1996

This act makes it illegal to cross over state lines to stalk a person. Specific punishment guidelines are in place: Crossing state lines for stalking purposes carries a penalty of five years in prison. The penalty increases to 10 years in those cases involving serious injury, or the use of a weapon. And 20 years is the punishment for permanent disfigurement, or a life-threatening injury. Life in prison is the result of those incidents that cause the victim's death.

(Note: Unlike some state antistalking laws, the victim doesn't have to have a restraining order against the stalker to press charges. Nor does the stalker have to commit an act of violence, or be a spouse or former intimate partner.)

(Title 18 USC Section 2261)

WEAPONS LAW OF 1996

Congress passed this law saying that anyone who is convicted of either misdemeanor or felony domestic violence is prohibited from owning, carrying, or transporting a gun.

(Note: The law has yet to figure out how this applies to police officers and military personnel who are guilty of domestic violence, since it interferes with their ability to make a living. The debate continues.)

APPENDIX

When I was going through my troubles in the late sixties and seventies, there were no women's shelters. Now, with a grassroots effort, there are several thousand service programs and shelters nationwide, offering 24-hour, 365 days a year crisis hotlines, emergency transportation, safety, secrecy, information, referral and self-help services revolving around personal, social, medical, and legal needs (TRO assistance, official forms, court accompaniment). Various counseling and support programs are available for victims, in addition to advocacy groups working to change societal attitudes and the law. The following represent the city, county, and national groups I became involved with, long after the fact. Research the groups available in your area to find those that fit with your needs (several of those listed below were helpful for information purposes only). Use their services, or donate much needed items, or money, or volunteer your time to assist other stalking and domestic violence victims.

City of Long Beach Organizations

Sexual Assault Crisis Agency (SACA), 1703 Termino Avenue, Suite 103, Long Beach, CA 90804. Office: (562) 494-5046; Fax: (562) 494-1741; TDD: (562) 597-5121;
24-hour hotline: (562) 597-2002 or (800) 656-HOPE.

National Organization for Women, Long Beach Chapter, P.O. Box 91294, Long Beach, CA, 90809; Toll-free: (866) 251-5167, ext. 3024; E-m: lbnow@onebox.com

Woman to Woman Domestic Violence Programs, 3750 Long Beach Blvd, Long Beach, CA 90807. Office: (562) 426-8262; Fax: (562) 426-5283; E-m: NCADDLBO1@aol.com

WomenShelter of Long Beach, P.O. Box 32107, Long Beach, CA 90832; Office: (310) 491-5362; Fax: (310) 436-4982; Hotline: (310) HER-HOME; E-m: 103633. 2644@compuserve.com

County of Los Angeles Organizations

Los Angeles Commission on Assaults Against Women (LACAAW), Office: (213) 955-9090; Fax: (213) 955-9093 TDD: (213) 955-9095; Self-Defense: (213) 955-9098; 24-hour Hotlines: (213) 626-3393; (310) 392-8381; (626) 793-3385; E-m: info@lacaaw.org; Web: LACAAW

National Organizations

Feminist Majority (FM), 1600 Wilson Blvd., #801, Arlington, VA, 22209; Office: (703) 522-2214; Web: www.feminist.org

National Coalition Against Domestic Violence (NCADV), P.O. Box 34103, Washington, DC, 20043-4103; (202) 638-6388

National Organization for Victim Assistance (NOVA), 1757 Park Road, N.W., Washington, D.C., 20010; (202) 232-6682; Hotline: (800) 879-6682; E-m: nova@access.digex.net

National Organization for Women (NOW),
733 15th Street, NW, Second Floor, Washington, DC, 20005; (202) 628-8669; E-m: now@now.org; Web: http://www.now.org

Rape, Abuse and Incest National Network (RAINN),
(800) 656-HOPE OR (800) 656-4673. This service will connect you to the crisis center nearest to you.

Second Amendment Sisters, Inc. (SAS), 900 R.R. 620 S, Suite C-101, Austin, TX. 78734; Toll-free: (877) 271-6216; Web: http://www.2asisters.org;
E-m: membership@2asisters.org

Sisters in Crime, Intnl., P.O. Box 442124, Lawrence, KS, 66044-8933; sistersincrime@juno.com The Local Chapters and Special Interest Groups of this mystery writers (and fans) organization provide programs, speeches, and support on a variety of issues, including criminal activity, law enforcement efforts, the courts, and changes in the law.

Survivors of Stalking (SOS), P.O. Box 173655, Tampa, Florida, 33672; Web: http://www.soshelp.org/

<u>Related Internet Links</u>

Antistalking
Antistalking web site
Armed Females of America
backgroundchecks.com
California Megan's Law
Christina Nealson's Home Page

Domestic Violence
Federal Bureau of Investigation
FindLaw.com
firstinc.com
Gun Owners of America
Love Me Not
Mothers Arms
National Center for Victims of Crime
National Crime Victimization Survey
National Rifle Association
National Violence Against Women (NVAW)
Office for Victims of Crime
Office of Community Oriented Policing Services
Paxton Quigley
Personal Protection
Privacy Rights Clearing House
Sourcebook of Criminal Justice Statistics
Stalkers
Stalking
Stalkingbehavior
Violence Against Women Office
Whoishe.com
Whoisshe.com

SELECTED BIBLIOGRAPHY

The materials listed below are only those that have been of use in the writing of this book. It is not a complete record of all resources on the subject of stalking. It merely indicates those books, periodicals, and Internet sites, that were the most helpful to me, or most clearly matched my experience. This selected bibliography is intended to serve as a convenience, for those readers who may wish to read more of what these informed sources have to say.

BOOKS

Amen, Daniel G. *Change Your Brain, Change Your Life: The Breakthrough Program for Conquering Anxiety, Depression, Obsessiveness, Anger, and Impulsiveness.* New York: Three Rivers Press, 1998.

American Psychiatric Association. *Diagnostic and Statistical Manual of Mental Disorders* (DSM-IV-TR). 4th ed, rev. Washington, D.C.: American Psychiatric Association, 2000.

Barnhill, John and R.K. Rosen. *Why Am I Still So Afraid? Understanding Post-Traumatic Stress Disorder.* New York: Dell,1999.

Beattie, Melody. *Codependent No More: How to Stop Controlling Others and Start Caring for Yourself.* San Francisco: Hazeldon, 1992.
———. *Beyond Codependency: And Getting Better All the Time.* San Francisco: Hazeldon, 1989.

Bernheim, Kayla F. and Richard R.J. Lewine, *Schizophrenia: Symptoms, Causes, and Treatments*. New York: Norton, 1979.

Berry, Dawn Bradley. *The Domestic Violence Sourcebook*. Los Angeles: Lowell House, 2000.

Braverman, Terry. *When the Going Gets Tough, the Tough Lighten Up! How to Be Happy in Spite of it All*. Los Angeles: Mental Floss Publications,1998.

Burgess, A.W. (ed). *Rape and Sexual Assault*, vol. 2. New York: Garland,1987.

Chopra, Deepak. *Ageless Body, Timeless Mind: The Quantum Alternative to Growing Old*. New York: Harmony, 1993.
———. *Unconditional Life: Discovering the Power to Fulfill Your Dreams*. New York: Bantam, 1992.

Chopra, Deepak and David Simon. *Grow Younger, Live Longer: Ten Steps to Reverse Aging*. New York: Harmony Books, 2001.

Cousins, Norman. *Anatomy of An Illness as Perceived by the Patient*. New York: Norton, 1979.

De Becker, Gavin. *The Gift of Fear: Survival Signals That Protect Us From Violence*. Boston: Little, Brown,1997.

Donnelly, John. *Suicide: Right or Wrong?* 2nd ed. New York: Prometheus Books,1998.

Durkheim, Emile. *Suicide: A Study in Society*. New York: Free Press, 1979.

Ford, Debbie. *The Dark Side of the Light Chasers.* New York: Riverhead Books, 1998.

Freud, Sigmund. *The Interpretation of Dreams.* Translated by A.A. Brill. New York: The Modern Library, 1994.
———. *On Dreams.* Translated by James Strachey, in collaboration with Anna Freud, assisted by Alix Strachey and Alan Tyson. New York: Norton, 1989.

Friedman, Sonya. *On a Clear Day You Can See Yourself: Turning the Life You Have Into the Life You Want.* New York: Ivy Books, 1991.
———. *Smart Cookies Don't Crumble: A Modern Woman's Guide to Living and Loving Her Own Life.* New York: Putnam, 1985.

Gelb, Michael J. *How to Think Like Leonardo da Vinci: Seven Steps to Genius Every Day.* New York: Delacorte Press, 1998.

Gladwell, Malcolm. *The Tipping Point: How Little Things Can Make a Big Difference.* Boston: Little, Brown, 2000.

Goodale, Renee. *Stalking and Harassment: Ending the Silence That Kills.* 2nd ed. Florida: Survivors of Stalking, Inc., 1996.

Hendricks, Gay. *Conscious Living: Finding Joy in the Real World.* San Francisco: Harper, 2000.

Herman, Judith Lewis. *Trauma and Recovery: The Aftermath of Violence—From Domestic Abuse to Political Terror.* New York: Basic Books, 1992.

Horn, Sam. *Tongue Fu! How to Deflect, Disarm, and Defuse Any Verbal Conflict.* New York: St. Martin's Griffin, 1996.

Johnson, Scott A. *When "I Love You" Turns Violent: Emotional and Physical Abuse in Dating Relationships.* New Jersey: New Horizon, 1993.

Jung, C.G. *Dreams.* Translated by R.F.C. Hull. Princeton, NJ: Princeton University Press, 1974).
———. *Memories, Dreams, Reflections.* Translated by Richard and Clara Winston. New York: Vintage Books, 1965.

Kabat-Zinn, Jon. *Wherever You Go, There You Are.* New York: Hyperion, 1994.
———. *Full Catastrophe Living: Using the Wisdom of Your Body and Mind to Face Stress, Pain, and Illness.* New York: Delta, 1990.

Keen, Sam. *Hymns to an Unknown God: Awakening the Spirit in Everyday Life.* New York: Bantam, 1994.

Khalsa, Dharma Singh. *Brain Longevity: The Breakthrough Medical Program That Improves Your Mind and Memory.* New York: Warner, 1999.

Koch-Sheras, Phyllis R., Amy Lemley, and Peter L. Sheras. *The Dream Sourcebook and Journal: A Guide to the Theory and Interpretation of Dreams.* New York: Barnes and Noble Books, 1998.

Kortge, Caroline Scott. *The Spirited Walker.* San Francisco: Harper, 1998.

Kubler-Ross, Elisabeth. *The Wheel of Life: A Memoir of Living and Dying.* New York: Scribner, 1997.
————. *On Death and Dying.* New York: Macmillan, 1969.

Landu, Elaine. *Stalking.* New York: Franklin Watts, 1996.

Lardner, Jr., George. *The Stalking of Kristin: A Father Investigates the Murder of His Daughter.* New York: Atlantic Monthly Press, 1995.

LaRoche, Loretta. *Life is Not a Stress Rehearsal: Bringing Yesterday's Sane Wisdom into Today's Insane World.* New York: Broadway Books, 2001.

Levine, Barbara Hoberman. *Your Body Believes Every Word You Say: The Language of the Body/Mind Connection.* Fairfield, CT: Aslon Publishing, 1991.

Lott, John. *More Guns, Less Crime: Understanding Crime and Gun Control Laws.* 2nd ed. Chicago: University of Chicago, 2000.

Maslow, Abraham H. *Motivation and Personality.* New York: Harper and Row, 1954, rev. 1971.

Meinberg, Sherry. *Be the Boss of Your Brain: Take Control of Your Life.* Minden, NV: Ripple Effect, 1999.

Meloy, J.R. (ed). *The Psychology of Stalking: Clinical and Forensic Perspectives.* San Diego: Academic Press, 1998.

Millman, Dan. *Everyday Enlightenment: The Twelve Gateways to Personal Growth.* New York: Warner Books, 1998.

————. *The Life You Were Born to Live: A Guide to Finding Your Life Purpose.* Tiburon, CA: H.J. Kramer, 1993.

Morris, Desmond. *Bodytalk: The Meaning of Human Gestures.* New York: Crown, 1995.
————. *Manwatching: A Field Guide to Human Behavior.* New York: Abrams, 1977.

Morris, Desmond, Peter Collett, Peter Marsh, and Marie O'Shaughnessy. *Gestures: Their Origins and Distribution.* New York: Stein and Day, 1979.

Mueser, Kim T. and Susan Gingerich. *Coping with Schizophrenia: A Guide for Families.* Oakland: New Harbinger, 1994.

Murphy, Patricia. *Making the Connections: Women, Work, and Abuse.* Winter Park, FL: GR Press, 1993.

Norwood, Robin. *Why Me, Why This, Why Now: A Guide to Answering Life's Toughest Questions.* New York: Carol Southern Books, 1994.

Null, Gary. *Gary Null's Guide to a Joyful, Healthy Life.* New York: Carroll & Graf, 2000.

Ochberg, Frank M. (ed). *Post-Traumatic Therapy and Victims of Violence.* New York: Brunner/Mazel, 1998.

Orion, Doreen. *I Know You Really Love Me: A Psychiatrist's Account of Stalking and Obsessive Love.* New York: Dell, 1997.

Osmond, Marie, Marcia Wilkie, and Judith Moore. *Behind the Smile: My Journey Out of Postpartum Depression.* New York: Time/Warner, 2001.

Pacetta, Frank and Roger Gittines. *Stop Whining—and Start Winning: Recharging People, Reigniting Passion, and Pumping Up Profits.* New York: HarperBusiness, 2000.

Quigley, Paxton. *Not An Easy Target: Self-Protection for Women.* New York: Fireside, 1995.
————. *Armed and Female.* New York: St. Martin's Paperbacks, 1989.

Resnick, Susan Kushner. *Sleepless Days: One Woman's Journey Through Postpartum Depression.* New York: St. Martin's Griffin, 2000.

Richardson, Cheryl. *Take Time for Your Life: A Personal Coach's Seven-Step Program for Creating the Life You Want.* New York: Broadway Books, 1999.

Richman, Linda. *I'd Rather Laugh: How to Be Happy Even When Life Has Other Plans for You.* New York: Warner, 2001.

Rasberry, Salli, and Padi Selwyn. *Living Your Life Out Loud: How to Unlock Your Creativity and Unleash Your Joy.* New York: Pocket Books, 1995.

Schaum, Melita and Karen Parrish. *Stalked: Breaking the Silence on theCrime of Stalking in America.* New York: Pocket Books, 1995.

Schwartz, Arthur and Ruth M. Schwartz. *Depression Theories and Treatments: Psychological, Biological, and Social Perspectives.* New York: Columbia University Press, 1993.

Skalias, La Vonne and Barbara Davis. *Stalked: A True Story.* New York: St. Martin's Paperbacks, 1994.

Small, Gary. *The Memory Bible: An Innovative Strategy for Keeping Your Brain Young.* New York: Hyperion, 2002.

Snow, Robert L. *Stopping a Stalker: A Cop's Guide to Making the System Work for You.* New York: Plenum Trade, 1998.

Stratton, Elizabeth. *Touching Spirit: A Journey of Healing and Personal Resurrection.* New York: Simon & Schuster, 1996.

Telushkin, Joseph. *Words That Hurt, Words That Heal: How to Choose Words Wisely and Well* New York: William Morrow, 1996.

Vendral, Joyce L. *Look In, Look Up, Look Out! Be the Person You Were Meant to Be.* New York: Warner, 1996.

Walker, Lenore. *The Battered Woman.* New York: Harper & Row, 1982.

Walsch, Neale Donald. *Moments of Grace: When God Touches Our Lives Unexpectedly.* Charlottesville, VA: Hampton Roads, 2001.

Wolpe, David. *Making Loss Matter: Creating Meaning in Difficult Times.* New York: Riverhead Books, 1999.

JOURNALS

Appel, J.W. & Beebe, G.W. "Preventative Psychiatry: An Epidemiological Approach," *Journal of American Medical Association,* 131 (1946): 1468–1471, quote on 1470.

Gottman, J.M., Jacobson, N.S., Rushe, R.H., Wu Short, J., Babcock, J., La Taillade, J.J., & Waltz, J., *Journal of Family Psychology* (1996): 9.

Harmon, R., Rosner, R., & Owens, H., "Obsesssional Harassment and Erotomania in a Criminal Court Population," *Journal of Forensic Sciences* 40 (1995): 188–196.

Johnsen, Paul, "When Creeps Come Calling," *Law Enforcement Quarterly,* February–April 1993, 9–32.

Meloy, J.R. & Gothard, S., "Demographic and Clinical Comparison of Obsessional Followers and Offenders with Mental Disorders," *American Journal of Psychiatry,* 152 (1995): 258–263.

Menzies, Robin P.D., Fedoroff, J.P., Green, C.M., & Isaacson, Kari, "Prediction of Dangerous Behavior in Male Erotomania," *British Journal of Psychiatry* 166 (1955) 529–536.

Morin, Karen S., "The Phenomenon of Stalking: Do Existing State Statutes Provide Adequate Protection?" *San Diego Justice Journal,* 1:23 (1993): 123–162.

Mullen, P. & Pathe, M., "Stalking and the Pathologies of Love," *Australian and New Zealand Journal of Psychiatry,* 28, (1994): 469–477.

Zona, M., Sharma K., & Lane, J. "A Comparative Study of Erotomanics and Obsessional Subjects in a Forensic Sample," *Journal of Forensic Sciences*, JFSCA 38 (1993): 894–903.

REPORTS AND SURVEYS

Koenig, Elizabeth, "Gender Gap in Police Brutality: Men Cost More," *Feminist Majority Report*, Vol. 14, No. 1 (Spring, 2002).

National Center for Women and Policing, "The fourth annual 2000 Status of Women in Policing Survey," *Feminist Majority Report*, Vol. 13, No. 2 (Summer, 2001), 8.

U.S. Department of Justice, Bureau of Justice Statistics, "National Crime Victimization Survey." This survey is administered yearly by the U.S. Census Bureau (since 1973) on behalf of the Justice Statistics. Accessed source: 29 September 2002.
<http://sss.ojp.usdoj.gov/bjs/cvict.htm>

National Violence Against Women (NVAW), "National Violence Against Women Survey." The National Institute of Justice and the Centers for Disease Control and Prevention cosponsored this national survey of 8,000 women and 8,000 men, 18 years and old. This project is supported by grant #98-WE-VX-KOO8, awarded by the Violence Against Women Office, Office of Justice Programs, U.S. Department of Justice, conducted between November 1995–May 1996. Accessed source: 29 September 2002.
<http://www.ncvc.org/src/Statistics/nvawsurvey.html>

MAGAZINES

Bidinotto, Robert James, "Revolving-Door Justice: Plague on America." *Reader's Digest*, February 1994, 33–39.

Edwards, Lynda, "Trespassers of the Heart." *Details*, December 1992, 34–40.

Ellis, D., "Nowhere to Hide." *People*, 17 May 1993, 63.

Meinberg, Sherry L., "Stalked!" *Voice*, Summer 1996, 38–39.

Nealson, Christina, "A Last Resort." *Voice of Reason*, Vol. 2, Issue 1, Spring/Summer 2002, 1–2.

Ratnesar, Romesh, "Should You Carry a Gun? A New Study Argues for Concealed Weapons." *Time*, 6 July 1998, 48.

Toobin, Jeffrey, "Stalking in L.A." *The New Yorker*, 24 February & 3 March 1997, 71–83.

NEWSPAPERS

Associated Press, "Tracking Sex Offenders to be Pricey." *(Long Beach) Press-Telegram,* 10 January 2003, A16.

Anderson, Troy, "Inmates Freed to Save Money." *(Long Beach) Press-Telegram, 21 June 2002, A3.*

Bluth, Alexa, "Prison Inmates May Be Released." *(Long Beach) Press-Telegram,* 24 December 2002.

City News Service, "DNA Testing Urged in Sexual Assault Probes." *(Long Beach) Press-Telegram,* 28 September 2002, A2.

Curtis, Kim, "Sexual Predators Missing." *(Long Beach) Press-Telegram,* 8 January 2003, A15.
_____, "Sex Offender Tracking Laws Ignored." (*Long Beach) Press-Telegram,* 31 January 2003, A5.

Editorial, *(Long Beach) Press-Telegram,* 12 January 2003, A14.

Jesdanun, Anick, "Are We Heading for a Surveillance Society?" *(Long Beach) Press-Telegram,* 2 September 2002, A24.

Kicklighter, Kirk, "Date Violence Reported at 5-10 Percent." *(Long Beach) Press-Telegram,* 27 August 2001, A12.

Lowry, Rich, "A Woman's Best Friend?" *(Long Beach) Press-Telegram,* 21 August 2002, A15.

McDowell, Amber, "Female Sex Offenders Get Life-Changing Help." *(Long Beach) Press-Telegram,* 4 September 2002, A18.

Russell, Wendy Thomas, "LBPD Shifting to Patrol." *(Long Beach) Press-Telegram*, 22 January 2003, A1

Wilborn, Paul, "Murder, Rape Evidence Feared Destroyed." *(Long Beach) Press-Telegram*, 3 April 2002.

INDEX

ABOUT THE AUTHOR

Considered to be the longest-stalked person in the nation, Dr. Sherry L. Meinberg is also a veteran educator of forty years, covering a wide range of experience: kindergarten through graduate classes, in public, private, and parochial schools, in urban and suburban settings. She wrote *Into the Hornet's Nest: An Incredible Look at Life in an Inner City School*, as the result of those experiences. Her second book was written for teenagers, entitled *Be the Boss of Your Brain: Take Control of Your Life*.

As a stalking survivor, teacher, and author, she has been the subject of various newsletter, newspaper, and magazine articles. In addition, she has been interviewed on local cable, national, and international television, along with hundreds of radio programs. She has been a speaker for numerous organizations, conferences, and conventions, on variety of issues, refusing to let her stalking experiences stand in her way, or slow her down.

Now, a core adjunct faculty member for National University, and a student-teacher supervisor, she continues to counsel stalking victims on a one-to-one basis. Recognizing that time is a limiting factor, she is now able to service a wider group of those in need, by sharing her personal experiences and suggestions in *The Bogeyman: Stalking and Its Aftermath*, with its companion how-to manual, *Toxic Attention: Keeping Safe from Stalkers, Muggers, and Intruders*.

Along with other awards, Dr. Sherry L. Meinberg was honored as a Community Hero at the Public Safety VI, 2000, and was deemed a "Cool Woman," by the Long Beach Chapter of the American Association of University Women (AAUW), in 2002.

0-595-26271-6

LaVergne, TN USA
08 December 2009
166375LV00006B/51/A